When All the Gods Trembled

American Intellectual Culture

Series Editors: Jean Bethke Elshtain, University of Chicago, Ted V. McAllister, Hillsdale College, Wilfred M. McClay, Tulane University

The books in the American Intellectual Culture series examine the place, identity, and public role of intellectuals and cultural elites in the United States, past, present, and future. Written by prominent historians, philosophers, and political theorists, these books will examine the influence of intellectuals on American political, social, and cultural life, paying particular attention to the characteristic forms, and evolving possibilities, of democratic intellect. The books will place special, but not exclusive, emphasis on the relationship between intellectuals and American public life. Because the books are intended to shape and contribute to scholarly and public debates about their respective topics, they will be concise, accessible, and provocative.

When All the Gods Trembled: Darwinism, Scopes, and American Intellectuals
  by Paul K. Conkin, Vanderbilt University

Heterophobia: Sexual Harassment and the Future of Feminism
  by Daphne Patai, University of Massachusetts at Amherst

Forthcoming Titles:

Modern Inconvenience: The Social Origins of Antifamily Thought
  by Elisabeth Lasch-Quinn, Syracuse University

Academic Politics: The Colonial Colleges and the Shaping of American Intellectual Culture
  by J. David Hoeveler, University of Wisconsin, Milwaukee

History and Public Memory in America
  by Wilfred M. McClay, Tulane University

Integrating the World: Cold War Intellectuals and the Politics of Identity
  by Christopher Shannon, the George Eastman House

A Pragmatist's Progress? Richard Rorty and American Intellectual History
  by John Pettegrew, Lehigh University

Ralph Waldo Emerson and the Problem of Democracy
  by Peter S. Field, Tennessee Technological University

The Murder of Joy: Paul Goodman and the American Battle over Maturity
  by Robert Oliver, University of Wisconsin, Madison

The Public and Protagonist: Tocqueville and American Intellectuals, 1835–2000
  by Matthew Mancini, Southwest Missouri State University

When All the Gods Trembled

Darwinism, Scopes, and American Intellectuals

Paul K. Conkin

ROWMAN & LITTLEFIELD PUBLISHERS, INC.
Lanham • Boulder • New York • Oxford

ROWMAN & LITTLEFIELD PUBLISHERS, INC.

Published in the United States of America
by Rowman & Littlefield Publishers, Inc.
4720 Boston Way, Lanham, Maryland 20706

12 Hid's Copse Road
Cumnor Hill, Oxford OX2 9JJ, England

British Library Cataloguing in Publication Information Available

Library of Congress Cataloging-in-Publication Data

Conkin, Paul Keith.
    When all the gods trembled : Darwinism, Scopes, and American
intellectuals / Paul K. Conkin
        p.   cm.—(American intellectual culture)
    Includes bibliographical references and index.
    ISBN 0–8476–9063–6 (cloth : alk. paper)
    1. Religion and science—United States—History—20th century.
2. United States—Intellectual life—20th century.   3. United States—
Religion—1901–1945.   4. Human evolution—Religious aspects—
Christianity—History—20th century.   5. Scopes, John Thomas—Trials,
litigation, etc.   6. Darwin, Charles, 1809–1882.   I. Title.   II. Series.
BL245.C66 1998
291.1'75—dc21   98-27694
                                                                          CIP

Printed in the United States of America

♾ ™ The paper used in this publication meets the minimum requirements of
American National Standard for Information Sciences—Permanence of Paper
for Printed Library Materials, ANSI Z39.48–1984.

CONTENTS

PREFACE

This is a book about gods, not a single god. Yet it is not a book about polytheists. Most of the people whose beliefs I summarize in this book were monotheists. Most were very much in the tradition of a mature Judaism. They believed that only one god existed, even when, according to various strategies, they tried to gain many of the benefits of polytheism (as when Christians use the Trinity doctrine to gain the solace of one divine Father and creator, of Jesus as a mediatorial and approachable Son, and of the Holy Spirit as a type of divine presence in the world). In fact, a monotheistic assumption is so deeply ingrained as to shape almost all talk about gods in the Christian West. Yet, on close investigation, various Christians have always held quite varied images or conceptions of what they assume to be the one and only God. In the early twentieth century, the number and diversity of such images and conceptions exploded. God talk had never been as confusing. But never had the array of gods faced more intimidating intellectual challenges. Quite literally, they all trembled.

What follows are six essays. They involve large, often cosmic issues. They involve a challengeable assumption—that the most foundational beliefs of Americans, almost all of which derive from the Judeo-Christian tradition, faced such an array of intellectual challenges in the late nineteenth and early twentieth centuries as to amount to a major crisis of faith. This crisis first climaxed in the mid-1920s, but the issues have remained at the very center of cultural conflict. The crisis involved the credentials of age-old beliefs in the existence of a god, in a world that exhibits some extrinsic or intrinsic purpose, in the divine origin and special destiny of humans, and in moral values that have some trans-human sanction.

My purpose is simple. In the first three chapters I have tried to show some aspects of a developing crisis involving these foundational beliefs.

I begin with what has to be a hurried introduction to the origins of these beliefs, particularly beliefs about the gods and about human origins, or beliefs that are common to the three great Semitic religions (for the sake of brevity, I refer to this as the "Semitic cosmology"). I also survey early challenges to these beliefs, particularly in biblical studies and the natural sciences. This leads to a chapter on Charles Darwin's thesis about the origin of organic species, and in particular the origin of self-conscious humans. My purpose is to break through most conventional, and often misleading, understandings of Darwin in order to probe the logical credential of his thesis and the exact implications it had for the Semitic cosmology. In retrospect, I believe his work, both when understood or even when blatantly misunderstood, had more impact on the erosion of this cosmology, at least among intellectuals, than any other innovation, although biblical criticism would be a close second and new developments in the physical sciences a distant third.

Among other consequences, the new understanding of the organic world helped aggravate developing tensions among American Christians, particularly Protestant Christians. The developing cleavages, between orthodox, evangelical, or fundamentalist Christians, on the one hand, and liberals or modernists, on the other, has remained, or even deepened, into a major cultural fault line at the end of the twentieth century. I try, in one chapter, to clarify the issues, to bare the definitional problems, and to set the stage for the so-called fundamentalist crusade of the twenties.

In an often confused way, these tensions helped create the enormous public interest in the Scopes trial of 1925. Finally, with the aid of some excellent recent scholarship, we now know almost everything there is to know about what happened in the small town of Dayton, in east Tennessee (I was born in east Tennessee just four years after this famous trial). I have tried to summarize the events of the trial and to offer an original perspective on it. I follow this with two essays on the intellectual debates that punctuated the twenties and that were often provoked by either Christian fundamentalism or by the Scopes trial. In the first of these two essays (Chapter 4), I develop a dialogue among the three most representative Christian intellectuals of the decade, an orthodox John Gresham Machen, a liberal Harry Emerson Fosdick, and a modernist Shailer Mathews. In the final chapter, I survey a somewhat more diverse group of intellectuals who rejected any version of theism and, in most cases, were particularly harsh in their evaluations of Christian modernism.

This is a book largely about intellectuals. This means that it fits the series of which it is a part. By "intellectuals," I refer to an unclearly bounded class, which includes individuals who are deeply involved in the life of the mind; who are at the forefront of developments in philosophy, the sciences, and the humanities; who teach in the leading universities or staff various research firms or think tanks; and who try to interpret intellectual innovations to a wider, literate public through the print media. Such intellectuals constitute a type of cultural elite. Therefore, this book is about elites. It is also, as some readers will note, a book almost entirely about white men. They were the ones involved with the issues that are central to this book. They made up all the prominent philosophers and theologians, and most scientists. Even though women outnumbered men in the churches, as late as the 1920s they rarely attended seminaries or held prominent leadership positions. I could find no influential woman modernist or fundamentalist, unless one somehow, and with limited justification, classifies Aimee Semple McPherson as a fundamentalist. Later, both women and blacks would reject such exclusion and become very much a part of contemporary debates about religious and philosophical issues, but this did not happen during or prior to the twenties.

I began this book, and to an extent finished it, with some disillusionment with the way American intellectuals treated the cultural conflict of the twenties. So much was at stake. In some sense, the foundations of Western civilization were crumbling. Honest people, no matter how reluctantly, had to give up on one consoling certainty after another. The loss was great, the possible gains for humanity unsure and precarious. This seems to me to define a tragic situation, in the sense that there were no good answers, no way out of a virtual trap created by what Walter Lippmann so aptly referred to as the "acids of modernity." But in the twenties, and even today, in a wide range of literature, I still most often meet an irresponsibly irenic response or apology. The new and the old, so the conventional message goes, when fully or properly understood, do not conflict. One can reconcile both. Or, in a language that reflects either stupidity or a deliberate refusal to define terms and think rigorously, I confront ad nauseam the assertion that "science" and "religion" do not conflict.

Such assertions are not necessarily wrong, since they beg a precise and necessarily stipulated definition of loaded terms, or exactly what I never find in such assertions. If one means by "religion" some traditional version of Christianity, and most protagonists seemed to have had such in mind, then it is obvious that, by 1925, a whole range of new, generally accepted knowledge undermined or subverted these traditional beliefs. In the sense of believability, of widespread acceptance, the gods were dying all around, even as clever theologians kept creating new ones, usually with an eye to what characteristics would be most consistent with new forms of historical or scientific knowledge or new philosophical or critical fashions.

As John Crowe Ransom argued in the twenties, reconciliationist strategies were almost conspiratorial. That is, an American intellectual establishment, made up of academics, working scientists, and modernist Christians, joined with one another to deny any basis of cultural conflict. They feared populistic reaction, for the victims would be intellectuals like themselves. Thus, instead of a carefully nuanced analysis of the issues at stake, they tried, through loose language and fuzzy logic, to glue together incompatibles and deny any basis for conflict. Part of this strategy required that they paint orthodox and traditional Christians as ill-informed or unenlightened. Then, in an often unintentional patronizing way, they tried to enlighten them. By my observation, such a strategy has remained dominant in textbooks, in most popular periodicals, and even in debates on college campuses. It has become more hypocritical as an increasing number of academic intellectuals have personally rejected any form of theism.

My purpose, in this little book, is to confront the issues as clearly as possible and to eschew easy or irenic answers. It makes no sense to talk about religion without clearly identifying a specific religion with its beliefs and practices. I try to do just this. It is useless, and almost always confusing, to refer to "God," without a very clear description of what god one means by that capitalized and singular term. I will consistently refer to gods. It is confusing to talk about scientific knowledge, unless one specifies exactly what forms of explanation, or what methods of verification, qualify any statement as scientific. I will make such distinctions, particularly in my explication of Darwin's *Origin of Species*. My task, in this largely interpretive effort, is to achieve a high level of analytic rigor and conceptual precision, not to introduce much new empirical knowledge. I hope to encourage new insights into, or new ways of understanding, very complex and vitally important issues.

I believe, with George Santayana, that almost all of the deepest secrets about our collective identity, in the West, lurk within the complex Judeo-Christian tradition. I also believe that this tradition is a font of beauty and wisdom. But many of the foundational beliefs, including the cosmology that once grounded this tradition, are simply no longer believable to an increasing number of people. For them, these lost beliefs have the status of myths. The beauty of these lost beliefs may remain a human adornment, but when based on recognized myths, the beauty often has a bittersweet quality. Much, even most, of the practical wisdom, the moral preferences, that guide our society derive from these beliefs. Yet to affirm that wisdom without the theistic foundations is to recognize that some of the assurance and certainty is thereby lost and that humans, if all alone in a world ever beyond their full understanding, have to take full responsibility for their moral standards. They cannot appeal to any authority. They live in a world without providential guidance, a world full of not only irony, but often also of tragedy, for it is a world that exhibits no purpose, moves toward no preordained goal, and provides no promise of human redemption.

INTRODUCTION:
CHRISTIAN COSMOLOGIES

Humans alone among mammals are self-conscious. They know themselves in relationship to other people and to the objects around them.
Their self-concept is shaped by what happened in the past, even when
unknown, and also by their perception of what happened. Much that
one never thinks about is nonetheless a product of the past, including
basic beliefs and preferences. Only when in doubt, or challenged, are
humans likely to spend much time thinking about who they are. At that
point they become historians, in the sense that they consciously look
back to the near or distant past. Only by doing this can they clarify their
own identity, as individuals, and as part of a family, clan, nation, or
religious community. Even the most primitive peoples have stories about
the origin and development of their clan. By the conventions of modern
scholarship, they may have insufficient evidence to support such stories.
But the scholarly standing of such recounted memories is a different
issue than the indispensable role they play in uniting people in communities. Such stories are often terribly important to people. They carefully
pass them on to children, or fight wars to defend them against competing

stories that, in some sense, subvert their own sense of roots, their moral self-complacency, or their fondest aspirations and goals.

Although rarely noted, the ability to arbitrate among competing perceptions of a group's past, or to control what young people learn about that past, is vitally important in any society. Look at the present Arab-Israeli conflict. Look at all the battles over history standards for the public schools. This control over understanding the past is most charged, seems most critical, when the issue is human origins, as exemplified in over a hundred years of debate in the United States over the teaching of evolutionary theories in our public schools. Here the problem of origins involves not only how humans understand their common identity, but, when the traditional understanding of origins dovetails with the central traditions of a great historic religion, even their chance for salvation.

For centuries, almost everyone within the cultural orbit of the three great Semitic religions (Judaism, Christianity, and Islam) found a rarely challenged, although not fully coherent, answer to questions about origins in the opening stories of the Book of Genesis in the Jewish Scriptures. We do not know who wrote and then later edited these stories, from what primitive sources the authors derived them, or even when the stories first assumed written form. But they are clearly rooted in the history of the ancient Jews.

The origins of Israel, of a people and a religion, is the subject of continuing scholarly controversy. The Jewish Scriptures, or what Christians somewhat unfairly denominate as an "Old Testament," contain detailed but often confused accounts. Scholars are unable to assess the accuracy of most of the biblical record before the era of Saul and David, or roughly 1000 B.C.E. From that point on, secular sources largely corroborate the overall sequence of personalities and events contained in the Jewish Bible. This does not mean that later Jewish editors, who selectively made use of older chronicles or official records, had factual accuracy as a controlling goal. They clearly shaped the historical account in behalf of later political and religious purposes. The process of selecting and editing lasted for centuries. Jewish scholars established the final Hebrew canon only after the beginnings of the Christian Era.

The first extant record of a Jewish people in Palestine dates from 1220 B.C.E. Egyptian troops reported the defeat of Israel. Clearly, by then, enclaves of Jews held territory in Palestine, alongside numerous Canaanite city-states. In the next two hundred years the Jews were able to gain reasonably secure control over about half of Palestine. Eventually it would be these Jews who would frame the stories about the origins of the earth, of life on earth, and of humans that are now encoded in the opening sections of the Book of Genesis.

Whatever their historical credentials, these two creation stories eventually became a critical heritage of the Jewish people, at the very heart of their sense of communal identity and of religious exceptionalism. The prehistorical parts of Genesis include not only the creation accounts but the saga of the first humans, Adam and Eve, and their banishment from a garden in Eden; the age of the long-lived patriarchs, particularly Noah, who survived a worldwide flood in his ark of deliverance; Noah's sons who became the founders of various nations; and the Tower of Babel and the fragmentation of languages. These accounts are mythical in several senses. They are not always specific as to place and never as to time; they are at points obviously symbolic; and they share much detail with other Mesopotamian religions, as best illustrated by numerous flood epics. In present form, few of these early sections of Genesis date from an early stage of Jewish religious development, although they may reflect very ancient myths.

What readers may easily overlook is that this mythic section of Genesis is about a period before the origins of Israel or the emergence of a Jewish religion. It is about people who had not yet received any covenant or promise from a god, had not yet received any law from Sinai, had not yet developed any organized religion with scriptures or rituals. Yet, at various places, the story is informed by a later Judaism. It is, in this sense, a peculiarly Jewish account of an ancient age.

The creation stories in Genesis are quite complex. It is impossible to identify authors or the time of composition for two quite different and extended opening accounts, as well as for several later biblical references to creation. Yet textual study by scholars has allowed some plausible speculations about the two main texts. The Book of Genesis, as a whole, reveals by language and content what seems to be at least three different merged texts. Because of the different name given to the deity in two of these, scholars have often identified E and J texts. In content and language, they seem very ancient. Some may draw upon oral traditions that date from the early conquests of Canaanite towns. In the E sections, the plural Canaanite term, "Elohim," is the name of the creator god. But the creation story in Genesis 1, which refers to the work of Elohim, is not one of the E texts, which appear only later in Genesis. Since this version of creation has so many Jewish markers, beginning with the Sabbatarian motif, scholars attribute it to later redactors or editors in the period of a more mature Judaism, or no earlier than the Babylonian exile (after 586 B.C.E.) and perhaps just after it. These priestly, or P, texts seem to reflect a true monotheism. The other more ancient Judean sections in Genesis, referred to as the "J texts," contain the four consonants (YHVH) in all references to a creator god (this title is often translated as Yahweh or, in English, as Jehovah). It is a J text that includes the creation story that begins at Genesis 2:5.

Genesis opens with the priestly (P) version of creation. It depicts the handiwork of a personal, masculine, and providential god—Elohim. Although the priestly editors clearly intended this plural name to refer to a single deity, it is possible that the E text that they drew from still reflected elements of Canaanite polytheism. This Elohim first created an earth dark and without form. Whether he did this during the first of six days of creation or long before is not clear from the text. In any case, in six frenzied days of artistry, he formed night and day, separated the land and the waters, filled the land with plants, formed the sun and moon to illumine the earth, added fish and birds and mammals, and on the sixth day formed the first but unnamed humans, male and female, in his own image. Elohim liked his work, and on the seventh day he rested.

What follows is the more ancient, or at least less edited, J story. This story contains neither six days of creation nor Sabbatarian motifs. After forming heaven and the earth, which was originally without vegetation and with no human to till the ground, Yahweh had a flood or mist from the ground come up and water the surface and form streams. He craved a garden. Since he needed someone to till his planned garden, he sculpted out of soil the first man, whom he called Adam, and breathed into him the breath of life. Yahweh then planted his first garden in Eden, apparently a geographic region of ancient Mesopotamia. Adam was to tend the trees and plants but not eat the fruit of one of two centrally located trees—that of knowledge of good and evil (the other tree was the tree of life, the fruit of which assured one immortality). Adam was lonely. So the master of Eden created birds and animals, which Adam named. Adam was still lonely, without a fitting companion. So the Lord took a rib from Adam and from it formed his companion, Eve.

Of the two accounts, the former—with its much more cosmic and less human-like god, its Sabbatarian themes, and its implied monotheism—has most influenced Western cosmologies. But the more primitive J story provides the setting—Eden—for the most dramatic story in Genesis: that of the temptation of Adam and Eve and their eating of the fruit of the tree of knowledge of good and evil. As Yahweh said, this made them like gods. As he walked in the cool of the evening, he became aware of their disobedience. Since he had assessed mortality as the cost of eating this fruit, he cast them from Eden before they could eat of the tree of life. Adam and Eve's disobedience enabled them to become human; they were now morally self-conscious and had to face death. Adam also had to till the earth by means of hard labor, and Eve, through pain, to bear children and begin filling the earth with people.

This story of expulsion from Eden has informed a range of critical Christian doctrines. Not all Christians view the expulsion as a fall or locate in it the source of original sin. Mormons honor Adam and rejoice in the opportunities that mortality offered humans. Questions remain. Why did the Lord of Eden warn Adam and Eve against eating the fruit of the tree of knowledge of good and evil? Was it to protect them? Possibly not. He knew what all students learn—that the sweet but dangerous fruit of knowledge is very addictive. If we feast long enough on it, we will join in killing all our tribal gods—that is, all personlike, willful, gendered gods. Thus, one logical answer is that Jehovah sought to preserve Adam and Eve's innocence, not out of solicitude for them, but in an effort to protect himself. Had Adam and Eve eaten of the tree of life, with its gift of immortality, and still retained their ability to procreate, Jehovah would indeed have been endangered.

The new earth, everywhere fertile and bountiful like Eden, sustained a race of very long-lived humans. Soon they fell into iniquity. Then Jehovah created rain and used a great flood to destroy the face of this first earth. Only Noah's family, and representatives of various species, survived in a big boat. After the flood, the earth soon lost most of its earlier fertility, and thus within a few generations human longevity declined to one-tenth of its former length. Noah's descendants began human history all over again. That history is our history.

These early chapters of Genesis make up the greatest story ever told, the most significant history ever written. Here is the most influential part of the Bible. Rooted here are some of the most basic assumptions of Western humankind, assumptions scarcely open even to doubt until the eighteenth and nineteenth centuries. Hardly anyone even loosely within one of the three Semitic religious traditions can fully divest herself of all the meanings tied to these Genesis accounts.

In no sense was this founding cosmology distinctively Christian. Christianity began with another story, one framed and shaped by this Semitic cosmology but not necessitated by it. This was a story about Jesus of Nazareth. His early disciples believed he was the Messiah (in Greek the Christ) foretold by Jewish prophets. This identity, plus stories about his sacrificial and atoning death and his resurrection from the dead, became the foundation of a new scheme of salvation and a new world religion. For the next 1,700 years, Christians argued, at times fought, over the exact details of this doctrinal and salvation religion. In the background remained the Genesis cosmology, undoubted and uncontested.

However divergent in details, the two creation stories in Genesis have much in common. Each is theistic if not clearly monotheistic. The masculine creator has the attributes of personality, of thought, will, purpose, and appetite. He is not a pure mind or spirit, whatever one means by "spirit." Early Jews did not believe in any separate mental or spiritual realm. This theistic perspective makes the physical universe dependent, contingent—"created" in the words of the Jews, or a way of thinking that survives to the present—but not in any sense accidental or without direction. As a created entity, it has a purpose given to it by the creator. Humans, as creatures, also fulfill a divine purpose, but they alone are self-conscious about these purposes and alone fulfill them through choices. For humans, time flows from meaning toward meaning. Events cumulate toward ends. All is providential. In the context of divine purpose, of a type of nonphysical necessity, events have significance based on when they occur. This is only to say that the worldview reflected in formative Jewish mythology was nontragic in its implications for humanity. It supported an emphatically moral or political outlook, as well as a very historically oriented outlook. One is a very exceptional person in the West who does not still reflect many of these beliefs.

One important commonality remained in what soon became a rich diversity of images or conceptions of a god or gods. Both creation stories involved an agent, with the humanlike qualities of will and purpose. Purpose implies self-consciousness and the ability to make plans and to carry them out. Thus only humans or gods can be true agents. They alone can purposefully manipulate and direct events toward chosen goals. In all versions of the Semitic cosmology, will and intent were present. Words like "creation," "providence," "design," and "selection" fit. In the most primitive, and still almost irresistible, sense of the word, what happened had a "cause," for behind all outcomes was an agent actively working in behalf of certain goals. Jehovah committed himself to certain causes, even as we commit ourselves to causes and try desperately to fulfill them. Gods, perhaps almost by definition, succeed. We often do not.

As written, the two Genesis stories of creation seem to involve two gods, Elohim and Jehovah. Yet the Jewish priests and scribes who ultimately compiled the Torah believed in the existence of only one god. For them, Elohim and Jehovah were simply two different names, and inadequate names, for a single deity. In all three Semitic religions, such a monotheistic understanding has prevailed. Yet the cosmic god depicted in Genesis 1 is very different than the lord of the plantation in Genesis 2. Thus, I suspect that the original stories reflected traditions about at least two Mesopotamian gods and that the Elohim passages may well have reflected Canaanite beliefs in a family of related gods, not one god.

One of the continuing legacies of this cosmology is a confusion in almost all popular language about gods—the common use of the generic term, "god," as if it were a proper name, or God. In our society, almost everyone, atheists as often as avowed theists, refer to "God," with the term always capitalized. A monotheistic assumption is built into this word use. People are often surprised, or even confused, when I ask which god they are talking about and what the name of the god they affirm, or deny, really is, if it or he or she has a name.

I find dozens of different gods among modern Christians. Some are closely related, have many overlapping characteristics. Others are not even cousins. I find no overlap, for example, between the Divine Spirit of Christian Science and the fully material deity of Adventists. Yet, both Christian Scientists and Adventists refer to their god by the singular, capitalized word, "God." I also find that most Christians, except Mormons, profess a belief in only one god, but in their worship and devotional life, they act like polytheists. That is, they relate to various divine beings, not only the three persons of their Trinity, but to Mary, or to guardian angels, or to saints, or, in a negative sense, to Satan. The exact identity of a single deity is often blurred, and for good reason. It is all but impossible to frame a fully coherent image of a god who is, at one and the same time, the ultimate reality, the creator of all phenomena, and also humanlike and gendered.

What does creation entail? Throughout the history of the Church, most Christians have affirmed that their god (various as the reference may be) created the universe and humans, not out of existing matter, but as they sometimes say, out of nothing (ex nihilo). If matter preceded divine creation, or set limits to it, then the creator was not all powerful, and thus in some sense had to be finite and limited (only Mormons accept this limitation). But "nothing" is beyond our comprehension. Thus, theologians by the time of Augustine, and under the influence of Greek philosophy, had moved to the mature form of theism that most Christian intellectuals still affirm—that their God is the eternal ground of being. He has no origins, was the product of nothing beyond himself. What he created, therefore, had to be an outflow, expression, communication, or extension of himself. If one does not interpret literally the heavily anthropomorphic and even gendered language, this position makes sense. But humans have no way to image such an eternal ground of being, except by reference to the types of objects we directly experience. Such an infinite and all-powerful god seems abstract and unapproachable. It seems misleading, if not impious, to refer to such a ground in terms that fit humans.

An infinite ground of being, the necessity that lies behind the contingency of all phenomena, also seems far removed from the creation stories of Genesis and especially from the gendered god of Eden. Tensions among various images of a god have helped account for the breadth and appeal of the Semitic religions. Only in the nineteenth century did most Christians have to confront these tensions, and the effort helped splinter Christianity in ways not directly related to competing schemes of salvation and worship but to the foundational theism that supports all such schemes. In the wake of Charles Darwin, Christians, from many divergent denominations, were forced to explore, as never before, what they meant by the word "god." The resulting god talk could be very confusing. It still is.

It is impossible to correlate the Genesis creation stories with the gradual development of a Jewish nation and religion. It is clear that the story in Genesis 1 was a product of a mature Judaism. The Jewish Scriptures contain a complex story of national and religious origins, stretching from a legendary Abram (Abraham), who moved from Mesopotamia into the land of the Canaanites, who promised faithfulness to Yahweh, and who by covenant gained a promise that his descendants would eventually gain title to the land of Canaan. Abraham remained a nomadic herdsman, as did his son Isaac and grandson Israel (or Jacob), father of twelve sons and in time twelve tribes. The older brothers sold one beloved son, Joseph, into slavery in Egypt, where he rose high in the court of the pharaoh. He was able, later, to welcome into Egypt his aged father and forgiven brothers. But after Joseph died, the children of Israel in Egypt become virtual slaves, now yearning to be back home in Canaan. Their new hero was one Moses, who negotiated with the pharaoh to gain permission for the now large tribe of Israel to return home to the promised land of Canaan. Jehovah intervened in the negotiations, so afflicted the Egyptians with curses that Moses was able to lead his people into the Sinai desert or wilderness, there to wander for forty years. Here, according to the legend, Moses received from Jehovah the Law for the people, including the summary obligations contained in the Ten Commandments, which resided on tables in a special ark or portable tabernacle.

Moses died just as the twelve tribes prepared to enter Canaan. But under his successor, Joshua (or Jesus in the Greek language, and thus a namesake of Jesus of Nazareth), the tribes conquered the land and divided it into tribal enclaves. During the next two centuries or so, Israel had no king, the tribes sometimes warred among themselves, and, at critical junctures, judges came forward to lead the people in their endless battles with Canaanite cities or the new sea people, the Philistines, who occupied the Mediterranean coastal areas. This prenational history ended when Jehovah reluctantly granted the wishes of the people and allowed Samuel, the last and greatest of the judges, to anoint a warrior chieftain, Saul, as the first king of Israel, late in the eleventh century b.c.e.

This story of national origins is legendary and impossible to confirm by sources outside the stories accumulated and later canonized by Jews. Historians are unable to complete the story, to verify a large body of Jews in thirteenth-century Egypt, to identify the pharaoh who let the children of Israel go and then drowned with his pursuing army in the Red Sea, to confirm most of the stories about Moses, to find much evidence of the sojourn in the Sinai, or to locate the sources of a slowly developing Jewish Law. Thus the exact mixture of fact and legend in these histories remains unclear and is a continued source of scholarly conflict.

Likewise impossible is any clear description of the early Jewish religion. The main doctrines, the key holy days, the codified Law all date from well into the national period. Even then, it seems from the biblical evidence, a small elite, soon led by priests and eventually centered in Jerusalem, fought with small success to woo the common people away from a popular polytheism. Only when the Jewish elite became captives of the Babylonians and lived among aliens did they finally codify their Law, at times heed the voice of inspired prophets, develop a nontemple or synagogue type of worship, and achieve, at least at times, a religion that was close to the type of Judaism practiced among at least most Jews at the birth of Christianity. The Genesis cosmology, with all of its internal complexity, was foundational for this mature Judaism and remained foundational for Christianity.

Not that Jewish conceptions of Yahweh did not change through time. It is all but impossible to develop a full description of a Jewish religion before the Babylonian exile. But the clues in historical books that at least draw upon records or memories that predate the exile, such as 1 and 2 Samuel, suggest a relatively small coterie of priests who struggled, with limited success, to establish a henotheistic religion of Jehovah. This primitive Jehovah required obedience to arbitrary and often very cruel demands. Central to obedience was ritual cleanliness or presentability, or the basis of later concepts of purity and holiness. For a time, the required rituals and sacrifices seemed unrelated to any ethical imperatives.

This primitive religion of Jehovah had changed little by the time of the early kingdom, or the age of David. By then, the epic of captivity and exodus and conquest had become central. The religion was already heavily sacrificial, with a developed priesthood, but one that still indulged in magic and divination. Before the building of Solomon's Temple the mobile ark and tabernacle served as a ceremonial center. To some extent, Jews already followed a code of cleanliness or presentability (women went through purification procedures after menstruation). But not present at this time, at least as revealed in the two Samuel accounts, was a codified Law, the major festivals, and any hint of true monotheism or universalism.

In the early kingdom period, Yahweh was still a very jealous, tribal, anthropomorphic god. He seemed oblivious to issues of justice, condemned the polytheism that remained normative among the masses of people, and dealt largely with the kings, whose behavior won or lost his favor, with the people either prospering or suffering. Up through the time of David and Solomon, polytheism remained widespread among the Jews. Even David's wives kept their household gods (idols) on their beds, and only later did prophets and priests denounce such gods and try to remove them from homes. Both Saul and David became involved in wild dances, in which they joined with ecstatic bands of prophets, even stripping off their clothes and dancing naked. Male prostitutes frequented rural shrines. Even the sons of the prophet Samuel had sexual intercourse with women who served at the entrance to the tabernacle that contained the ark of the covenant (this means that the early religion still featured temple prostitution, like many of the Canaanite cults). Ghosts and spirits abounded. Oblique references suggest the late survival of human sacrifices. The leading men of Israel married numerous wives or bought or captured concubines. Above all, Ashtoreth and Baal, plus other goddesses and gods, retained an irresistible appeal, as did the high places, the totemic poles, and all manner of idols that accompanied the rich polytheistic religion of Canaan.

Then came the Prophets. Beginning just before the fall of the northern half of the now divided Jewish lands (the kingdom of Israel) to Assyria in 721, a group of denunciatory teachers or preachers, now known as the "literary prophets" (their teachings have survived), began to reform the early religion. They stressed Jehovah's demands for justice, thus giving ethical content to the religion. In times of adversity, they dreamed of a restored kingdom, thus adding a utopian motif. As the Babylonians successfully besieged and twice captured Jerusalem, thus ending the independence of the small kingdom of Judah, the prophet Jeremiah began to emphasize a personal, rather than a communal or national relationship with Jehovah. During the captivity of the leading intellectuals and politicians in Babylon, prophets in the tradition of Jeremiah helped begin the synagogue tradition, a type of teaching and worship to substitute for the temple and sacrifices. Finally, as the new Persian empire allowed captive peoples, such as the Jews, to return home and restore their traditional religions, a few prophets began to move Judaism toward a universalist outlook, or to a true monotheism. By then, the exile intellectuals had fully codified the Jewish Law and had probably collected and edited the first five books of the later Jewish canon (the Torah) into something close to their present form.

After some, but never all, the captive Jewish elite returned to Palestine, Judaism would have two intellectual centers: Jerusalem and Babylon. The exiles, in defensive isolation, had created the first mature Judaism. Back home, they had difficulty gaining an expected level of zeal and orthodoxy among the people of the land, the ordinary folk who remained in Judah during the time of the exile. At times, the elite moved toward a very nationalistic and exclusive emphasis, with losing efforts to stamp out intermarriage with non-Jews. But at least a few Jews now wanted the religion of Jehovah to be a world religion and came to conceive of Jehovah as the god of all people, not just the Jews. The beautiful story of Ruth, the faithful Moabite daughter-in-law, and the parable of Jonah both taught an openness to other peoples. Most of all, an eloquent, poetic prophet, whose writing makes up chapters 40–55 of the Book of Isaiah, reinterpreted the motif of a chosen people. Now, at a time of redemption, he argued that Israel had been chosen by Jehovah to nurture and mature a religion for all humankind. Through cycles of obedience and disobedience, it had completed this task. Jehovah was the god of all peoples on earth; and, by implication, the religious insights of Israel, as matured by the Prophets, would now be shared with the whole world. It did not happen that way. The late prophets kept the universalist outlook but with a much more begrudging attitude toward Gentiles. But it would be the reinterpreted message of this Isaiah that most influenced a later Christianity and that also provided an understanding of the sacrificial role or mission of Jesus of Nazareth.

For two centuries, Judea survived as a Persian province. We have so few records from this period that it is impossible to chart any changes in the Jewish conception of a deity. In 331 B.C.E. Alexander the Great conquered Palestine, and from then until a successful revolt after 168 B.C.E., Judea remained under Greek control. In this Hellenistic period, the Jewish religion fragmented into competing sects or factions, and Jewish intellectuals assimilated Greek ideas. For the first time, Jews adopted motifs from mystery religions, including a belief in the resurrection of the righteous to live again in a new, Davidic kingdom, one to be ushered in by a divine deliverer or Messiah. This resurrection doctrine, almost normative by the time of Jesus, found its first expression in a new literary genre, apocalyptic writings.

Apocalyptic writers expressed, or expanded upon, such late prophetic themes as an omnipotent and cosmic deity who catered not just to the Jews, but to the righteous in all nations. In fact, apocalyptic writers introduced a more general vocabulary into their theology and typically turned to nature and all its wonders to illustrate God's power. Yahweh seems an inappropriate name for a cosmic deity who presides over the starry heavens and works his will through horrible natural catastrophes, who plays not only with empires and nations but with the orbits of suns and moons. Apocalyptic writers moved far from the governmental deity of ancient Israel, the god who above all else issued commands and asked for dutiful obedience.

Early Christians did not inherit any one, precise conception of a god from the Jews. Cosmological issues were too much in flux in the Hellenistic age, and various religious and cultural traditions too interactive, for any one view to dominate. What Christians had was a rich but complex tradition, with only a few essential characteristics. By the early Christian Era, Jews in all the competing factions were fervent monotheists. They believed only one god existed, however many gods the Gentiles professed. This god was, at least to some extent, still personal and masculine. Although Hellenistic Jews interacted with Greek philosophers, particularly in Alexandria, they had not yet clearly accepted Greek beliefs in a fully separable mind or soul. Thus, whatever the difference in details, their god was still a person. Above all, he was still the creator and governor of the whole world. The creative and providential motifs of Genesis

1 remained. He was also a god who directly intervened in human affairs, as he had done constantly in the history of Israel. Differently expressed, he was a god of miracles or special providences. He was also a god with a special relationship to humans. He accepted their sacrifices, listened to their prayers.

Most of these Jewish themes would continue in the Christian Church, or at least in the Church that matured by the fourth century. But not without challenges. In the second century, a widespread but never unified group of Christians reflected many of the world-weary themes of Greek mystery religions and thus could not identify with the creator and governing deity of the Jews. These so-called Gnostic Christians often repudiated the Jewish Scriptures and either rejected the Jehovah of Judaism or conceived of him as an evil god, one responsible for an evil world. They divinized the Christ, often by minimizing his human traits. The Gnostics lost. If they had won, Christianity would have been a very different religion, and the Genesis stories, the basic Jewish view of origins, would never have become central to the new religion.

Complicating the images of god even more was the intimidating role of Greek philosophy. The Greeks, more than earlier peoples, began asking probing questions about the nature of reality. Some flirted with a deep skepticism about any truth claims. Many turned away, in disbelief, from the polytheistic gods of Olympus. Some, such as the Stoics, created a type of philosophical religion, austere in its moral demands. Most enduring would be the closely related beliefs of Plato and Aristotle. In a sense, they created the two most important metaphysical traditions in the ancient world, traditions that inescapably influenced the development of Christian theology, or attempts to rationalize critical Christian doctrines, particularly those relating to Jehovah and Jesus. Yet neither Plato nor Aristotle identified ultimate reality with a personal god. But both did believe in a reality above the physical world (unlike Greek materialistic philosophers).

Plato believed that the highest reality transcended the imperfect world of existence. Timeless, universal essences or ideas did provide the form for imperfect objects in the material world. Humans, because of mind or self-consciousness, shared in the higher reality of these pure forms and in a type of intuition, or even a type of recall of what their minds had once known directly, they could grasp at least some of these ideas. These ideas, at the most simple level, consisted in the forms that gave an identity to objects (they were the nouns in our language). But more important were relational forms or ideas and, finally, unifying or normative ideas, with the "good" the most regulative. The world of material objects makes up a shadow world, a reflection of universal ideas. Experience of things, or empirical knowledge, though useful for fulfilling animal needs, never in itself leads to the highest truth. In various forms, this Platonic theory of ideas would be parent of almost all Western forms of idealism.

Aristotle agreed with Plato on the priority of ideas or forms. But he believed human apprehension of them came, in the way of inferences, from experience, from an encounter with the world of objects. He embraced no form of intuitive truth. But knowledge of our experienced world, all the way up to celestial bodies, led him to infer an ultimate object, perfect and luminous, that pulled all objects toward its perfection. This teleological mover, or divine mind, capped his system of philosophy. By the time of the early Church, latter-day disciples of Plato (middle Platonists) had conflated Aristotle and Plato. The ideas of Aristotle's prime mover were identified with the Platonic ideals. This brought Platonic thought closer to a type of rarified theism, since the perfect ideas now cohered with a thinking mind. But note that no one in this classic philosophical tradition identified these conceptions of ultimate reality with a personal god.

Christian theologians would made this connection. Intimations of it are present in Paul and even more in the Gospel of John. In fact, some aspects of Platonic thought, although possibly derived most directly from Jewish intellectuals at Alexandria, proved indispensable in rationalizing later Trinitarian doctrines (Jesus was by then identified with the ideas of a creator god, ideas that provided the blueprint or form or soul for all the created world, or what some called the Logos). But the ultimate ideas identified by Plato, the prime mover of Aristotle, the world soul or Logos of middle Platonists, or the later, infinite One of Neoplatonists had little apparent relationship to the personal god of the Jews or, for that matter to the various deities present in the myriad religions of the Greco-Roman world. Yet the philosophers did set a task for the Church, one rejected as unnecessary by many early Church fathers, but one almost necessarily embraced in the battle against Gnostics and other perceived heretics: finding ways of rationalizing, or even demonstrating or proving, the central beliefs of the Church. Christianity not only became a heavily doctrinal religion (much more so than Judaism), but also one that would spawn several theological traditions.

Pre-Hellenistic Jews, at least as far as their literature reveals, never developed, perhaps never felt the need for, any systematic justification of their belief in Jehovah. Their literature is rich in images of their god and, in this sense, theologically pregnant. But Jehovah seemed so much a reality in their life and experience that they did not need to prove his existence, although on occasion they tried to demonstrate his superiority over Canaanite deities. Hellenistic Jews, as they divided into factions, or tried to come to terms with Greek culture, had to begin the theological enterprise. Most of this appeared in wisdom literature. Also, in the heterogeneous mix of cultures, deep doubts surfaced. Some of these doubts even made it into the Jewish canon, such as Job's profound doubts, not about Jehovah's existence, but about his righteousness and the possibility of any final justice, and the deep, cynical skepticism reflected by the unknown author of Ecclesiastes. By the time Paul wrote his critical letter to the Romans, in the mid-first century, justification of what one believed already seemed necessary. He drew upon Greek philosophical tools in his vindication of the power and justice of his god. He tried to make the new Christian religion respectable among gentile intellectuals. In this sense, he was the first Christian theologian.

From the Greeks until Immanuel Kant, in the late eighteenth century, most Western philosophers had not only believed in the existence of a god, but believed they could frame rational proofs for such existence. The strategies varied. But in all cases the proofs were for the existence of a prime mover or first cause, for a final goal, for some ground of being, for the necessity that lay behind contingency. Such rational proofs had little relevance for most believers, whose interaction with a god required no more vindication than one's dealing with a parent. More important, the ultimate principles justified, whether by compelling logic or not, were far removed from the personal, masculine Jehovah of the Jewish tradition, let alone the complex Trinitarian God of the fourth-century Church. The champion of theistic proofs, Thomas Aquinas, acknowledged that the god of philosophical reasoning was not, by any principle of reason, the God of the Church. Only direct divine revelation, in Scripture, or the Holy Spirit, or the teachings of the Church, or intimate personal religious experience enabled the Christian to affirm that the rational principle and the personal deity were one.

Thus, the images that early Christians had of their God were quite varied. Some of the subtle differences are clear even in the New Testament. Theological discourse simply amplified the differences. All that one can do is set certain parameters for a Christian God. To do this is arbitrary, given the wide range of theistic beliefs among avowed Christians. As understood by most Christians before the nineteenth century, in various doctrinal traditions, the Christian God was the ultimate or highest reality, unbounded, eternal, beyond full human comprehension. He was also the source or creator of all finite being and in full control of all history. Yet the Christian God was also personal, in the sense of having a will and purpose, and thus anthropomorphic or humanlike. As the pronoun suggests, he was masculine, whatever masculinity entails. The Christian God, by being a person, could not be a pure mind or spirit, whatever one means by such. Yet, paradoxically, he could not be limited by any materiality, which would restrict him to some place and subordinate him to the material components that he shares with earthly creatures. The Christian God had a special relationship with humans, unlike that with other of his creatures. He had taken an active role in their career on earth, had shown special solicitude to at least some humans, and had revealed himself to humans in a special way. Finally, he had promised some form of salvation to faithful or obedient humans, whatever "salvation" means.

One may protest that such a complex concept of god is incoherent, full of tensions or even contradictions. This is true. It is impossible to merge an infinite ground of being, even if it is in some sense mindlike, with a manlike God who is a father to humans, concerned about the life of every individual, and even willing to answer petitionary prayers. As Reinhold Niebuhr confessed, the Christian God does not match any rational criteria. But it is the very richness, whatever the tensions, that has characterized Christian views of a god and that has helped account for the diverse appeal of various versions of Christian theism. Jesus, as a mediating Son of God, helped bridge some of the tensions. But the relationship of Jesus to the traditional Jewish God raised such an array of new issues as to make most Christian views of God even more complex, as demonstrated in the three-hundred-year effort to mature an acceptable Trinity formula.

Today, many people who use the label "Christian" as a mark of self identity obviously do not believe in a supernatural god who reflects even the minimal characteristics listed above. In fact, one almost defining trait of "modernists" has been their rejection of some of these traits, such as the elements of corporeality and gender that were part of the traditional definition. Such dissent from tradition does not necessarily mean that modernists are not Christian (this depends on how one defines "Christian"). Note that the above characterization of the traditional Christian God sets only very broad and general boundaries. Unitarians and Trinitarians, Roman Catholics and Protestants, Calvinists and Arminians have all affirmed these minimal defining traits. Note also that the above definitional boundaries derive from, and are consistent with, at least most of the images of God in the Jewish Scriptures and in the Christian New Testament, but, although biblically grounded, this definitional framework does not require any literal or inerrant view of the Bible.

Belief in a God who created the earth and humans, and who determined the course of historical events, remained the most central or defining belief of the Christian West until at least the nineteenth century. This foundational belief was shared with Jews and Moslems. Christian conceptions of Jesus and the salvation he offered made up the distinctively Christian superstructure. Most divisions within the Western Church implicated subtly different conceptions of this creator God, but they were ostensibly tied to controversies about distinctively Christian beliefs, including the scheme of salvation. Only in the eighteenth century did any large or influential number of intellectuals challenge the distinctive beliefs of Christianity. Self-proclaimed rationalists rejected the miracles of the New Testament and could neither understand nor believe the more subtle doctrines of the Church, which they viewed as superstitious or overly subtle and abstract. Some did admire the moral teachings of Jesus. Notably, with very few exceptions, these rationalists retained a belief in a creator God, and some used the label "deist" to denote this retained theism. But such a theism, although in a sense shaped by the distant cosmology of Genesis, did not involve any literal acceptance of the two creation stories in Genesis. In one form or another, the continued belief in a god primarily rested upon the design argument—the quite intricate world around us required some purposeful creator. Otherwise, it was inexplicable. Secondary to this was a widely perceived need for rewards and punishments after death, both to fulfill the principle of ultimate justice and as a support for human moral systems.

In the eighteenth century trained historians first began to question the biblical cosmology. Bible scholars asked critical and soon very disturbing questions about the Genesis stories, and also about the Bible itself. In the nineteenth century, they began to fill in an ever more complex story about the authors of the varied biblical books, about the cultural assumptions that informed their content, about likely sources and guiding literary conventions, about the time of the original composition and of later editing, about the tortured path to an authorized Jewish and Christian canon, and about all the internal problems that surround the earliest extant texts. The unsettled dilemmas that plague such scholarship, the paucity of evidence on many subjects, means that scholarly judgments had to remain tentative and in flux. But the lack of certainty is quite distinct from the fact that we now know, with a reasonable degree of assurance, a great deal not known even a hundred years ago. The scholarly game, even though never infallible or complete, has opened up a thousand questions that anyone willing to take the Bible seriously, who wants to understand it, has to confront. It is not a settled game, but an enormously unsettling one.

At the same time, natural historians told new stories about the earth's development though time. By 1830 it was clear that the earth was very old, thousands of times older than suggested by the biblical genealogies. Over aeons of time, plants and animals had died and left organic deposits, some of which survived as fossils. These fossils, as revealed in layers of sedimentary rock, most of which began as mud on the bottom of ancient oceans, made clear that life-forms varied from age to age. Soon, distinctive layers of flora and fauna provided a way of ordering the historical sequence of rocks. Tectonic forces had meantime heaved and folded the strata, even as erosive forces had furrowed surfaces. But the sequence or column of life-forms was everywhere exemplified. Most past species were now extinct. Many present species were distinctive to our age, including a very recent emergent in the fossil record: homo sapiens. It was by then clear to most naturalists that Noah's flood never inundated the whole earth and that the two Genesis stories of creation were wonderful fables but misordered or incorrect in almost every detail.

Nineteenth-century naturalists did not easily come up with an alternative to the Semitic cosmology. One reason why this was so was the intimidating power of the older cosmology, which continued, and today continues, to condition almost everyone's understanding of origins. It has shaped our language. Even physicists now refer to the big bang as a "creation." Until after 1830, no natural historian was able to offer a widely accepted explanation for the by then well-documented past changes in flora and fauna. Thus, geologists, who were usually devout Christians, continued to rely upon a modified Genesis account to explain the origin of new species. A god created them. Thus, in this one area of natural history, naturalists still appealed to a teleological view of the universe and introduced agency and purpose, or final causes, into their accounts.

This was an old habit. Isaac Newton, who founded a new mechanics based on invariant laws of motion, never doubted that the Christian God made it so. If one wanted, not descriptions of regularities in matter but a causal explanation of why nature was as it had proved to be, one still had to turn to the Genesis cosmology. Fortunately for Christians such as Newton, such newly discovered regularities or laws did not conflict directly with any biblical histories. As Christian geologists filled in their story of successive ages of plant and animal life, they recognized a conflict with the biblical stories but generally finessed these difficulties. They tried to salvage the Genesis stories, to explain away their seeming opposition to accepted knowledge. The two most influential general strategies developed long before Darwin: the day-age theory (the six days of creation were really geological ages), and the gap theory (a vast expanse of time separated the original creation of the universe and the six days of Genesis).

At first, it was not clear that life continued from one geologic age to the next, after the possibly catastrophic extinctions that seemed to mark the boundaries between ages. Indeed, some seemingly identical species were present in successive ages. But since so many were not, it was easy to assume that a god recreated the recurring species along with all the new and appropriate species that marked each new age. Unlike in physics, where an act of creation could be singular and at the beginning, it now seemed necessary to appeal to agency and providence to account for multiple origins of life. Biologists by 1840 were out of line with physical scientists, both in the sense of major discontinuities in their stories and in their appeal to a god that seemed, at least periodically, to intervene in the earth and set life off in new directions. An appeal to causes, to agents at work, seemed to be the deus ex machina that preserved some degree of coherence in theories about organic phenomena.

Indeed, soon after 1800, such naturalists knew of evolutionary theories that preserved a principle of continuity. Most of these involved idealistic philosophies or forms of pantheism, and thus an all-pervasive teleology. Emergents in all areas, including the organic, simply reflected the outward manifestations of a divine mind. Quite different were the fully naturalistic theories of Jean Lamarck, the French zoologist, but his theories, announced as early as 1809, involved a soon outdated belief in the spontaneous origin of microscopic life, the direct shaping impact of environments upon simple forms of life, an inherent tendency toward greater complexity, and the role of acquired characteristics in altering more complex organisms. He also, with what now appears as preternatural wisdom, denied any real or objective species. In this he subverted the heart themes, not only of a classic chain of being, but also of the classifications developed by a century of work by naturalists such as Carolus Linnaeus.

This was the setting for Charles Darwin as he took up the species problem in about 1837. By 1844 he had identified what he believed was a pattern of development in organic life, and he spent the next fifteen years in perfecting and amplifying his theory. Dozens of people anticipated his theory. Alfred Wallace came to the same conclusions on his own before Darwin published the *Origin of Species*. Even at his death, Darwin did not have direct verifying evidence for his hypotheses. Nonetheless, his *Origin* would have enormous significance. He wrought much more than he knew. From the perspective of the present, it was the complex arguments in Darwin's *Origin* and *The Descent of Man* that, more than any other intellectual development in the modern era of Western history, began to erode crucial, foundational beliefs in a controlling deity behind all history, and a deity who, above all else, created humans in his own image.

1

WHAT DARWIN WROUGHT

The literature on Charles Darwin is immense. We now know about every aspect of his life. Biographies abound. We know about his numerous predecessors and anticipators, his major disciples, and his impact upon contemporaries. It is not my purpose to retell any of that story. Instead, what I want to do is look very closely at Darwin's arguments in both the *Origin of Species* and *The Descent of Man*. What type of explanations did he offer? What logical form did they take? What evidential support did they have? And, perhaps above all, what were the exact implications of his theories, particularly as they relate to Christian theism and human origins?

In a sense, Darwin came to class after the first recess. He did not create any of the new earth history. It was largely in place. He did not discover evolution. Even by 1850, thousands of people believed in the emergence of new species through time. What he tried to do was find a way of understanding changes in life-forms that would support continuity and dispense with any need for direct divine intervention. Long before 1859, he thought he had an explanation, one borrowed in large part from plant and animal breeders and from such political economists as Thomas Malthus.

Darwin engaged a historical problem: how did new species originate? How did the present diversity of plants and animals develop through time? He at first had a very simple answer, one that he complicated by subsequent revisions. In normally scarce environments, ones in which few progeny survive, some inherited and inheritable variations slightly enhance the chance for lucky individuals to survive and reproduce. In time, cumulative variations may lead to major modifications. In a very long time, such cumulative variations may account for so many modifications to one or a few original organisms as to lead to all present life-forms. He thus identified a pattern of change in organic life, one that led to cumulative and designlike outcomes, such as highly specialized organisms that almost perfectly fit a given environment, or such a specialization and coordination of parts in organisms as to enable them to adapt to varied environments (he called these "higher species").

It is very important to keep the historical context in mind, for if one tries to assimilate the work of Darwin to that of physical scientists one reaps only confusion. As do many historians, Darwin began with present outcomes and looked back in order to identify some critically necessary conditions for such outcomes. Since his object, even in *The Descent of Man*, was to account for the origin of new species, his work fits within natural, rather than human, history. That is, he did not try to understand acculturated activity by humans, or activity at least in part conditioned by systems of verbal meaning. Human history involves self-conscious purposes or goals. Natural history does not. But natural history, in every formal sense, is still a type of history. Is it, therefore, outside the domain of "science"? That depends on how one uses the word "science." By the conventions of his day, Darwin was a naturalist or a natural historian. He carried out careful inquiries, documented his findings, and added to the store of human knowledge. So did historians of human societies.

Today, the word "science" refers variously. Of course, there is no entity called "science." All references to what science has achieved or what science does are, at best, metaphorical. Nothing is there, any more than in the case of a reified "history" that is always proving this or that. But people do inquire, and some of these people prefer to call themselves "scientists," either because of the subject matter of their inquiry or the methods they use. One convention, today, is to restrict the word "science" to areas of inquiry that lead to generalizable knowledge. Then one talks about laws. Physics becomes the archetypal science. Even organic phenomena (not the physical correlates involved in biophysics) are not fully determinant or lawful. Because of the nature of his subject (how new species emerge), Darwin could not appeal to any laws that could explain emergent species. He discovered none. His outcomes—

new species—were not predictable. He could locate no sufficient conditions for any new species. He could only cite certain conditions that were necessary for specific change, which allowed cumulative outcomes over time. In this he was a typical historian.

Darwin, by reputation, discovered something called "evolution," a word he did not use in the first edition of the *Origin*. By the 1920s, everyone talked about an evolutionary controversy. Some even personified the word and talked about what evolution had wrought. This type of talk is either metaphorical or simply nonsensical, since there is no evolution at work in the world. Change is continuous, and at times it seems to be directional, at least in the perspective of the humans who conceptualize what they bump into. Perhaps any gradual change, in any phenomenon, that leads to some cumulative or progressive outcome is an example of evolution. If so generalized, the word loses most of its discriminatory power. In Darwin's era everyone conceded such change, even in biology. Animal and plant breeders, in a single lifetime, had been able to accumulate several changes in organisms, leading to what most people conceded to be new varieties. The modified characteristics that emerged in this process did not break the hereditary connection of offspring to their progenitors. This was a type of evolution. Darwin believed such organic change, such cumulative divergence of offspring from parents, took place in nature, but without any guidance and thus at a much slower pace. What was revolutionary in his *Origin* was his claim that, at some point, the modified individuals were so different from often distant progenitors as to make up, not new varieties, but new species.

But what is a species? Once again, definitions are most of the game. The French naturalist Jean Lamarck had concluded by the early nineteenth century that the word "species" was simply a useful and always in some sense arbitrary class term developed by humans. It joined other classes, from varieties below species, to genera and families above. One can define a species any way she wants and, if she remains consistent, can communicate effectively by using such a class term. In the early nineteenth century almost no one was willing to buy in to Lamarck's extreme nominalism, and thus give up on any real or objective species. In fact, Darwin so loosened the meaning of the word as virtually to agree with Lamarck. He stressed the arbitrary and conventional status of the word "species." Yet he did not give up on at least loose objective criteria for identifying what he called "good and true" species, or "well marked and permanent varieties."

The word "species," more than any other, confused almost all the debates over Darwin's simple thesis. Darwin did not help. He frequently referred to the mutability of species and denied any precise boundary between varieties and species. Of course, if it is a useful class term, a species cannot connote something imprecise or mutable. Individuals fit within a given species if they have certain defining characteristics. If they do not, they are members of some other species. If modifications, generation after generation, eventually eliminate even one defining characteristic, then at that point the newly emergent individual moves out of the class. Species do not change. Individuals do, and class specifications may be very useful in correctly identifying an individual. Those who believed in fixed types, tied to the creative intent of a god or to an architectonic structure in nature, rightly denied mutability. It made no sense. By definition, any characteristics that changed over time were not specific but incidental; these might help identify varieties.

Darwin's "explanation" of how new species emerge was both disarmingly simple and yet quite novel. He appealed neither to physical laws nor to efficient or final causes, although his loose language often suggested otherwise. He began with inherited and heritable variations. Animal breeding revealed how such normal variations could accumulate in such a way as to eventuate in quite dissimilar varieties, all tied to an original progenitor. But in this case an outside agent, with goals and purposes, contrived such outcomes. They selected. But apart from human breeders, nature contains no agents who can do any selecting, unless one believes a god behind the scenes directs events, or unless nature itself is humanlike, with its own goals. Without an agent to select, any cumulative or progressive change had to be a nonteleological outcome of interactive factors present in nature. For Darwin, working in the wake of Malthusian population theories and concepts of diminishing returns among political economists, the substitute for an agent was a characteristic that seemed general everywhere in nature—such a scarcity of the means of subsistence that most offspring face an early death or fail to reproduce. In such a context, survival and reproductive success were so precarious that any new variations that even slightly improved the odds for individuals had something more than a random probability of surviving in the population. Differential survival rates thus took the place of agency and accounted for designlike outcomes, or outcomes that Darwin celebrated because they were so similar to the best laid plans of a wise god.

In fact, these celebrations make up the most passionate interludes in the *Origin*. Even as early as 1857, in a letter, Darwin set the theme for a series of celebrations, most in the critical fourth chapter of the *Origin* (on natural selection). He compared what he already called "natural selection" with earlier images of the Christian God. He asked what a being who did not judge by external appearances, who could study the whole internal organization of organisms, who was never capricious, and who could go on selecting for one goal during millions of generations might not effect. He concluded that there was such an "unerring power at work in *Natural Selection*, . . . which selects exclusively for the good of each organic being." In the *Origin*, he noted that "Nature" cares "nothing for appearances, except as they are useful to any being." It cares only for "the being which she tends." How poor are the efforts of human breeders compared to those produced by Nature, whose productions are "infinitely adapted to the most complex conditions of life and should plainly bear the stamp of far higher workmanship." Nature is daily and hourly scrutinizing the slightest variations, "rejecting those that are bad, preserving and adding up all those that are good . . ." This is the language of natural theology, a language he learned in divinity courses at Cambridge University. Nature or natural selection simply takes the place of a god. Nothing is more revealing in Darwin than how continuously he used such causal or teleological language, language that came directly out of his own religious heritage.

Since this language appeared even before publication of the *Origin* and remained in all six editions, one cannot tie it to Darwin's increasing awareness and concern about the waste and cruelty present in nature. This aspect of organic change bothered him, perhaps contributed to his increasing doubts about the existence of a creative and providential deity. But in this celebratory and anthropomorphic language, he revealed what amounted to a natural theodicy, or a vindication or justification of the ways of nature. The seemingly cruel process was necessary to gain the designlike outcomes, and thus a subject for celebration. In much the same sense, Thomas Malthus had rebuffed those who saw, in his population theories, such an awful fate for most people that the only consistent response was to curse a god who made it so. Malthus argued just the opposite—that it was the cruel implications of natural scarcity that led some people to new levels of prudence and to a higher form of civilization. God did it right, much in the same sense that Darwin personified Nature and approved of her handiwork.

Darwin also continued to attribute the origins of life to a creator. Eventually, this was probably only a verbal convenience or a way of

deflecting Christian critics. But his theistic strategy, joined with his celebrations of what nature achieved, provided an opening for most American disciples, who continued to appeal to divine design. Surely a process,
productive of the wonderful outcomes celebrated by Darwin, had to
reflect, not only some original divine intent, but also the guidance of an
immanent god behind the proximate workings of nature. As a careful
scientist, Darwin identified only the proximate conditions that led to
new and at times higher species. But surely, argued many American
disciples, he recognized the elements of intent and purpose behind what
he simply referred to as "nature" or "natural selection." In this way,
Darwin's avowed American disciples continued to claim him for Christianity, although without consulting Darwin. They distinguished him
from such agnostic disciples as Thomas Huxley, or they tried to separate
Darwin from a broader philosophy that they called "Darwinism," a philosophy that was materialistic and mechanistic in its assumptions and
blatantly immoral in its social implications. Thus, many liberal and modernist Christians, instead of finding a challenge to their theism in Darwin, professed to find just the opposite. By the twentieth century, a
Shailer Mathews would find his only justification of a belief in a god in
Darwin (see Chapter 4). Had such Christian apologists more carefully
read Darwin's *Descent*, they would have been much less sanguine.

What Darwin contributed to biology was much more simple and
mundane than any insights into the goodness of nature. His central insight involved the consequences of variation and scarcity. As he later
acknowledged, others had come close to the same insight. In a sense, he
only generalized Malthus's theories about human populations. Alfred
Wallace, a zoologist working in New Guinea, came to the same conclusions and forced Darwin to publish the *Origin* before he thought it ready.
His thesis began with certain givens: the fact of variation, the self-evident fecundity of known plants and animals, and thus the population-
controlling effects of a scarcity that was inevitable when organisms occupied a given environment for any extended length of time. Darwin used
the loaded word "competition" for the effect of such scarcity, while
Herbert Spencer talked about the "survival of the fittest." Such loose
references impeded much more than they helped readers gain an understanding of Darwin's theory, although not nearly as much as the label
Darwin gave to his patterned or nonmechanistic explanation of how
new species at least usually emerged in nature—"natural selection."

Why Darwin fell in love with this label is not completely clear. He
drew the language from animal and plant breeders, who on occasion

attributed desirable but unchosen traits to nature (much like we attribute a tornado to Mother Nature). But much more than he suspected, the explanation probably lay in his earlier theological training and his openness to the language of agency. Or the choice may have reflected only a type of linguistic need. In a sense, his "natural selection" served him well. The label caught on and continues in use to this day. It may be that the label, more than the simple logic of his explanation, helped account for Darwin's fame. For complex reasons, most of his audience needed a label, needed what passed as a cause, or even what took on the role of an agent at work. But it was nonetheless a very misleading label. It clearly involved a completely false analogy with plant and animal breeding, or what Darwin sometimes referred to as "artificial selection." The very word "selection," with its suggestion of guiding purposes, was alien to the logic of Darwin's explanation.

One way to clarify some confusions introduced by natural selection is to probe the multiple meanings that people give to the word "cause." If cause means a necessary condition for an outcome, Darwin identified such a cause. Without variability in inheritance, no cumulative processes would be possible. Thus, in this sense, variation was one cause of organic change. Darwin had to take variation as a given. His speculations about what we would later call "genetics" were generally mistaken, uninformed about the early work on particulate inheritance already published by Gregor Mendel. Darwin did believe that certain hidden physical regularities might explain variations, and in this sense "explain" would have meant sufficient conditions for outcomes. One might call such sufficient conditions a "cause." Here he broached physical processes that correlated with biological observations. But Darwin knew of no such regularities, and in none of his work on organic evolution was he ever able to appeal to physical laws. Even our present knowledge of the molecular structure of genes does not allow any prior prediction of reproductive outcomes. In cell division (mitosis), copying errors along strands of DNA seem completely random, while in the more complex process (meiosis) in sex cells that leads to new gametes (eggs and sperm in mammals), the breaks in strands of DNA that make possible multiple recombinations are also random.

"Natural selection," as Darwin used the phrase, was not a cause in the sense of either necessary or sufficient conditions. Rather, it functioned, at least verbally, as a cause in the sense that a human choice or action is the cause of an outcome, or, even better, in the sense that divine agency is the cause of what takes place in nature. He knew that there was no such entity as natural selection; in rare moments of self-criticism (beginning with the third edition of the *Origin*) he even acknowledged natural selection as a shorthand figure of speech, or a metaphor. But he would not give up on the phrase and at times found satisfying its appeal to many readers. For them, it must have been a familiar handle. Those who had attributed perfect adaptations and intricate complexity to a god now attributed them to the workings of natural selection. In the teleological meaning that most people give to the word "cause," in the sense that most people answer "why" questions, Darwin provided a cause. Even today, from the normal language of serious scientists to popularized natural history series on television, nature or natural selection or even evolution continue to function as causes, to provide bogus answers to questions about why or how new species emerged or why existing species exhibit certain traits. Perhaps because of the way humans make choices in behalf of chosen goals, it is difficult for them to speak of natural events without reverting to the language of agency or causation. Thus, people constantly appeal to hidden "forces" or personify natural processes. Darwin did this all the time. Such personifications always involve mystifications, since nothing is there. But such verbal mystifications are not unique to biology. Note how often economists appeal to the accomplishments of a nonexistent market.

Darwin's inability to offer a physical, and thus lawlike, explanation for variations has led to endless confusion. In ways he could never have anticipated, it opened the door for some of the most persuasive arguments against Darwin by modern creationists. Darwin talked, very loosely, about laws. Historians have often credited Darwin, not with the discovery of evolution, but as the first to offer a mechanism to explain it. Such language, freely indulged by present-day biologists and historians of science, suggests an explanation of a type that was foreclosed to Darwin, as it is for almost all historians. He could not appeal to any known regularities, any covering laws, that allowed one, given certain initial conditions, to deduce outcomes, such as any new species. If scientific explanation requires such an explanation, and with it the possibility of prediction and even control, then Darwin did not offer a proper scientific explanation for new species. The patterns he appealed to could not serve this role. Thus, if one expects such an explanation from Darwin, he failed. If one attributes such to him, one simply profoundly misunderstands the logic of his theory. If one so defines "scientific explanation" as to require covering laws and the possibility of prediction, then Darwin was not a scientist. Creationists like to cite these facts to

discredit Darwin. They subtly hint that, lacking such scientific credentials, Darwin's conclusions remain unscientific and speculative. They are
no more credible, have no more scientific standing, than teleological
explanations, such as an appeal to a god who made it so.

To point out the absence of any scientific explanation for any new
species is beside the point, a way of denying that Darwin achieved what
he always admitted was, at least in his time, impossible. To make Darwin
responsible for lawlike explanations duplicates the mistaken effort to
characterize him as a generalizing scientist rather than a natural historian.
Although Darwin could not explain, in the sense of sufficient conditions, the emergence of any particular species (he thought that unknown
physical structures in organisms might someday provide such an explanation), he devoted himself to what was clearly a much more important
issue. It is at this point that one has to be very careful in explicating some
rather complicated logical issues. More often than not, Darwin seemed
to explain emergents as the work of nature or natural selection. But his
language in these cases had to be a loose verbal substitute for what he
actually achieved. The context invited his recourse to the language of
agency and causation, for the central goal of his *Origin* was to describe a
naturalistic substitute for the Semitic cosmology. In fact, he was so captive to the language, and to the logical form, taken by this traditional
cosmology that he easily fell back into its form over and over again.
Thus, ironically, much of the secret of the language of the *Origin* lay
hidden in the very Semitic cosmology he did so much to overthrow.

Much popular misunderstanding of Darwin, even today, derives from
the teleological nature of Darwin's language. What Darwin tried to explain was not individual emergents, but a pattern of emergence. Just as a
Christian appealed to God to account for a designed and purposeful
universe, so Darwin appealed to a dynamic process in nature to account
for designlike but undesigned outcomes. The critical concept here is
"designlike." Differential survival rates among inherited variations in a
context of resource scarcity seemed, to him, to assure such outcomes.
This process led, necessarily, to more specialized adaptation, to more
internally complex organisms, and to ecological richness. Yet the process
was random, not mechanistic. In fact, it depended on randomness, even
as it led to cumulative but never fully determined outcomes. From a
purely logical perspective, this was one of the more subtle and fascinating explanations in the history of human inquiry. What made it such a
powerful and persuasive explanation was the very fact that its outcomes
so closely duplicated the work formerly attributed to a creative and pur-

poseful deity, although the process itself seemed, at times even to Darwin, to be very wasteful and cruel. The outcomes were such that one could rightly say that "it was as if" nature were an agent and chose such effects.

Darwin postponed publication of his theories as long as possible, in part because he could not cite direct evidence for specific change. His best firsthand observations involved animal and plant breeders, but in no clear case could Darwin argue that they had ever so selected variations as to gain a new "species," at least as people conventionally used that loaded word. He agonized about the problem. He noted, correctly, that animal breeders knew the departure point for new, developed varieties. In visible ways, the distance between a Pekinese and a Great Dane was far greater than that separating any number of bird populations that all naturalists agreed were separate species. When the ancestors were known, as Darwin lamented, naturalists usually denominated all the modified descendants as mere varieties. When no ancestors were known, when there were no clear linkages, they usually classified a distinctive population as a species. This seemed to make the popular use of the term "species" completely arbitrary or contextual. But not quite so, since even quite divergent breeds of dogs and pigeons can interbreed, while many seemingly close species in nature do not, or cannot, interbreed. Darwin would have rejoiced if some pigeon fancier, like himself, could have developed a breed that was reproductively isolated from its ancestors. None ever did.

Since, as he understood it, speciation in nature is too slow for direct observation, all the indirect evidence he could look for was paleontological. And he confessed that this data was as yet too thin to bear the burden of proof. Even in his later years, as paleontologists began to assemble some impressive fossil series, it was again impossible to be sure that any modified descendants were more than new varieties. Of course, much of the problem resided in the concept of "real" species. Those who believed in fixed species were quick to deny that identified changes over time as revealed by fossil discoveries reflected any specific change. They knew this all along. Those, like Louis Agassiz, who believed in divine intervention at the beginning of each new geological age simply introduced new ages when it seemed clear that major organic changes, of the magnitude that suggested new species, occurred within a formerly identified age. This game had no limit and, in a sense, made fossil evidence of new species impossible in principle. Thus, in all his editions of the *Origin*, Darwin used his wide knowledge of the biological sciences to demonstrate why verifying evidence was so far unavailable.

This lack of directly confirming evidence does not mean that Darwin's *Origin* lacked data. It was full of data, some very rich. He drew from every developing speciality that in any way related to the species problem, and during the years before publication of the *Origin*, he corresponded with hundreds of naturalists, subtly drawing them into his developing theory. He had great promotional or political skills. But all the collected data had to serve other than a direct confirming role. Instead of citing verifying evidence, Darwin stressed how well his theory cohered with existing knowledge, how well it correlated with new theories in geology, how well it fit with the known distribution of species, how inherently plausible his theory was, how much it unified the biological sciences, how many new research agendas it clarified, and, perhaps most important, the lack of any plausible alternative, even as he admitted the multiple impediments to any early confirmation. Correctly described, the *Origin* contained a rich but as yet an unprovable hypothesis about a historical pattern in nature, a pattern that Darwin, despite the looseness of his language, defended so persuasively as to win over most naturalists before his death.

Later, the word "theory" would occasion multiple confusions. Once again, one has to navigate among loose terms. Darwin, with some false modesty, presented the *Origin* as a preliminary sketch. In it he offered a hypothesis. From what had to be some highly speculative reasoning, he identified a pattern in organic life that led to new species but did not "cause" new species either in the sense of sufficient conditions or some controlling agent. The pattern guaranteed continuous organic change, at least in the context of ever changing environments. In 1859, these speculations were persuasive, as events proved, but quite general in nature, loose in conceptualization, and without proof. It made sense to call his arguments a "theory," and it still does even today. In the same sense, other competing explanations of how new species emerged, from multiple divine interventions after catastrophic extinctions, to Lamarck's emphasis upon acquired characteristics, to philosophical idealists' insistence upon the progressive concretions of an immanent divine mind, also lacked any proof and were in that sense unproved hypotheses or theories, although only Lamarck's was an empirical theory of the same type as Darwin's.

What Darwin would not have called "theoretical" was what, by 1859, had long seemed to be well-verified knowledge. This was the geological column, tied to the evidence in sedimentary deposits. That life-forms had changed, dramatically, through time was not an issue of debate among naturalists. It was the "how" that still puzzled, and this was the object of Darwin's work. He is correctly identified as the most important catalyst for a new understanding of organic change and for expunging from all proximate explanations of new species any direct intervention by a divine creator. He won this degree of consensus not only not only because of his explanation, but also because of the range of investigations he pursued, his argumentative skills, his metaphysical restraint, his political savvy, and his well-deserved reputation based on investigations and publications on several other topics.

It is almost impossible to evaluate Darwin without recourse to present genetic understanding. What he observed as normal in nature— inherited and heritable variations—now make sense at the correlative level of physical processes. Copying errors in DNA replication (mutations) during gamete formation provide a continuing foundation for variation, in the sense of introducing new possibilities. But most of the variations noted by Darwin were proximately determined by recombination (the cutting and splicing and thus mixing or crossing of strands of DNA during meiosis). In complex organisms, those in which each gene may contain several slightly different codes (alleles), the lottery of reproduction, because of recombination, has what might seem an almost infinite range of possibilities, but not infinite because of the constraints of the existing gene pool. Mutations introduce novelties into that pool, and thus make new recombinations possible.

Although Darwin continued until his death in 1882 to work at the theory he called "natural selection," his first edition of the *Origin* has fared better than the later editions. In response to criticism, he gradually qualified the role of differential survival, with greater and greater stress on sexual selection, with its Lamarckian intimations of voluntary choice. He also placed more and more emphasis on use and disuse. Finally, he even backed away from completely random variations. By his sixth and last edition, it was increasingly unclear what role he still attributed to purely random variations in a context of scarcity. What has survived best was what Darwin first achieved, but without a full appreciation of the fact: a coherent historical hypothesis about the critical necessary conditions that made possible a pattern of historical development in the organic world. Unfortunately, his teleological language, his misleading emphasis upon "selection" and "competition," obscured this central argument.

In some sense, most of the competing evolutionary theories of 1870 contained valuable insights. For example, much more than Darwin ever conceded, catastrophic extinctions have occurred in the past, including one around 65 million years ago. Consistent with contemporary genetic knowledge, we now know that the pace of organic change can be very rapid after such environmental debacles. The rapidity of speciation in certain circumstances (in small, isolated, or remnant populations in a new environment, such as the volcano-created Galapagos Islands) comes close to confirming the belief of Christian evolutionists in the early appearance of a whole new flora and fauna at the beginning of each new age. Likewise, the slow pace of organic change within stable environments vindicates their almost correct belief that no specific changes take place during each age (of course, their metaphysical use of the word "species" assured that this was so). At the same time, we now understand how, sooner or later, some acquired and very beneficial characteristics may become hereditary. That is, some rare recombination, or some needed copying mistake in a gene, may assimilate the formerly nonheritable modifications. Not only Lamarck, but Darwin as well, was correct in noting the seeming role of use and disuse, but neither had the genetic knowledge to explain what happened. Because of the blending theory of inheritance that Darwin usually assumed, and thus the enormous time that would elapse before random variations could alter a population (successive blendings would soon all but obliterate the effects of a single variation), Darwin moved closer to Lamarck by his final edition of the *Origin*. By then he believed that new environmental conditions may directly trigger similar variations in multiple individuals, thus speeding the process of change (had he had a theory of particulate inheritance, he would not have needed this concession).

Darwin's openness to the role of use and disuse meant that he was not exclusive. He never argued that differential survival rates in normally scare environments accounted for all new species. This meant that his nonexclusive explanation was impossible to falsify by citing exceptions to what he called "natural selection." Also, some naturalists, such as Agassiz, agreed with Darwin that differential survival explained the origin of new *varieties* within clearly demarcated geological ages.

It was not variation that led many to dissent from Darwin, but what he meant, sometimes not too clearly, by natural selection. The dynamic in his theory, the explanation of continuous "advances" toward better adaptation or greater complexity, was what he described as the "screening" role of "nature." This language, once again, had to be metaphoric, but one has to concede that it is difficult to talk about what happens without such a teleological language. The same is true when one refers to the "unfit" who do not survive or reproduce and the "fit" who do. Darwin seemed at first to believe (some present-day disciples believe even more firmly) that most enduring changes in life-forms reflect adaptively advantageous variations "preserved" by nature. This gave a teleological color to the language of later Darwinists. Note some novel trait in an animal, or even some cultural trait in humans, and they will immediately attribute it to natural selection, with an assurance that the trait has to have survival or mate-procuring benefits.

It is almost impossible to translate such misleading language into precise description. What seems to be the working assumption is that life, possibly from the point of origin (if it had a point of beginning), has certain built-in characteristics that assure cumulative or designlike developments. These characteristics involve usually stable replication or reproduction, but with room for some variation, and also a type of reproductive excess that assures a type of functional scarcity. In such a "competitive" context, life-enhancing variations make possible continuous change and adaptation. In stable environments, highly specialized organisms achieve an almost perfect fit in some life-sustaining niche and may change little over time. In this environment, variations, which continue to occur, cannot have beneficial effects, and thus most do not survive. Some evidence even suggests that, in enduringly stable environments, the rate of mutations slows. To what extent incidental (with no clear survival value) variations can accumulate in such an environment was unclear to Darwin, but he did find such "neutral" change in what he called "polymorphic species" and in certain cosmetic traits of birds that he believed enhanced the chance for neither survival nor for successful mate procurement.

If this is a correct interpretation, then cumulative developments are inherent in life itself, whatever the exact source of variations. This means that Darwin, in one sense of the word, "explained" outcomes in nature without recourse to controlling laws and without introducing a purposeful agent. The only earlier explanation of this type that I am aware of came in the opening sections of Adam Smith's *Wealth of Nations*. He introduced what he called a "law of progress." Given certain characteristics of humans (he appealed to human nature), in a context of freedom, they would barter with one another, specialize in their productions, become ever more inventive with such specialization, and thus over time produce more and more. Any nation would become wealthy. This internal dynamic required no outside force or agency, no guiding hand, yet it represented a type of progress. Much as Darwin did later, Smith worried about how too much goal-directed human intervention in this almost magical system might mess it all up and preclude the best possible outcomes.

Today, it is difficult to relate Darwin to various new twists in evolutionary theory. Those biologists who believe that much organic change is random and not always related to any functional or competitive advantage may seem to disagree with Darwin. Those who emphasize the rapidity of speciation (punctuational evolution) in certain contexts may seem to reject Darwin's emphasis upon a gradual and continuous process of change. But the issue in either case is not that clear, in part because Darwin kept changing his mind. He speculated frequently, and sometimes with prescience, about the conditions that abet or retard speciation, and in his fascinating work on sexual selection, he certainly emphasized variations that have no direct tie to subsistence and in some cases even impede it. In an amazing concession to critics, in chapter 2 of the *Descent*, he admitted that in early editions of the *Origin* he was so under the sway of natural theologians, who attributed to God every structural detail in an organism, that he fell into the same pattern and attributed all to natural selection. He had believed all surviving variations contributed a functional advantage, but, by 1871, he confessed that many peculiarities of structure were probably not of any service to an organism.

Most biologists assume that life developed on earth at some time in the past. It may not have. It could have migrated to earth on a meteorite or on the newly discovered small, water-impregnated comets that enter our atmosphere. In any case, we have a record of living organisms that go back nearly four billion years. Maybe the earliest or most primitive life-forms were little more than a few strands of DNA. Maybe replication, at first by cell division, was always robust, with a rapid multiplication of organisms assured so long as an environmental niche could support them (present bacteria support this view). If so, almost by definition, life has always assured scarcity. If so, then life and a type of evolutionary development entail each other, and what Darwin did was simply elaborate upon one defining characteristic of life itself. Certainly one characteristic is what we very easily but figuratively describe as a "will to live," a certain inherent and urgent bent to keep life going. Darwin thus identified certain inherent properties in living matter that assured, through time, that every niche in nature capable of supporting life would gain life (a rich ecology); that some populations would, through adventitious but fortunate variations, come to fit each niche (specialized organisms); and that other populations would become so complex, through the internal specialization of parts, elaborate feedback mechanisms, and a central directorate or brain, that they could adapt to many different environments. Newton believed a god made physical laws. Darwin at least suggested that it would be a great compliment to a god to argue that it so contrived life as to assure these long-term outcomes.

In what ways did Darwin's theory (or theories) about how new species originate challenge traditional beliefs, and particularly the Semitic cosmology? This question implicates Darwin's *Descent* even more than his *Origin*. By the end of the nineteenth century, in the wake of Darwin, almost everyone seemed to talk about some conflict between science and religion or science and theology. Such talk only added more confusion to a range of issues. I have already suggested that Darwin's explanation of speciation in nature was more nearly a historical than a scientific explanation, at least if one restricts the label "scientific" to generalizable knowledge. But however classified, his explanation, despite the misleading implications of his language, did not involve any agency. He did not answer any big "why" about nature, and he carefully avoided the issue of how life originates in nature.

Questions about ultimate origins were, from Darwin's perspective, simply not open to the type of inquiry, or even to the type of hypothetical reasoning, that characterized natural history or any of the biological sciences. In a sense, these were causal questions in areas of inquiry where causes do not fit but where structural regularities or historical patterns are the object of knowledge. Nothing in his *Origin* or *Descent* precluded a causal explanation of the phenomena that fascinated him. But such an explanation, as was obvious to Darwin, was of a different order, part of a quite different form of discourse, with different conventions or rules. Maybe all patterns or regularities in the world that we bump into have a cause, serve some end, eventuate in some predetermined outcome. Newton thought so. But whether they do or not, we are still left with the same problem of trying to determine what those regularities or patterns are. Darwin restricted himself, more rigorously than almost any of his contemporaries, to this limited, foreground problem. Others obviously did not, and thus Darwin had to confront challenges tied to Christian beliefs, even as some of his least-examined assumptions reflected his own Christian background.

How did his theory relate to religion? That depends upon what one means by the loaded word "religion." I have great difficulty finding any conflict with Hinduism and Buddhism, even as Darwin was often an inspiration to some creators of types of religious humanism in the twentieth century. Nor do Darwin's theories necessarily conflict with certain types of theistic religion. As later chapters will make clear, some Christian intellectuals thought they found in Darwin a needed support for theism. Once again, the existence of a god or gods is not directly challenged by any of Darwin's theories, for theistic theories simply address quite different issues and quite different modes of knowledge. Thus, the issue is not one of conflict between either science, whatever that is, and religion, whatever that is, but rather how, and in what ways, Darwin's theories challenged specific religious beliefs. In the United States, the conflict, as perceived on both sides, usually involved versions of one particular religion, Christianity. It involved a subclass, not the class.

In some respects, Darwin's tentative explanation of how new species could develop in nature did not add much to the already existing challenges to Christianity. Most of the debates that, purportedly, involved Darwinism actually also involved almost all the competing theories about the evolution or emergence of new species through time. That is, Darwin only added to challenges already raised by geologists or by Lamarckian theories about speciation. Of course, Darwin described a process of emergence that contradicted any literal understanding of the Genesis accounts of creation. But so did even those bitter opponents of Darwin, such as Agassiz, who believed in the multiple origins of life, and thus numerous creative acts by a god. Almost none of the new geological knowledge, about the great age of the earth, about past extinctions and new emergents, and about tectonic and erosive changes in the earth's surface, was consistent with the historical parts of the Christian Bible. If the danger perceived by Christians was a lessened respect for the Bible, particularly as an authority on ancient history and on astronomy and physics, then Darwin was only one among thousands of enemies. He did ratify much of this new geological knowledge by showing how consistent it was with a proper understanding of speciation.

Those naturalists who still believed in fixed species were, indeed, closer to the biblical understanding than those who accepted Darwin. But they too accepted emergents in time. A belief in multiple creations meant, observationally, that a whole repertoire of appropriate new species simply appeared at the beginning of each new geological age. If one accepted Darwin's narrow conception of empirical inquiry, then the idea of multiple creations was simply a metaphysical window dressing for spontaneous generation. And spontaneous generation is, in a sense, a verbal camouflage for unexplained phenomena. Thus, those who argued for multiple creations had no empirically meaningful explanation for emerging species. Contemporary creationists, who have tried to establish the legitimacy of "creation science," totally apart from any religious belief that may lie behind it, have acknowledged just this point and often refer to their theory as one involving "complex initial appearances," or what everyone in the nineteenth century called "spontaneous generation." But those who continued to believe in direct divine creation were, empirically, in no worse a position than was Darwin on the issue of the beginnings of life itself. In the absence of an explanation of life, at least of the type he offered in the *Origin* for the emergence of successive life-forms, Darwin also at times took the habitual route and appealed to a creator (one whose existence he personally doubted), which means that he also, from an empirical perspective, sometimes appealed to spontaneous origins. Such appeals to an external, supernatural cause added nothing to the developing natural sciences. Thus, such appeals, in a sense, were markers for the limits of any empirical ordering and patterning of phenomena.

If Darwin was a thorn in the sides of biblical literalists, so were almost all nineteenth century naturalists. But he did explore new ground in suggesting a fully natural explanation of emergent species, given the existence of life, hereditary variations, and natural scarcity. Until someone offered a persuasive explanation of such emergence, as something coherent with other natural processes, then Christians had been able, at the very least, to note phenomena that seemed inexplicable on empirical grounds. The very incompleteness of natural explanations left space for a continued appeal beyond natural processes to some purposeful agent who was outside or superior to nature. The very intricacy of adaptations gave support to natural theology, or one particular use of the design argument to justify belief in the existence of a creator god. Particularly in Britain, where forms of natural theology were deeply entrenched, Darwin's work seemed most dangerous. In Germany, where transcendental theology was widely accepted, Darwin not only seemed to pose no problem, but offered a developmental explanation that seemed complementary to their belief in the continuous unfolding of an immanent divine mind.

Asa Gray, the very able Harvard botanist, wrote the most perceptive early review of the *Origin*. Typical of most American disciples, or near disciples, of Darwin, he emphasized that nothing in the *Origin* refuted design and teleology. He stressed Darwin's references to the creation of life itself. He did not believe that what Darwin called "natural selection" could explain self-conscious humans, and thus he wanted to exempt them from the now-clarified pattern of organic development (as did Alfred Wallace). Otherwise, he had to agree with Darwin and work in America to defuse what many saw as the anti-Christian implications of Darwin's simple theory. But Gray was also aware that the Genesis account of creation was symbolically but not literally correct. He suggested three new cosmologies that were consistent with Darwin. One was the earlier deistic view of a god who designed a perfect world and then withdrew to let it follow its own predetermined trajectory. A second view, one we have seen to be very popular both before and right after the publication of the *Origin*, was that of a god who usually let the universe proceed according to fixed laws but at a few points had intervened directly to introduce life-forms appropriate to each new age, or, in a position that marked the eventual and most obliging Roman Catholic concession, at least intervened at one subsequent point—to create the human soul. Finally, Gray was aware of the dominant theological trends of the mid-nineteenth century, particularly among German Protestants and New England transcendentalists. From their perspective, a god was immanent in all that happened in nature, and this god was the ultimate cause of all that happened, whatever proximate means effected its purposes.

Gray correctly perceived that the third was by far the best strategy for Christians, but it was a strategy that stripped much of the Bible of any literal authority. In some sense, the justification for belief would have to switch from nature or from history to human experience, and thus to an authority immune from the ravages of biblical criticism or new understandings of nature. New England transcendentalists, such as Theodore Parker, had already recognized the necessity of such a switch. A Christianity tied to a literal reading of biblical texts was already doomed; the blows delivered by geologists were only a straw in the wind, small intimations of the blows that would come later. Parker advised Christians to turn from ancient texts to the nature of human consciousness as a partial window into divinity. Parker was so conversant with nineteenth-century idealist philosophy that he never doubted the existence of a divine mind whose purposes guided all history.

Such an idealist turn proved the one Christian approach most immune to threats from Darwin, or from any scholarship or scientific discovery. But was this strategy loyal enough to the traditions of the Church to earn the label "Christian"? Charles Hodge, an old curmudgeon at

Princeton and a latter-day disciple of John Calvin, appreciated the appeal of various versions of religious idealism, which he labeled "pantheism," but at the same time he noted that such humanly appealing religions were not Christian, not tied to the authority of the Bible, not consistent with the major doctrines of the Church. For him, as for many other prominent theologians, evolutionary theories, if at all acceptable to evangelical Christians, might indeed require a new understanding of biblical truths and the teachings of the Church, but they could not contradict these truths. As Hodge understood the implications of Darwin's theory, Christians had either to reject Darwin or give up on their most basic beliefs. Hodge felt, quite correctly, that Darwinism, even as promulgated in the melioristic language of the *Origin* and not in the more militant terms of Huxley, was inherently inconsistent with the heart themes of Christianity and not merely with the creation stories of Genesis. Hodge grasped the deeper challenge posed by Darwin—to supernaturalism and to most forms of theism. In this sense, Hodge argued that Darwinism was a form of atheism. Although overstated, this charge had in it a grain of truth.

I am confident that Darwin never recognized these atheistic implications. He probably did become an agnostic on the issue of theism. He did not know whether gods existed or not, and he did not seem overly concerned about the issue. This again documented his amazing metaphysical restraint, his aloofness from the questions that agitated almost everyone in the nineteenth century. His great challenge to Christianity was in his *Descent of Man*, not in the *Origin*. But Darwin did not present his key arguments as such and apparently did not grasp their significance.

In the *Descent*, Darwin tackled a problem that he had finessed in the *Origin*. Could his explanation of speciation account for the emergence of a self-conscious, moral, religious, rational species? He believed it could, in the sense of defining the necessary conditions for such an emergent, not by providing any sufficient conditions. No species reflected any hard necessities. None had to appear. Even were one able to replay the natural history of the earth, one would have no reason to expect the same array of species that now exists on earth. The process had too much randomness for that. Thus, in a replay, one could not expect or predict the emergence of humans. If life exists on other planets, in our own or in other galaxies, one cannot be confident that organic change there will lead to self-consciousness or that complexity there will take anything like the form that it has on earth, even should the environment be as conducive as our own to complex forms of life.

Asa Gray reflected a widespread doubt that Darwin could explain what is most distinctive to humans. This was not largely, or perhaps at all, a defensive human reaction to kinship with "lower" life-forms but rather a recognition of how vast are the differences between humans and all other species, including closely related primates. Darwin did not deny the differences, although in certain respects he narrowed the gulf, at least in such areas as morality. He spent much of the *Descent* in proving what is now self-evident: the anatomical and embryonic developmental similarities of humans and other mammals. Given the prevalent racial theories of his time (Darwin was conventional on such issues), he saw a much broader spectrum of abilities among humans than we now know to be justified. At times his Hottentots seemed only slightly advanced orang-utans. But from his contact with aboriginal Americans, he conceded that humans, even the most "degraded," possessed all distinctive human traits, including self-consciousness and rationality. They could learn all the arts of civilization. Despite the anatomical similarities, they were functionally so far above primates as to mark what seemed a difference, not of degree, but of kind. It was Darwin's purpose to prove that a difference of degree, in the brain and nervous system, was sufficient to explain the profound functional differences.

Darwin became fascinated with the emotional traits of animals and wrote a book on the quite similar role of emotions in man and animals. He found in higher mammals many bases for the so-called higher attributes of humans, including the types of empathy that underlie human moral systems. He was fascinated with the display of feeling, the complex learning, even the seemingly rational decision making that he found in animals. But, admittedly, the use of such skills became self-conscious only in humans, who are able to plan, project, and set up rules. Darwin sought help in accounting for human "self-consciousness," a word that expressed many, if not most, of the meanings traditionally intended by such words as "mind," "spirit," or "soul." An American admirer, the lay philosopher Chauncey Wright, tried to help Darwin. He wrote a long, turgid essay on human self-consciousness, in which he tried to demonstrate that what distinguished humans from other animals was not the use of signs or types of language, but a unique ability to recall, and distinguish, internal images that mediate between sensory inputs and an active response. These internal images are the foundation of human concepts, of general or class terms, and are retrievable and distinguishable because of the acuity of human memory, which enables humans to note the internal images, and this in turn requires an ability to articulate and understand words. Only humans have developed external symbols to encode internal images. In brief, the great tool enjoyed by humans is a symbolic language.

Darwin incorporated this insight and acknowledged the work of Wright, but he certainly did not emphasize it. In one awkward, passive, but pregnant sentence in the second (1874) edition of *Descent*, he summarized what would become the most revolutionary implication of all his work: "Through his [man's] powers of intellect, articulate language has been evolved, and on this his wonderful advancement largely depended." One would expect, if human advance "largely depended" on language, that Darwin would have made it the centerpiece of his *Descent*. He did not, although at times he referred to the "general propositions" used by advanced or educated humans (not, he thought, by primitive or savage humans). An incautious reader might miss these brief references to language and thought, while enjoying pages devoted to such minor human differences as a limited amount of hair. Yet only language could account for the type of systematized moral systems and even religious beliefs that distinguished a human culture. Perhaps because of his fascination with the shared traits of humans and higher animals, and his belief that no "fundamental" differences separated their mental traits, Darwin was very reluctant to talk in any detail about human cultural achievements.

Darwin's borrowed and never fully assimilated insight about language had monumental significance, but again he apparently recognized little of this. Here was the one area in which he began to subvert even the idealistic or immanent forms of theism that had most easily accommodated his evolutionary theory. In the Genesis stories, a manlike god had deliberately made the earth and all that is on it, in behalf of his own hidden purposes. In idealistic theologies, a divine spirit is immanent in the world and in human history, even realizing its own purposes in the world. In both cases, plans or ideas precede and guide creativity and history. Mind is formally, if not temporally, prior to things. Darwin began to reverse this order. In his *Descent*, mind is a very late emergent, a nonnecessary but yet not purely accidental outcome of random variations in a context of scarcity. It is not accidental because of the constraining role of particular environments. By making mind, or self-consciousness or thought, an emergent in nature, Darwin seemed to leave no phenomena outside nature. He naturalized mind. But, one has to note that, in doing so, he ennobled nature with attributes of purpose, with the teleology present wherever mind is at work. In no sense did Darwin suggest a completely "mechanistic" and "materialistic" universe.

For philosophers such as John Dewey, this naturalizing of mind, although only tentative and undeveloped in Darwin, was the most revolutionary implication of organic evolution. Now, it seemed, no experienced phenomenon was beyond the scope of proximate empirical understanding, albeit in many cases not open to a mechanistic or fully determinate model of explanation. This did not mean that one had to give up a belief in a cause behind all empirical phenomena. That remained an option; but from the standpoint of proximate understanding such a cause was unneeded and irrelevant and, in this sense, more gratuitous than ever before. Such a cause was clearly beyond nature, or beyond physics and, in a literal sense supernatural and metaphysical, even as what had seemed to be types of nonnatural or spiritual phenomena were now fully assimilated to other phenomena in nature. The two universes of discourse, causal on one hand, structural on the other, heretofore so often intermingled, were now completely separate.

The implications of this insight were almost beyond calculation. They were most profound and fruitful in a discipline that soon began to separate from philosophy, psychology. Now, of course, Darwin was not alone or even primarily responsible for the emergence of physiological, functional, and behavioral schools of psychology. People like Chauncey Wright would have moved in this direction without Darwin's influence. But such psychologists could, and often did, cite the influence of Darwin, and they gladly identified with such an eminent person. Of all disciplines, psychology owed the most to Darwin. This was not evident for a long time, particularly because of the many evolutionary themes that emerged in sociology and anthropology, or these that were already present in political economy (here the path was from economists to Darwin, not the other way around). But these evolutionary themes, on close investigation, almost always reflected the influence of the cosmic evolutionary theories of Herbert Spencer or the abstract free market model of David Ricardo and John Stuart Mill, not the very restrained theories of Darwin. Philosophers with ties to the new psychology, and most particularly John Dewey, found in Darwin a road map beyond all forms of supernaturalism, but at the same time to a much richer and more nuanced understanding of nature than had prevailed in the past.

For Christians, the challenge of Darwin varied widely according to what each viewed as critical in the Christian tradition and according to how they understood Darwin's theories about organic evolution. Although unjustified in doing so, many Christian apologists used the word "Darwinism" to encompass a range of knowledge and theory in geology as well as biology. Thus, they made Darwin the center of their concern to uphold the literal truthfulness of the first eleven chapters of Genesis. Their concern involved much more than the origin of life-forms, for at times Noah's flood was as much at the center of debate as the two stories of creation, and even more so for modern "creationists." Debates on all these issues preceded publication of the *Origin*, even as some pre-1859 debates involved pre-Darwinian theories of evolution. From 1859 to the present, those who affirm an error-free Bible, have had no alternative but to reject almost all the new knowledge in geology and biology gained in the nineteenth century. Day-age and gap theories, almost universally accepted in some form by most late-nineteenth-century evangelical Protestants in America, at least offered a loose way to finesse the problem of the earth's age. In no sense could either theory do full justice to the history recorded in Genesis 1–11 and at the same time remain loyal to the new geological and biological knowledge. Also, such interpretations of the language of Genesis failed to do justice to the ancient authors and to the message they most likely wanted to communicate by their stories.

Since Darwin added nothing distinctive to these issues, the real problem he posed to Christians was at another, and much more critical, level. This involved, not necessarily the reasons that people believed in gods, but the type of justification they could offer for such belief. At the popular level, then and now, theists most often offered one or another version of the design argument to justify belief in a god or gods. The argument is very persuasive. Given an intricate earth, and in particular the great range of well-adapted species, and perhaps above all given humans and their minds, how could one doubt creative design? Did such phenomena come about by accident? It had long seemed almost beyond doubt that such seeming artistry demanded an artist. To many people, the fact of design is still truistic. Neither geologists nor Darwin provided an explanation for the origin of the earth, one at first not hospitable to any form of life. But they did identify proximate conditions necessary for the subsequent development of the earth (such as tectonic and gradational forces). They did not offer explanations for the origin of life, but given life, they had an explanation of how such life radiated out in multiple directions to eventuate in the present flora and fauna. The fact of existence, of the earth being here, of its regularities, of life beginning—all these, for a certain type of mind, still beg a causal accounting, and thus can still legitimately lead one to seek out an agent that made it so. But none of the details, none of the specific adaptations, require such a cause. In this sense Darwin helped attenuate earlier design arguments and make such arguments seem more ad hoc or challengeable. He did this, most of all, by his assimilation of human self-consciousness to the same processes that led to all but some original life-form or forms.

In brief, Christians faced two issues: the Bible and theistic belief. For a large subset of American Christians, the Bible issue remained in the forefront. After all, bound up in the Bible, in their estimate, was the evidence for the existence of their God, or the proof of their God's veracity. Other Christians, often deemed liberal or modernist, reluctantly gave up on an inerrant, if not yet on a divinely inspired, Bible. But they too remained theists and often found in parts of the Bible the authority for their beliefs and values. They used the received Scriptures selectively, and did so in order to keep all the consolations of Christianity as they understood it. They saw a kernel of truth in the Genesis accounts. A creative god willed that the earth and humans come into being. A providential god somehow directed events toward a final redemption. And the most essential truths in the Bible did not involve creation stories or even the legendary history of the early Jews. They involved the moral insights of the Prophets and above all the accounts of Jesus the Christ, his atoning death and his resurrection, and the hope of salvation for humans who found themselves loving this God and consenting to his plan. None of these New Testament doctrines had anything to do with Darwin or his theory.

But, as the orthodox protested, such views, usually labelled liberal or modernist, involved new gods and a new religion. In fact, Darwin's *Origin*, and the controversies that swirled around it, proved a great stimulus to theological workshops, which began to turn out new gods, or new versions of the Christian God, almost every year. In the United States, the most bitter conflict was not that between Christians and non-Christians but that among competing Christians. These conflicts very rarely involved competing denominations, but complex divisions within denominations, divisions that soon gained labels. Among these labels were new ones that have remained in use all the way to the present— "modernism" and "fundamentalism." Hidden in the ambiguities of such loaded terms are many of the keys to unraveling the cultural significance of Darwin's theories.

Reading Guide

For over twenty years, I have struggled to understand Darwin's arguments in the *Origin* and *Descent*. Obviously, these two books are the most important source for this chapter. But the single most important key to my reading of Darwin lies outside any Darwinian sources—in the philosophy of science and of history. I do not think anyone can understand Darwin's arguments without attending very carefully to the logical form exemplified by what people, in various disciplines, refer to as "explanation." This issues implicates a vast, growing literature. My fullest effort to clarify these issues, an effort at many points informed by my work on Darwin, appears in a chapter entitled "History and the Generalizing Sciences," in Paul K. Conkin and Roland N. Stromberg, *Heritage and Challenge: The History and Theory of History* (Arlington Heights, IL: Forum Press, 1989), pp. 149–69.

The work on Darwin is enormous. The modern phase of that scholarship arguably began in 1958 with Loren Eisley's *Darwin's Century: Evolution and the Men Who Discovered It* (New York: Doubleday) and in 1964 with Gavin R. De Beer's *Charles Darwin: Evolution by Natural Selection* (New York: Doubleday). Both were ardent admirers of Darwin and what he achieved. They embraced his central arguments in the *Origin* without much critical analysis and emphasized how much contemporary genetics had confirmed his central insights. Darwin was one of the great scientists of all time, and his triumphs were now evident in the marriage of modern genetics with his great and enduring insight: natural selection. I find it difficult, today, to read such triumphant and Whiggish accounts.

The more critical turn began with Gertrude Himmelfarb's *Darwin and the Darwinian Revolution* (New York: Norton, 1959). In this very literate and very readable book, Himmelfarb dispenses with celebrations of Darwin's greatness, surveys the complexity of his life, adds little in the technical understanding of his theories, but surveys, with elements of misgiving, the influence Darwin exerted in several areas of social thought. Her doubts and concerns reflect some earlier cautions advanced by Jacques Barzun in *Darwin, Marx, and Wagner* (New York: Doubleday, 1958).

Among contemporary Darwin scholars, Peter J. Bowler has probably had the greatest impact, in a series of interpretive books and an introductory biography and text, *Charles Darwin: The Man and His Influence* (London: Blackwell, 1990). Bowler offers very complex, at times what I find idiosyncratic, interpretations, but interpretations keyed to a very intensive analysis of the larger intellectual community in which Darwin participated. A much less interpretive but more personal or domestic biography is by John Bowlby, *Charles Darwin: A New Life* (New York: Norton, 1990). In process is what will become the definitive personal biography by Janet Browne; the completed first volume, *Charles Darwin: Voyaging* (London: Jonathan Cape, 1995), brings the story up to the eve of the publication of the *Origin* but duplicates Bowlby except that it has twice the details.

More specialized books support some of the key themes in the above essay. Closest in perspective is a group of wide-ranging essays by Robert M. Young, *Darwin's Metaphor: Nature's Place in Victorian Culture* (Cambridge and New York: Cambridge University Press, 1985). In a key chapter, on Darwin's use or misuse of the phrase "natural selection," Young brilliantly analyzes the logical credentials of Darwin's major contribution to biology and demonstrates his lack of any coherent mechanism or any justification for his anthropomorphic and teleological language. Although at times a tedious book, keyed to paradigms or epistemes, Neal C. Gillespie's *Charles Darwin and the Problem of Creation* (Chicago: University of Chicago Press, 1979), documents the critical role of natural theology in shaping his theories. So does Doe Ospovat, in *The Development of Darwin's Theory: Natural History, Natural Theology, and Natural Selection* (Cambridge and New York: Cambridge University Press, 1981). Darwin himself, in what his granddaughter would later compile as *The Autobiography of Charles Darwin*, Nora Barlow, ed. (New York: Norton, 1958), reveals his running dialogue with religious issues. Here, late in life, he confesses that he had come to an agnostic position on such issues as the existence of a god and on human immortality.

2

EVANGELICALS, FUNDAMENTALISTS, AND MODERNISTS

Only after World War I did a large body of Christians mobilize against the teaching of something called "evolution" in the public schools. Long before this, despite competing explanations of how it happened, an acceptance of organic evolution had become so consensual among biologists that it was almost impossible to find any informed advocate of fixed types or specific creation. Even late-nineteenth-century high school textbooks in zoology, botany, or geology all contained sections on evolution, as did the early-twentieth-century texts written to guide the popular new synthetic courses in biology. This does not mean that the issues involved—either in the battle between orthodox Darwinians and geneticists, or between those who advocated competing evolutionary theories—were widely understood by the American public. The issues could be very complex. Even the high school texts invited a very superficial understanding. And only after 1900 did a growing number of state-supported secondary schools make a high school education an option for other than a few wealthy or well-located youth.

Since 1859 Darwinism or evolution had been one among many issues that divided Christians, particularly those in the center, evangelical de-

49

nominations. By 1920, with the formation of new fundamentalist organizations and the decision by William Jennings Bryan to lead a crusade
against the teaching of evolution in public schools, the so-called evolution issue rapidly became, at least for about seven years, a critical ingredient in battles among Christians who often disagreed profoundly about
what seemed to them critical religious beliefs, beliefs only partly identified by such labels as "modernist" and "fundamentalist." Even to utilize
such labels is already to engage major definitional issues. The largest
number of Americans who, on grounds of Christian beliefs, rejected
various aspects of evolutionary theory were reasonably orthodox Christians, but not part of any fundamentalist crusade. Such Christians were
in Roman Catholic, Lutheran, Wesleyan, or quite varied Reformed or
Calvinist denominations, or the traditional churches with European
roots. Others were members of new Christian movements with largely
American roots, such as the Restoration Movement, Seventh-day Adventists, Mormons, and Pentecostals.

By the 1920s, the most outspoken opponents of something called
"Darwinism," and particularly its inclusion in high school courses, were
self-acclaimed evangelical Christians. Some of these adopted, as a label
of self-identity, a newly popular word, "fundamentalist." "Evangelical,"
by almost any definition, whether as a label of self-identity or as a scholarly concept, by then denominated an often very self-conscious body of
Christians who, whatever the commonalities that justified the label, still
disagreed among themselves on fine points of doctrine, patterns of worship, social commitments, and moral standards. The word "fundamentalist" was even more treacherous, since it often had a very different
connotation for those who proudly claimed it as a label of self-identity
than for the many on the outside who used it, often pejoratively, to
characterize certain categories of Christians. For some journalists in the
twenties, such as H. L. Mencken, the word "fundamentalism" was almost as inclusive as the word "Christian." Anyone who affirmed the
traditional doctrines of the Church, in any denomination, was for him a
fundamentalist.

As I will use the labels, "evangelical" is the class and "fundamentalist"
a subclass. The words "evangel" and "evangelical" are part of the total
history of Christianity. The root word simply means good news, a news
associated with the New Testament gospels. This broad meaning of
evangelical is common to all Christians, Roman Catholic, Eastern Orthodox, and Protestant. But both Martin Luther and the founders of
various Reformed confessions placed a new emphasis upon "evangeli-

cal," a word that they used to distinguish their churches from the Church of Rome. Thus, Lutherans generally, and Reformed Christians often, used the label "evangelical" in the title of their churches, as do almost all American Lutherans today. For a Luther or a John Calvin, "evangelical" identified their central claim: that justification was by faith alone and not by sacramental works. Closely tied to this was the special role of Scripture, the Word, when informed by the Holy Spirit, and also the convicting role of the Spirit in leading individuals to conversion or in aiding them to move toward sanctification within the Church. This meant a ministry of the Word and Spirit to replace that of priests and of sacraments detached from faith.

Modern evangelicals all accept these definitions and fault mainline churches that have displaced the centrality of either Word or Spirit. But they mean much more than this by the label "evangelical." From the seventeenth century on, the Lutheran and Reformed churches of Europe faced internal reform or revitalization movements. These gained the label "pietist" among continental Lutherans, "puritan" within England. In each case, the reformers remained within the state church, at least for a time, and fought for a deeper and purer religion, one of heart as well as mind, and one farther removed from a religion of works or from Roman Catholicism. They wanted a purer church, one less corrupted by worldly concerns; they wanted a simpler but more heartfelt form of worship. They celebrated very rigorous, even abstentious, moral standards and struggled for a life informed by the third person of the Trinity. They wanted an able, conscientious, and clearly converted ministry. They tried to stop short of enthusiasm (claims of direct inspiration from God), but they still wanted a warm and experiential religion.

By the eighteenth century, such reformers had a much more clear quarrel with the established churches, in an age of religious rationalism, latitudinarianism, and worldly accommodation. Sporadic awakenings of religion, both in Britain and America, led to new revival techniques, to a new morphology of conversion, and to what was by then a religious stance almost everywhere called "evangelical," both by those who affirmed the label and by those who were its targets. In this sense, the label "evangelical" began to distinguish a part, but not all, of mainline Protestantism. After the 1740 awakening in America and the Wesley revivals in England, self-proclaimed evangelicals distinguished themselves from other Christians by four emphases. First and most central was their insistence upon a climactic and crisislike rebirth experience; second was their effort to cultivate affectionate and Spirit-filled forms of worship and devotion; third was their strong commitment to spreading the gospel and saving souls both at home and abroad, often through new revival and missionary institutions; and fourth was their demand for a very austere and nonworldly moral stance, one conducive to personal holiness and purity. Up through the mid-nineteenth century, those who held to these positions almost monopolized the label "evangelical."

Of course, certain doctrines lay behind such evangelical commitments. All evangelicals were heirs of the Reformation. All believed in the Pauline scheme of salvation—in justification by faith and in the atoning role of Jesus' death. All believed in an inspired Bible as the final authority on matters of faith and practice. Beyond such consensual beliefs, evangelicals honored their own specific denominational commitments. In this sense, they agreed to differ.

Evangelicals, so defined, made up a majority within such mainline Reformed denominations as Presbyterian and Congregational, and they fully dominated Methodists and Baptists. Even within the Episcopal Church, such evangelicals grew in strength up through the Civil War and came close to a majority by the fifties. The early, soon Americanized Lutherans and Dutch and German Reformed confessions largely capitulated to such an evangelical form of Christianity, at least up until conservative immigrants in the mid-nineteenth century shifted these denominations toward a more sacramental and liturgical form of Christianity. In other words, this evangelical outlook was dominant or hegemonic in the pre-Civil War years, so hegemonic that aspects of a near evangelical consensus (particularly conceptions of conversion, the use of revival methods, and a very abstentious morality) infiltrated such nonevangelical groups as Quakers, Mennonites, and the Church of the Brethren.

Resistance to such a hegemonic evangelicalism remained strong among a minority of Congregationalists and Old School Presbyterians as well as a growing majority of Lutherans. Except briefly at midcentury, the Episcopal Church remained predominantly nonevangelical. The new Restoration churches (Disciples, Christians) replaced a crisislike conversion by a series of rational decisions, although otherwise they remained close to evangelicals. Nonevangelicals did not require or at least emphasize a crisis rebirth experience, opposed the more overt new revival techniques or distrusted the emotionalism of revivals, stressed a moralistic more than an affectional understanding of regeneration, usually preferred a more formal or sacramental form of worship, and permitted a more relaxed and accommodating moral stance.

Even before the Civil War, the mainstream evangelical denominations faced small revolts within their own ranks. With cultural ascendancy, with growth, with greater educational sophistication, such former evangelical denominations as the Congregationalists, and to a lesser extent northern Presbyterians, Methodists, and even Baptists, seemed to critics to be losing their evangelical soul. Some congregations softened demands for an explosive conversion, watered down their revivals or dropped them altogether, became embarrassed by too much emotion in worship, and began to allow members to own slaves, attend the theater or dances, adopt changing fashions in dress and diet, and join in an open quest for wealth. In other words, formerly evangelical denominations, or those still such by profession, had slipped from the older standards. This complaint became more widespread after the Civil War, as new doctrinal dilemmas, occasioned by biblical scholarship and new evolutionary theories, forced more sophisticated evangelicals to abandon an earlier, almost reflexive biblicalism, and thus to become more latitudinarian in doctrine, even as some experimented with new liturgical forms. Note that those who so shifted their beliefs, and who soon gained the label "liberal," were part of the evangelical mainstream and in many respects still honored that tradition.

But with the developing divisions within traditional, mainline, and still avowedly evangelical denominations, the word "evangelical," at least in common use, gradually took on a more reactive or restrictive meaning. It continued to identify the four defining traits of late-eighteenth and early-nineteenth-century evangelicalism, but now with a defensive emphasis. What had been new in the early nineteenth century, and in many cases without clear scriptural justification—sudden, public conversions; new and rousing hymns of invitation; the open solicitations of sinners by laypeople; Sunday schools; summer camps and weekly prayer meetings; prayers at the anxious bench; and even a new class of ministers (those who devoted their career to revival preaching)— became by 1900 the essence of what some evangelicals called the "old-time religion."

"Fundamentalism" is a more tricky label than even "evangelicalism." Here the conventions are so varied, the popular use so ambiguous, that one has to stipulate clearly, and with a sense of being almost perversely arbitrary. Many people throughout the history of Christianity, when challenged, have tried to identify the most basic or fundamental beliefs of the Church. Words such as "fundamental" were descriptive but designated no distinct class of Christians. That changed soon after 1900, when some evangelicals began emphasizing certain widely shared beliefs and values as essential to being Christian and as a way of distinguishing themselves from other, purported Christians who had rejected or compromised some of the fundamental beliefs as they defined them. Thus, phrases such as "fundamentals of the faith" became a label of self-identity after 1910, chosen by more and more Christians and soon incorporated into publications and interdenominational organizations. Of course, those who adopted such labels for themselves varied greatly in doctrines, polity, and worship, but those who rallied around the fundamentals, or joined in causes or organizations to support them, assumed, correctly or not, that there were a few beliefs and moral values that any authentic Christian had to affirm and that those who affirmed such fundamentals now made up a distinct and beleaguered class among all those in America who claimed to be Christian.

So far, these emerging fundamentalists were orthodox, concerned with upholding traditional doctrines that they believed essential. As evangelicals, and all were in the sense of my definition, they joined their defense of the experiential and moral dimensions of their traditions with a doctrinal one, and in both cases in opposition to what seemed to them deviant developments within their traditional denominations. In fact, I would restrict the label "fundamentalist" to those evangelical Christians who became aware of, even obsessed with, doctrinal compromises or biblical deviations or moral laxity among other Christians, those whom they often called "liberals" and "modernists." As I define fundamentalism, it had a dialectical content, for it was shaped by its opposite. Before modernists, there could be no fundamentalists.

What is modernism? I am not going to pin it down very precisely (see chapter 4 for more details), for I suspect that the label never functioned very precisely among either those who condemned modernism or even among a very few theologians and ministers who adopted the label for themselves. I will follow some historians, such as William Hutchison, who have used liberalism as an encompassing class and made modernism a subclass, or a parallel to evangelicalism and fundamentalism. Liberals were those Christians who rejected narrow interpretations of creeds or doctrinal statements, were generous and inclusive in setting standards of membership, and, most important, were open and responsive to the need for rethinking or reformulating doctrines in the light of new biblical and scientific knowledge. They were, to this extent, heirs of eighteenth-century latitudinarians. Most came from an evangelical heritage, and because of that some were attracted to idealistic forms of theology, those that made the foundation of religious conviction not reason or

Scripture but inward experience. Implicit in such liberalism was an opening to major doctrinal revisions or compromises, and a selective and imaginative, rather than a comprehensive and literal, interpretation of the Bible. It is important to note that most such nineteenth-century liberals were basically conservative, in the sense that they sought ways of preserving the essentials of the older faith, and that most such liberals still claimed the label "evangelical" for themselves, even as they gladly conceded it to their more literalist opponents.

Modernists, by such a classification, were a small but more radical subbranch of liberals. Instead of struggling to accommodate new knowledge, modernists avidly greeted it. They accepted a progressive conception of revelation, tied to a God much more immanent than transcendent. Thus, one could argue that all new knowledge, all new insights, all new scientific theories progressively revealed more about divinity. In their conception, God was not supernatural or transcendent, but a spirit or mind or force that was in the world and guided the processes of nature. Older beliefs, tied to a different understanding of the world or rooted in different social organizations, were by definition provisional, limited by time and place, and thus never properly dogmatized or frozen into creeds and confessions. Thus the word "modern" generally stood for what was better, higher, or more truthful.

As ideal types, such a defined liberalism and modernism are useful for historians and for the sake of clarity. Yet I doubt that many self-proclaimed fundamentalists, in their denunciations of either liberalism or modernism, were quite so precise and discriminating. They often used the labels synonymously and, in each case, pejoratively. What they condemned was any deviation from what they saw as the minimal essentials of Christianity, which, from their perspective, meant some version of the Pauline, Augustinian scheme of salvation, whether interpreted from a Calvinist or an Arminian perspective, and, in each case, doctrines rooted in the full and complete authority of an inspired and error-free Bible. Even small deviations led to charges of heresy. They also bemoaned the loss of the experiential and moral content of the older faith.

It is important to emphasize that the laypeople who identified themselves as fundamentalists, or joined in fundamentalist crusades, were not academic theologians or even able dialecticians. They indeed emphasized beliefs, but they tended to reduce the essential beliefs to a few, including some that became focal largely because they seemed most threatened by liberals and modernists. What fundamentalists could agree on was the full authority of the Bible, the literal historicity of events stretching back through Noah to Adam and Eve, the Jewish Scriptures as prophetic of a coming Messiah, Jesus as that Messiah, his virgin birth, the truth of the gospel accounts of his many miracles and above all of his resurrection, his early return to earth to establish a millennial kingdom, and the absolute nature of a fully Christian or biblically grounded morality. The one most common appeal was to an inerrant Bible.

One final feature of fundamentalism, as I define it, involved more than beliefs. Just as fundamentalists defined themselves by what they opposed and identified the common or rallying doctrines and moral values that "modernists" threatened, so they distinguished themselves from other orthodox, doctrinally concerned evangelicals by their willingness to join in militant crusades against modernism in order to preserve or reestablish the old verities, or to cleanse churches or the larger society of heresy and immorality. They were fighting evangelicals. They were very defensive, both on doctrinal and moral issues, and to the extent that they felt threatened they were willing to fight back.

This activist bent spurred fundamentalist involvement in public policy issues. Fundamentalists tried to legislate what they saw as a biblical morality (including an endorsement of conventional roles for women and strong support for prohibition), to outlaw evolutionary theories or, later, to gain an equal hearing for creationist beliefs; to screen textbooks and control local curricula or, if this failed, to organize separate parochial schools; and, more recently, to organize political action groups in order to infiltrate or control local political parties or to elect friendly candidates to key positions in local or even state and national governments. At the same time, they tried to build defensive fortifications against the erosive effect of American higher education through a huge national network of Bible institutes and small evangelical and fundamentalist four-year colleges, as well as through periodicals, alliances, mission teams, youth groups, radio and television evangelists, summer camps and retreats, and conferences. Just like other visible minorities, such as blacks and Jews, fundamentalists in many parts of the country voted as a bloc and could often swing elections by their massed power. This activism completes my necessarily arbitrary definition of fundamentalism: *a very defensive coalition of evangelicals (that is, born-again, spiritually-minded, mission-oriented, and morally rigorous Protestants) who affirm a few common and clearly endangered doctrines, who bow before the binding authority of an inerrant Bible and its moral teachings, and who actively crusade in the public arena against their many identified and allegedly liberal and modernist enemies.*

In the nineteenth century, the challenges to Protestant orthodoxy were multiple. Biblical criticism was at first even more threatening than the new geology or various evolutionary theories that competed for acceptance from 1800 on. But the major denominations held firm on biblical authority and on either a Calvinist or an Arminian scheme of salvation. Internal debates raged on almost every issue, such as the revival techniques introduced by Charles Finney. New and very distinctive sects, such as Adventists and Mormons, posed a more immediate challenge than did scholarship or science, while the great competitive challenge to Protestants was the deluge of Roman Catholic immigrants. But fissures within the evangelical camp were prophetic.

In 1857–58, evangelical Protestants enjoyed the last widespread, synchronized revival in American history, although even it was limited largely to the North and flourished most of all in larger cities. It was very different from the awakenings of the past, with prominent leadership from Episcopalians, with businessmen taking the lead, and with a clear dominance by affluent and educated laypeople. This was an evangelism from the top down, and thus a revival that scarcely touched the South or many rural areas. Its promise proved ephemeral, as the nation plunged into the Civil War. Never again would such hopes revive. In the postwar years, evangelical Christians lost any sense of clear identity, lost power and influence to nonevangelical Christians, and, most depressing of all, fell into a confusing factionalism among themselves. In the northern denominations, it would be evangelical leaders, in major urban pulpits or in the best seminaries, who would move toward greater inclusiveness doctrinally, toward liturgical reforms, and toward accommodations with biblical scholarship and the new biology. But until the twentieth century, even among Episcopalians and Congregationalists, the liberals were a minority, well ahead of a majority of either clergy or laypeople. This meant opportunities for effective appeals to members by those ministers or intellectuals who were resistant to innovations in worship or revisions in doctrine. In all the major denominations, the conservative factions, or moderates willing to support them, were able to hold on to denominational policy, meaning that avowed liberals remained a resented minority, although they gained increased strength in northern seminaries. This power alignment gradually shifted toward liberals and moderates in the twentieth century, at least in the North. It would be the newly self-identified fundamentalists who would fight a rearguard action to prevent these liberal shifts.

The divisions in the late nineteenth century were complex. It is all too easy to assert a disjunctive alignment, between orthodox and liberal.

Within the two Methodist Episcopal Churches (North and South), still the largest Protestant confession, the cleavage developed, not overtly around confessional issues but around the issue of sanctification or holiness. Among Calvinists it usually involved doctrine and, in some cases, adherence to the Westminster Confession. Prominent ministers became identified as liberal or as orthodox. The loosely defined factions fought battles in denominational conferences or conventions, in periodicals, and in seminaries. In almost all contested cases, including five or six well-publicized trials for what amounted to heresy, the orthodox won. But with each passing year the liberal side seemed to grow. Clearly, the intellectual trends favored liberalism in the North and in the best seminaries.

In the developing controversies within Calvinist denominations, two issues slowly rose to centrality in the last decades of the nineteenth century. Neither was new, but both took on new meaning because of the context. These were the related issues of biblical infallibility and eschatological expectations. In complex ways, these often overlapped with the debates over Darwin or Darwinism, but many of the orthodox believed that a day-age or gap interpretation could reconcile the Genesis accounts with some form of Christian or theistic evolution.

Until the nineteenth century, biblical authority had been so nearly consensual among Protestants that it occasioned few controversies. An inspired Bible, and its ultimate authority in matters of belief and practice, had always been a background assumption of Christians in all confessional traditions, although Christians disagreed, often violently, on the correct interpretation of Scriptures. They even had different canons, or conceptions of what was scriptural and what not. It was clear that the Christian Bible, in Protestant or Catholic versions, was a complex body of writings, composed over a long period of time. Such was the richness of content that Christians had no alternative but to try their best to interpret the meaning of different books. Whether acknowledged or not, these interpretations were varied and always selective. But the fact that all sides appealed to the Bible establishes the critical point: they accepted it not only as binding on issues of doctrine and practice, but as a textbook on history and the laws of the physical universe.

Behind the near-universal appeal to an inspired Bible were huge problems of interpretation, and even equivocal understanding of what inspiration meant. Only a few radical Unitarians, and especially transcendentalists in that movement, such as Theodore Parker, essayed a complete break from either natural or biblical authority for religious belief and practice. Such lonely voices were literally crying in the wilderness. After the Civil War, many intellectually honest Christians simply could not accept all parts of the Bible as equally authoritative or see the whole as internally coherent and divinely inspired. Yet those who tried to formulate a different attitude toward Scripture, or to escape into idealistic theologies that made experience or inward understanding the foundation of religious belief, faced condemnation or even expulsion from all save Unitarian and some Episcopal pulpits. For the orthodox, the full and binding authority of Scripture was clearly the most critical issue, for biblical authority lay behind all the essential doctrines of the Church as they understood them. Thus, biblical infallibility gradually became the most crucial test of what, after 1910, conservative evangelicals would call the "fundamentals of the faith." But such a view of the Bible was increasingly challenged by almost every intellectual development of the new century.

What if all parts of the Bible were not true? What if, in fact, it contained a large component of fable and myth? What if it were internally inconsistent, often contradictory, and always conditioned by the time and place and cultural assumptions of its varied authors? Today, almost every educated person makes assumptions about the natural universe, and about human history, that are radically inconsistent with any literal understanding of parts of the Bible. This is a fact, one documented by almost every textbook taught in the schools, by every television program on natural history, even by popular fiction or movies. Children grow up with some conception of the antiquity of the earth, with its relative position in a galaxy and in the ever expanding universe, with theories about the big bang as an elusive explanation of the origins of our universe, with a fascination with dinosaurs and other extinct species, with some grasp of the enormous variety of religions and religiously based scriptures, and with a belief that, in some sense, later and higher species have a genetic connection to earlier and at times more primitive ones. Early in their education, children come to understand that no physical theory can account for a worldwide flood, that no ark could begin to contain members of every species, and that humans did not originate quite recently in a Mesopotamian Eden but evolved from humanoid species in Africa. This is all common knowledge, not thereby infallible or beyond challenge and revision, but so much a part of self-understanding as to be basic to individual identity. That this is so, that the understanding of the world absorbed by most people in our society has changed so dramatically in the last two hundred years, is a fact of life, and one that offered a powerful challenge to fundamentalists.

Before World War I, another issue that eventually became a mark, or a test, of the largest and most clearly fundamentalist wing of evangelicalism was what protagonists called "premillennialism." For anyone who took the Bible literally, it was clear that Jesus had promised to return to finish building his kingdom. This doctrine is spread throughout the New Testament. The exact scenario of his return is less clear, for the intimations vary somewhat in detail. These scenarios are variously hinted at in apocalyptic segments in the Gospels, in Acts, and at a few points in the Epistles of Paul. The only elaborately detailed scenario of the advent is in chapters 20 and 21 of Revelation. It makes clear that Jesus will return to earth only after a great period of troubles among world empires. The returning Christ will defeat the enemies of God and chain Satan for a thousand years (hence the word "millennium"), during which the Christ reigns, presumably here on earth, carrying out a great judgment and assisted by resurrected martyrs and saints. A final resurrection, and a final judgment, follows this millennium. The New Jerusalem descends from the heavens to become the capital of God's Kingdom, now on a newly cleansed earth.

This is the literal account in Revelation. Notably, many Christians have chosen to ignore such a version of last things. Others, by use of various biblical passages, have embellished the main story, and in a fascinating variety of ways. Both Luther and Calvin were leery of extreme chiliasts; the Augsburg Confession has an article condemning literal advent doctrines. Yet the promise of Jesus' return, and images of a millennial age, have remained central to Protestants. It was the details that varied. Calvinists typically avoided dogma at this point, leaving such mysteries to God. But beginning in the late eighteenth century, the apocalyptic texts in the Bible led to dozens of theories and scenarios. American Adventists made the Revelation account central but added to their expectation of an immanent Advent such unorthodox doctrines as soul sleep and annihilationism. More influential among American evangelicals were the prophetic theories of an Englishman, John Nelson Darby, who founded a primitive, restoration fellowship, made up of completely independent congregations and known as the Plymouth Brethren. Darby worked out the seven ages of human history, or what he called the "dispensations of God." The first five ranged from the Garden of Eden though the period before the flood, to the age from Noah to Abraham, to the age of the patriarchs, and finally to the dispensation of the Law in Israel. Each age ended in catastrophes. The present age, that of grace or the church, will also end in the tribulations that precede the millennial age.

Most Christians had thought in terms of ages or dispensations, but not with the formal details of Darby. Yet it was not the seven dispensations that proved important in America but Darby's pessimistic view of contemporary events and his emphasis upon the period of troubles that would precede what he believed to be the early Advent. He believed that when Jesus prepared to return to earth, living Christians would escape a final, seven years of woeful tribulation, because they would enjoy a secret or invisible rapture just before the suffering (his rapture doctrine, unlike his general scenario of last things, was based not on any literal reading of biblical texts, but a very idiosyncratic interpretation of biblical prophecy, leading to intramural debates that continue to this day over pre- or post- or even intra-tribulation doctrines). The rapture, a doctrine that still percolates widely among evangelicals and fundamentalists, gives to living Christians a hope that, either when the Christ comes or just before, they will ascend to meet him. By the end of the nineteenth century, most self-conscious evangelicals except those out of Methodism had at least accepted some version of premillennialism, but far from all accepted a schematic form of dispensationalism. They simply believed that God directly controlled all historical events, that he dealt differently with humans in each age, that a time of troubles would precede the Advent, and that the millennium would rest upon the work of the returning Christ and not upon any human achievement.

Since in all these predictions about the future, Jesus would return at the beginning of the thousand years, evangelicals began to emphasize the "pre" in the label "premillennialism." If one accepted Darby's full system, then one was a dispensational premillennialist. Actually, premillennialism was the only position consistent with a literal reading of the Bible. Thus biblical literalism and premillennialism joined as identifying doctrines of conservative, orthodox evangelicals. But those more clearly in a confessional tradition—Episcopal, Presbyterian, or Lutheran—had to reject any schematic dispensationalism, for at many points it was inconsistent with their confessions or their doctrinal or theological traditions.

What was most persuasive in a formalized premillennialist position, one affirmed by Adventists and Mormons as well as Darbyites, was a realistic or pessimistic perspective on contemporary history. In the language of the developing controversy, something called "postmillennialism" was the inverse of premillennialism. The label was very imprecise

or misleading. What is true is that American evangelicals had, in the pre-
Civil War period, looked forward to such an expansion of the Church,
and of evangelical Protestantism, not only in America but in the world,
that they believed something close to the promised millennial kingdom
might be realized in the present age, or before the return of Jesus. Rarely
did such hopeful Christians view such a golden age of the Church as a
thousand years in duration, or even as an alternative to the scenarios of
Revelation, which they often found too obscure to take literally. The
label "postmillennialism" rarely identified a clear alternative to premillennialism but rather a more optimistic outlook on the immediate future
of the Church or, in some cases, of the United States. From Jonathan
Edwards on, many of the leading Calvinist theologians had used millennial images to talk about the possible effects of great revivals, but in most
cases they used these images in a figurative and not a literal sense. If
challenged, most might have conceded that Jesus would return to inau-
gurate a special thousand-year period, for it was impossible to get this
out of the Bible. I suspect few American evangelical Christians, before
the late nineteenth century, ever worked out a fully coherent or dogmatic view of last things. This is what Darbyites contributed, and with
a vengeance. It was in this sense that even an insistence on dogmatic
premillennialism, totally apart from the special rigidities of dispensationalism, represented an innovative new departure among American evangelicals.

Premillennialism served a vital role among culturally beleaguered
evangelicals. It documented a new apocalyptic outlook. It symbolized a
loss of faith in the potential for human achievement, located the cause
of significant historical change in divine agency, and shifted the primary
goal of Christians from building the kingdom to salvaging as many souls
as possible from all the impending calamities that loomed ahead. This
saving remnant mentality was characteristic of a people living in a confused, Hellenistic age. One implication was a new perspective on Christian reform, or on efforts to clean up this old world and make it as
respectable as possible. The great heresy tied to postmillennialism was an
impious expectation that humans could build the kingdom by their own
efforts. Although nineteenth-century evangelicals had often taken the
lead in trying to ameliorate the problems of the larger society (they were
more likely to oppose slavery, to struggle to control vice or alcoholism,
to open missions or Sunday schools for the poor or oppressed than more
confessional or liturgical Christians), they had kept their priority on winning souls.

This remained true of the new evangelicals, but with a critical difference. The pessimism tied to their premillennial scenarios, perhaps reinforced by their increased cultural isolation, led more and more evangelicals to repudiate what became known as a "social gospel." The label is one of the most imprecise in American history, and it has impeded the understanding of Church history more than any other simplistic concept. Of all Protestant groups, it would be the fundamentalists who adopted the broadest social agenda and who fought more aggressively to achieve it. But scholars, usually, denote by social gospel a few latter-day, and often doctrinally liberal, evangelicals who tried to find a solution to some of the manifest problems of cities or the types of dependency involved in wage employment. Joined with this, at times, was an optimism about the possibilities of reform and a decreased emphasis upon conversion and piety. From the perspective of conservative Christians, the whole Pauline scheme of salvation had given way to conceptions of moral effort, social reform, and utopian achievements, or a diversion from all the heart themes and doctrines of the historic Church. In this one respect, the new evangelicals anticipated the more realistic social analysis of a later Reinhold Niebuhr. The crisis theology or new orthodoxy of the thirties and the World War II era had some affinities with such an earlier premillennialism, but with critical differences. The neo-orthodox theologians rested their faith, not upon a literal or inerrant Bible, but upon the congruence of certain biblical themes with human experience, or a blending of the Word, which was both more and less than the Bible, with some of the experiential themes that had always characterized evangelicalism. Reinhod Niebuhr, for example, emphasized a Biblically based Christian philosophy, one that involved a realistic view of humans and of history, but he did not view the Bible as a textbook on nature or history.

By the early twentieth century, various conservative evangelicals had already created their infrastructure. Out of dispensationalist premillennialism came an influential series of annual prophecy conferences, which first began in 1876. In 1909, C. I. Scofield, the most influential advocate of a Darby-like form of dispensationalism, published the *Scofield Reference Bible*, in actuality a heavily annotated King James text, with the annotations so guiding Bible students as to lead them to dispensationalist conclusions. After 1882 holiness advocates began moving out of Methodism and into independent congregations. In the new century these began to coalesce into national denominations. Some of the leading revivalists, in the tradition of Dwight L. Moody, merged forms of holiness doctrine with Calvinist doctrines and formed separate colleges or, in one case, a new denomination, the Christian and Missionary Alliance. Conservative revival preachers formed a national network, as they interacted at summer encampments and at conferences. Thus, in the new century, one could identify an emerging coalition of a few dozen key leaders, all revivalistic, strictly evangelical, biblically oriented, and, in most but not all cases, premillennial. These leaders eventually became identified fundamentalists when they launched a major attack upon modernist heresies in the mainline churches, Darwinism, and secular trends and moral degeneracy in the larger society.

Fundamentalism, as an organized protest movement, had two early forms. One was the effort, within a few denominations, by conservative ministers or seminarians to purge liberals and modernists and to save their churches for orthodoxy. This was a movement fought within the governing agencies of major denominations, among a ministerial and in some cases scholarly elite, and centered almost entirely in the North, although a surprising number of fundamentalist protagonists were born and reared in the South. Paralleling this was a more popular crusade, against not only modernist heresies, but even more against Darwinism and moral trends in the larger society. This crusade often involved less academic or less scholarly preachers, such as the almost exhibitionist showman J. Frank Norris or even the popular evangelist Billy Sunday, plus such lay frontmen as William Jennings Bryan. Joining the two into a loose coalition were an overlapping leadership and a growing appreciation on both sides that, whatever the differences of style, both had common enemies.

One symbolic date for the beginnings of this crusade was 1910. In that year, the General Assembly of the Presbyterian Church in the United States of America (northern) adopted a five-point platform, one pushed upon it by those most concerned about the orthodoxy of professors and students in Presbyterian theological seminaries. Ministers already subscribed to the doctrinally rigorous Westminster Confession. Notably, the five points in the declaration clearly reflected some concerns of recent vintage: the inerrancy of Scripture, the virgin birth, a substitutionary atonement, the bodily resurrection of the Christ, and the authenticity of biblical miracles. This would have seemed a strange declaration to early Calvinists, involving as it did what had formerly seemed either truisms or issues peripheral to the important doctrines of the Church. Times had changed. Of the five issues, inerrancy figured largest in this and subsequent Presbyterian conflicts. Many later fundamentalists would adopt the first four points but make premillennialism, not biblical miracles (inerrancy took care of this issue), the fifth. Confessional Presbyterians could not accept dispensationalism or any rigid premillennial scenarios. Not only did this Presbyterian declaration include a strange, doctrinally nonparallel series of points, but it was a platform that was general enough to appeal to conservative evangelicals in Methodist or other traditional Arminian denominations, or the enemies of the past. In a sense, the Presbyterians flirted with dogmatic softness.

Also in 1910, a wealthy California oilman subsidized the publication over the next five years of twelve paperback books, collectively titled *The Fundamentals*. Each edited book contained a series of essays, some scholarly, some more popular, on the critical issues raised by liberals or modernists. Each writer gave his own testimony to the truth, meaning that the books had no one coherent thesis. Many committed dispensationalists contributed, but this was not an issue pushed by the volumes. The authors of the essays reflected a rather broad spectrum of American and British evangelical spokespersons. The most addressed issue was the status of the Bible, but not all authors adhered to a narrow conception of inerrancy. Neither did all reject Christianized versions of evolution. Some reflected what had so far been a degree of flexibility on the chronology of creation, a flexibility present even among British dispensationalists. All identified ministers, missionaries, seminary professors, Sunday school superintendents, and religious editors in Britain and America received free copies of these subsidized essays. What impact they had is impossible to gauge. They surely reinforced orthodox beliefs, but such was the sophistication of some that they may have made older ministers or lay leaders aware of challenging issues that they had not heretofore had to face. In time, these volumes probably (there is no direct connection) helped lead the defenders of the old order to adopt the label "fundamentalist" at the end of World War I (apparently the first expansion of the word "fundamentals" into "fundamentalism" came in 1919).

The internal crusade came to a head in the early twenties, as liberal and orthodox ministers and professors fought for the soul of northern Presbyterian and Baptist denominations and the avowedly nondenominational Disciples of Christ. For the Presbyterian Church, the conservative protagonists ranged from a very scholarly and professorial John Gresham Machen at Princeton Seminary, to such a denominational politician and pastor as Clarence E. Macartney, to the best-known Presbyterian layman, William Jennings Bryan. Their enemies were not as well-identified, although in time one Baptist clergyman, Harry Emerson

Fosdick, who had a pastoral appointment in the liberal First Presbyterian Church in New York City, became the devil of the orthodox. Fosdick was a perfect foil, not only because he reflected an almost caricatured version of liberalism (for his beliefs, see Chapter 4), but because he openly bearded the fundamentalists and did so with enough verve, eloquence, and cleverness to win many moderates to his side.

Machen became a spokesman for Presbyterian fundamentalists in 1923, with a very polemical but brilliant book, *Christianity and Liberalism* (for a detailed survey of this book, see Chapter 4). Machen and other orthodox spokespersons made Fosdick the target of several charges and, in the General Assembly, succeeded in an indirect tactic to force him from his Presbyterian pulpit in 1925 (they required that he join the Presbyterian Church, which meant that he would have to subscribe to the Westminster Confession). But in their now well-publicized effort to control the General Assembly, the orthodox faction failed. This northern wing of Presbyterianism had gradually moved from a narrowly confessional body to a moderate and inclusive fellowship. No doubt a majority of members agreed with the orthodox position, but it was not clear that they wanted a new series of heresy trials or such restrictive standards for ordination as to force liberal ministers out of the church. Such inclusiveness, or doctrinal flabbiness, paralleled the virtual disappearance of church disciplinary procedures against errant members in congregations. The General Assembly, in 1903, had approved amendments to its confession (a version of Westminster) that so softened its Calvinism as to enable a 1906 merger with the near-Arminian Cumberland Presbyterians. Even the five points of 1910 accommodated the perspective of the still fully evangelical Cumberlands. By the 1924 General Assembly, the new fundamentalist crusade threatened to split the denomination. The assembly elected as moderator one of the church's most powerful ministers and an ally of Machen, Macartney, who had led the fight against Fosdick.

It seemed that the orthodox would now win, but it was not to be. A large group of liberal (in the sense of inclusive) ministers drafted a resolution (the Auburn Affirmation) that challenged the right of the assembly to do what it had voted to do not only in 1910 but twice thereafter: to make the five points of 1910 a requirement for ordination. The liberals correctly pointed out that the points were not clearly biblical or confessional and that to make them obligatory would require amendments to the discipline of the church (its constitution). The logic was impeccable, and the resolution passed.

In the tense 1925 assembly, a moderate colleague of Machen, Charles Erdman, won in the ballot for moderator against Bryan (this was just before Bryan's appearance in the Scopes trial and his early death in Dayton, Tennessee). The assembly, rather than bringing the more sensitive issues to a vote, appointed a committee of inquiry to report at the next assembly. It did so, and with recommendations that variously appeased both sides. This strategy, in effect, deflected the fundamentalist challenge. From 1926 on it was clear that the denomination, probably supported by a majority of laypersons, would remain flexible on such issues as inerrancy (it still required subscription to its revised Westminster Confession) and inclusive enough to accommodate liberal ministers and seminarians. Most of the conservatives accepted such mediatorial compromises, but not Machen (see Chapter 4).

Equally racked by a fundamentalist–liberal controversy was the Northern Baptist Convention. Northern Baptists split with their southern brethren in 1844 over the slavery issue. What remained, in both regions, was a type of missionary organization. Southern Baptists first converted this into a rather tightly organized service organization for what remained legally independent congregations. Northern Baptists followed in 1908 with a Northern Baptist Convention modeled on that of the South, but again one with no legal authority over congregations. The convention was thus a voluntary fellowship, but one that supported missions, colleges, seminaries, and publications. In its annual meetings, delegates debated and voted upon doctrinal and other issues, again with only an advisory role. Yet the convention's effective power was considerable, although not as controlling as in the present Southern Baptist Convention. It was in this loose, but focused, institutional context that northern Baptists fought the same battles as the Presbyterians, and with the same outcome—the more inclusive or liberal factions won, not on the disputed points of doctrine, but on the preservation of a typically Baptist commitment to personal religious freedom, local autonomy, and a type of inclusiveness or pluralism.

The most effective leaders of the fundamentalist movement in the Northern Baptist Convention were powerful preachers, each a pastor of a large urban congregation. Most influential in the larger fundamentalist movement, but less attached to the convention, was William Bell Riley, for almost fifty years the minister of the largest Baptist church in Minnesota, First Baptist in Minneapolis. Joining him in efforts to purge the denomination of liberals was J. C. Massee, pastor in the twenties of the Tremont Temple Baptist Church in Boston, and John Roach Straton, a biting, sharp orator and nemesis of Fosdick when pastor of the Calvary Baptist Church in New York City and a close ally of Bryan and Riley in the battle against evolution. Massee and Straton were born in the Confederate South, while Riley grew up in Kentucky. All three gained their ministerial training at the Southern Baptist Seminary in Louisville, and all had at one time or other connections with Southern Baptist congregations. On doctrinal issues, they were in full agreement. In addition to the standard beliefs of evangelicals, all three affirmed both inerrancy and a type of premillennialism.

Riley was arguably the most influential of the early fundamentalist leaders. In a sense, he even invented the label and the movement. He stood midway between scholarly advocates such as Machen or even Macartney and the more popular crusaders such as Norris and Bryan. He built an evangelical empire in Minneapolis, including his own periodicals and his Northwestern Bible Institute, Northwestern Seminary, and, just before his death, a liberal arts college. By permission of his congregation he devoted four months each year to evangelism. He eschewed the showmanship of Billy Sunday, but perfected techniques for winning converts in carefully organized urban crusades, or a ministry that presaged that of his selected successor (but not really a close disciple either in style or social outlook), Billy Graham. From his college training on, Riley preached a conventional form of evangelical Christianity, and in sermons (most published in a series of books), he fought against both the liberalism that grew out of the higher criticism and the humanism that derived from the teaching of evolutionary theories. He epitomized evangelical culture in his puritanical moralism and in his condemnation of modern vices and diversions. He was often denunciatory, confrontational, and divisive, an angry prophet bringing God's condemnation to all aspects of modernism. He lacked the scholarly pretension of Machen but excelled at proof-text apologetics and, like Machen, continuously invited the liberals to move out of the Church, for what they taught was simply inconsistent with Baptist traditions. He could be anti-intellectualist, as in his running attacks upon Shailer Mathews and the Divinity School of the University of Chicago and upon professors generally, in his efforts to purge unwanted liberals from all Baptist colleges, and in his attempts to secure an anti-evolution bill for Minnesota (he failed for the last time in 1928).

During World War I, Riley joined with Reuben A. Torrey, a disciple of Dwight L. Moody and then head of the Bible Institute of Los Angeles (Biola College) and one of the most outspoken, holiness-oriented evangelicals in America, to launch an organized fundamentalist movement. The first discussions began in 1918 and matured into an organization—the World's Christian Fundamentals Association (WCFA)—in 1919. Conservative evangelicals had reacted in horror to abortive liberal and ecumenical efforts to found a World Church Union as a counterpart to the League of Nations, or what many premillennialists believed to be the beast of Revelation 20. They succeeded in reversing early Northern Baptist Convention involvement and formed their own counter organization. Established to fight liberalism, the WCFA had its own fundamentalist platform and, under Riley's leadership, soon devoted most of its efforts to the battles against evolution. It enlisted William Jennings Bryan to join the prosecution in the Scopes trial of 1925. The WCFA began with a conference of already networked evangelical leaders, most from Baptist churches and Bible institutes, and all but a handful from Canada and the United States. Because of its morbid preoccupation with evolution, and the inability of highly independent and egotistic fundamentalist ministers to cooperate, the WCFA never lived up to the lofty expectations of Riley. By 1928 Riley was also a defeated dissident in his own denomination. The old man became a virulent anti-Semite and right-wing fascist sympathizer in the thirties and, in the last years of his life, he formed a separate Baptist association in Minnesota.

It was Massee and Straton who took the lead in efforts to purge and purify the Northern Baptist Convention. They convened a meeting of like-minded Baptist ministers in New York City and again in a conference before the meeting of the 1921 convention in Buffalo. The conference tried to find a way to preserve the "fundamentals" of the Baptist faith. Riley gave a sermon on the menace of modernism, directed mostly at avowedly modernist professors in Baptist universities and seminaries. This led to a conference-sponsored resolution, introduced by Massee, requiring an investigation of colleges and seminaries as to their adherence to the central doctrines of the Church. A committee of nine carried out this inquiry but professed to find no problems with most of the now frightened teachers and students. While it reflected concerns about the biblicalism of some professors, it left all discipline up to the institution (actually, it had few alternatives). The resolution, and the bitter debate, placed the fundamentalists in the position of obstructionists. Straton, in particular, was sharp and scurrilous in his attacks on the majority in the convention. Having suffered a legislative victory, yet a complete failure to gain their goals, the fundamentalists after 1921 set as their goal the acceptance by the convention of an orthodox confession as a basis of congregational fellowhip in the convention (of course, the convention could not force any congregation to accept such a creed but it could refuse to seat its delegates). The new Fundamentalist Federation drafted a confession, but it failed to get consideration because of what seemed a likely joint confession under development by both the Southern and Northern Conventions. At the 1922 convention, Massee and Riley moved the adoption of the new confession, yet they lost when an opponent moved a cleverly worded resolution to make the New Testament as a whole the basis of faith and practice. Some supported this alternative in principle, others saw a strategy to prevent deeper divisions in the church. Massee, unhappy with this result but increasingly dismayed by the extremist language of Straton and Riley, began to move toward a more mediatorial stance and slowly lost the support of the extreme fundamentalists.

The final battle in the denomination, and a decisive defeat for fundamentalists, came in 1924. Straton and fellow fundamentalists in the New York area now demanded a right to examine all official correspondence with foreign missionaries, in order to detect the virus of liberalism. They wanted, in effect, to set up a test of doctrinal orthodoxy for all missionaries (unlike minsters in local congregations, they were directly responsible to the convention). Massee deserted the extremists on this, and helped engineer another investigating commission, which in effect deflected the purge effort. By 1925, the Baptists were more divided than the Presbyterians, with not only a liberal-fundamentalist split, but a growing division between extreme fundamentalists, with their aggressive and abusive tactics, and doctrinal conservatives like Massee, who still hoped to find ways of holding the denomination together. The Fundamentalist Federation, which Massee helped organize and then headed, was now upstaged by a more radical Baptist Bible Union. Massee resigned his presidency of the federation. In the 1926 convention, to help defuse fundamentalist efforts to keep congregations practicing open membership from having a right to send delegates, Massee proposed, unsuccessfully, a six-month truce between the opposing sides, while the denomination launched an ambitious new evangelical effort (Baptists could all agree on efforts to save souls or gain members). Even as they reviled Massee as an apostate, Riley and Straton recognized that they could not win within the denomination, and thus began working largely within their own fundamentalist organizations.

These tensions within Baptism led to schismatic new denominations. In 1932 a remnant of the Baptist Bible Union, by now embarrassed by scandals affecting one of its ministers, formed a new General Association of Regular Baptists. Appropriately, it adoped the same confession rejected in 1922 by the convention and added a premillennial clause. Today, this conservative Baptist denomination claims over 200,000 members. Riley did not join this splinter, but in the war years he effectively separated the Minnesota state convention from the national denomination, formed a separate missionary society, and fought unsuccessfully for its recognition by the Northern Baptist Convention. When this failed, and after a nasty battle within the convention, in which the fundamentalists lost in their efforts to get the convention out of the Federal Council of Churches and to set up very narrow doctrinal tests for missionaries, he and his followers withdrew to form the Conservative Baptist Association. Today, this denomination also claims over 200,000 members. At this point, Riley died. He had softened some of his anti-Semitism during the war, and at its end he was so impressed with the work of the evangelist Billy Graham that he persuaded the reluctant young man to succeed him as head of his three educational institutions. Graham, who never personally moved to Minneapolis, and who preferred his evangelical work to the management of institutions, was not an effective replacement for the dictatorial Riley. He resigned in 1952, just before the institute and seminary began a fatal decline, and before the college faced suspension and reorganization. But this brief tie with Riley led the Billy Graham Evangelistic Association to continue its headquarters in Minneapolis.

The Christian Churches (Disciples of Christ) suffered divisions that rivaled those in northern Presbyterian and Baptist denominations. It had already suffered the exodus, by 1907, of a strongly anti-institutional, largely southern splinter, or congregations that became the Churches of Christ. From the turn of the century until a climactic struggle in the mid-twenties, the Disciples suffered increasing tensions between liberal innovators and defenders of the purity of the old Restoration movement. A new leadership developed among Disciples, one tied to young and better-educated ministers. Young men attended major universities, such as Yale or the new University of Chicago. They responded to intellectual trends, identified with colleagues in other mainline denominations, and were increasingly embarrassed by the more sectarian or divisive aspects of their movement. They absorbed new, scholarly information about the Bible. They sought ways to reconcile New Testament Christianity with theories about evolution. Out of honesty, they could not accept the commonsense biblicalism of such founders as Barton W. Stone and Alexander Campbell. They wanted a more inclusive movement, and they wanted to fulfill the old goal of Christian unity through different forms of cooperation with other Christians. As in most denominations, the ministers moved far ahead of the majority of the laity and at times practiced a type of duplicity in camouflaging what they were about. They gathered at their new seminary, the Divinity House at the University of Chicago, and formed an elite or exclusive theological discussion group, the Campbell Society. As they gained leadership roles, a gulf developed between the leading agencies of an emerging denomination and the broader constituency the agencies were supposed to represent, but, in fact, a constituency they tried to lead and mold in new ways.

Soon the signs of controversy were all about. Among the Disciples, the one most potent symbol of change, or what conservatives saw as betrayal, was open membership, meaning the admission to fellowship of people who had not received proper baptism. This issue focused the problem of biblical authority, since the movement had always argued that baptism by immersion, for the remission of sins, was a critical aspect of the New Testament plan of salvation. If there were any essential doctrines, surely this was one of them. Only a few congregations practiced open membership before 1910, but others reflected an ecumenism that clearly pointed in that direction. Disciples led in the successful effort to form the Federal Council of Churches and won convention support for membership in it. Disciples missionaries in China formed working alliances with other Protestants. Socially active Disciples joined in broader moral reforms, beginning with temperance. One of the most prominent of many Disciples journalists, Charles C. Morrison, took over a small periodical, renamed it the *Christian Century*, and turned it into the leading proponent of Protestant liberalism and unity.

By 1919, the leading conservative periodical, the *Standard*, began rallying effective opposition to what its editors saw as modernist trends in the central agencies of the Disciples. Some of the leaders of a developing revolt had close ties to evangelicals and fundamentalists. Bryan gave an anti-evolution speech to one of their preconvention congresses. But the smoking gun, from the conservative viewpoint, consisted of policies sanctioned by a newly unified mission agency, the United Christian Missionary Society (UCMS). It seemed that in China, at least, missionaries had adopted an open membership position. Beginning in 1919, the conservatives, who undoubtedly reflected the majority view of laypeople, began meeting in congresses before the International Convention. A pattern soon developed. They introduced resolutions upholding the traditional membership standards, the convention as a whole voted in their favor, but then the various agencies always seemed to find ways of diluting their intent. From the standpoint of those who headed the agencies and boards, and particularly the UCMS, such resolutions came perilously close to creedal tests and violated the principle of free conscience. Thus, they found ways to allow individual missionaries to evade the policies of the convention. In a pattern that duplicated the Presbyterian and Baptist conflicts, investigations, committees, reports, and divisive resolutions dominated the annual conventions, with the level of bitterness increasing almost yearly.

The climax came in 1925 and 1926, at the same time and with the same result as in northern Baptist and Presbyterian denominations. The "liberals" won. In 1925, the conservatives planned carefully, packed the convention floor, and won passage of seemingly clear resolutions requiring closed membership in the agencies of the church (they could not do anything about individual congregations). But the leadership diluted the impact of such resolutions, carefully planned the 1926 meeting at Memphis, politically outmaneuvered the conservatives, and, despite some verbal compromises, clearly won the battle in behalf of greater membership inclusiveness. From this point on, many of the leading conservatives did not actively participate in the International Convention, although some joined in commissions that sought means of healing the informal split. After 1926, the conservatives withdrew support from most of the official agencies of the denomination and began creating their own "free" organizations, those supported informally by members and congregations. By 1930, the Disciples movement effectively had a dual organizational system, with little contact between the two groups (separate colleges, mission efforts, periodicals, and publishers). In 1927, the "independents," as they now began to call themselves, organized the first North American Christian Convention. It met periodically until 1950, when it became a carefully planned annual assembly, the one most visible symbol of unity in what became by the sixties a separate fellowship, Christian Churches and Churches of Christ.

At least in the perception of the larger public, the more dramatic fundamentalist crusades were not those that divided largely northern denominations, but those that involved broader cultural issues. Much more than it deserves, this perception drew upon the Scopes trial and controversies involving evolution. At the popular level, it was people like the ex-baseball star Billy Sunday, and his great revivals, or the flamboyant Fort Worth evangelist, J. Frank Norris, who symbolized fundamentalism. Norris used sharp and blunt language, held revivals in large tents, shot to death one of his enemies (avowedly in self-defense), and launched a national campaign to block the election of Al Smith (more because of his antiprohibition stance than his Catholicism). Norris early became a critic of his own Southern Baptist Convention, largely because of his resentment of any centralized control, but also because of its ecumenical involvements and what he alleged was the modernism and Darwinism among Baptist professors at Baylor University and elsewhere. His personal attacks on denominational leaders led to censure and, ultimately, the denial of fellowship to his congregations and to himself. In 1931, he organized his own Baptist fellowship, appropriately denominated the Premillennial, Fundamental, Missionary Fellowship. Today, this is the World Baptist Fellowship, now the largest of all the fundamentalist splinter denominations to derive from the controversies of the 1920s.

Norris was untypical in his confrontations with fellow southern Baptists. The early fundamentalist crusade was almost entirely centered in the North. The reason is simple: only in northern churches or seminaries had liberals and modernists gained a position of power. Here the fundamentalist crusaders were on the way to representing a minority subculture. They felt threatened. Not so in the South. The warm evangelical religion that northern fundamentalists endorsed remained dominant in the South, and evangelicals still controlled the mainstream southern denominations. An infallible Bible had all along been the unchallenged basis of religious authority, while premillennialism well reflected a more pessimistic view of modern culture that had become almost consensual among southern whites after the Civil War. Thus, while organized fundamentalism developed in the North, the underlying beliefs and values of such fundamentalists had broad support in the South. Within denominations, comparable battles in the South would develop much later during the controversies that preceded the merger of both southern Methodists and Presbyterians with their northern counterparts. These battles left as a legacy many resisting congregations that are now in such splinter denominations as the Southern Methodists and the Presbyterian Church in America. For southern Baptists, the great battle now rages, with the early victories almost entirely won by evangelicals and fundamentalists in the Southern Baptist Convention, making possible the defection by minority "moderates," as they now designate themselves.

Outside the churches, fundamentalist efforts to prevent the teaching of evolution in schools, to defend and preserve prohibition, and to resist almost every secular trend in the larger society had the broadest popular appeal within the South. The legislative successes came here, including three anti-evolution bills. Because of this, and because of the images conveyed by journalists, Americans came to identify fundamentalism with the South. This identification was usually undiscriminating. The older, warm, revivalistic forms of Protestantism endured in a South in which over half of church membership was Baptist (in black and white denominations) and almost a third Methodist. Among blacks, Baptists and Methodists had almost a complete monopoly; in their separate denominations a warm, revivalistic, and very spontaneous religious style dominated. The faith, for whites and blacks, was biblical, conversion oriented, premillennial, and puritanical in profession if not always in achievement. What is not clear is to what extent the emerging issues in the North, such as biblical criticism or the implications of Darwinism, became focal or important among southern evangelicals, at least below the level of seminaries or denominational bureaucracies. We know least about this among the third of southern Christians in black denominations. Clearly, southerners were predominantly evangelical in their religious beliefs and style, and when alerted to controversial issues, or when issues such as the teaching of something called "evolution" became a sharply contested political issue, one could easily anticipate how southern evangelicals would vote. Also, when holiness or fundamentalist splinter denominations developed within Baptism and Methodism, these had a disproportionate appeal within the South, or among southern migrants, with holiness and later Pentecostal sects most appealing to blacks, new fundamentalist sects most appealing to whites.

If southern Christians had long ignored evolutionary theories, or confronted few modernists, this changed rather abruptly after 1919. It changed, in large part, because of the fundamentalist organizations formed by Riley and others. These were most successful in a carefully organized effort to get states to enact laws against the teaching of evolution in the public schools. And, by far, the most effective spokesman for this new crusade was the old commoner and three-time Democratic presidential candidate William Jennings Bryan. Bryan had retired to Florida, accumulated a fortune, in part from promoting Florida real estate, and after 1920 spent most of his time in writing and speaking against the evils of evolution, by which he meant any theories that traced human descent to animals, or that abetted the types of nationalism that led to World War I, the eugenics movement and other assaults on the sanctity of human life, and a competitive capitalism that had led to monopolistic trusts. He was particularly effective in well-publicized addresses before state legislatures, and as early as 1921 he secured a strongly worded resolution from the Florida legislature (it did not involve teachers) and, in 1922, the near adoption of a very stringent Kentucky act against the teaching of such theories. Oklahoma enacted a law that forbade evolutionary theories in textbooks adopted within the state. It is not clear that these successful crusades, so influential among legislators, filtered down to the larger public, but at least the publicity surrounding the legislative action, and the very popular tracts and lectures by Bryan, very quickly placed the issue of evolution, whatever this meant, on the broader public agenda. It is possible that the belated spread of high schools, particularly in a South that had long underfunded even elementary schools, created new fears among parents, for in most high schools students at least had the option of taking courses in biology. Out of such fears came the Butler Act in Tennessee and the famous Scopes trial.

Reading Guide

Many of the difficulties of understanding conflict among Christians involve the lack of a common vocabulary. Labels abound, but no firm semantic conventions govern their use. Perhaps this confusion of tongues has been greatest for "modernism" and "fundamentalism." In the preceding essay, I have stipulated the way I choose to use the two terms, consistent with definitions of evangelicalism that I first introduced in my book *The Uneasy Center: Reformed Christianity in Antebellum America* (Chapel Hill: University of North Carolina Press, 1995). I can only recommend such a tactic to others. So often, historians fall into what I call the "essentialist fallacy." They assume that there is some religious phenomenon that should match the word "fundamentalist," and then they try to locate and correctly describe and classify this phenomenon. This turns a formal or definitional issue into an empirical one. Then one debates, endlessly, about who has described fundamentalism correctly. Such a tactic can lead only to confusion, for the labels we use are not empirical issues at all, but choices about word use. If well-established conventions exist, if everyone uses certain words to denote the same object, then communication is easy. When no conventions guide use, careful stipulation alone can allow communication, provided, of course, that listeners are willing to suspend their own word preferences and follow the definitions offered by a writer.

The two classic books on modernism and fundamentalism address definitional problems, at times with a degree of subtlety, but both continue to confuse descriptive and formal issues. The first of these was William R. Hutchison's *The Modernist Impulse in American Protestantism* (Cambridge, Mass.: Harvard University Press, 1976). Hutchison defined modernists as a subclass of Protestant or evangelical liberalism. He focused on about a dozen theologians from major northern seminaries, most all but forgotten by the mid-twentieth century. On the other side is a book by George M. Marsden, *Fundamentalism and American Culture: The Shaping of Twentieth-Century Evangelicalism, 1870–1925* (New York: Oxford University Press, 1980). As the two labels in his title indicate, this book necessarily engages, and at times begs, a series of definitional issues. Marsden provides the fullest story of the major battles within the northern Baptist and Presbyterian denominations, and he emphasizes, not the rarified intellectuals written about by Hutchison, but broader social and cultural themes. This remains the most coherent and revealing book about those various Christians who now lay an almost monopolistic claim to the word "evangelical." Unfortunately, no such comprehensive survey continues the story from 1925 to the present.

The most prominent, self-denominated fundamentalists of the twenties have not found many sympathetic biographers. By far the best introduction to such leaders as Straton, Riley, Massee, Norris, and Macartney is Charles A. Russell's *Voices of American Fundamentalism: Seven Biographical Studies* (Philadelphia: Westminster Press, 1976). William V. Trollinger has completed a very perceptive biography of Riley: *God's Empire: William Bell Riley and Midwestern Fundamentalism* (Madison: University of Wisconsin Press, 1990).

3

THE SCOPES TRIAL

After 1920, the new but rapidly growing fundamentalist movement invaded the South. The major crusaders, John Roach Straton, William Bell Riley, and above all William Jennings Bryan, found very receptive audiences. By then, their one common theme was the evils of evolution in the classroom. Their agitation led to a nearly successful bill that would have banned the teaching of evolution in Kentucky in 1922. In the same years, legislators in Tennessee introduced similar bills, but with little public attention and no success. This all changed with the Butler Act of 1925, in part because of its timing. This was the first successful anti-evolution bill to include criminal penalties (Bryan had opposed any fines).

John Washington Butler first gained election to the Tennessee House of Representatives in 1922. He was a moderately successful farmer in Macon County, in the hilly country of the highland rim, along the Kentucky border and about sixty miles northeast of Nashville. With only a few years of elementary education, he nonetheless had taught a few sessions in the small local schools, read more broadly than most of his neighbors, and was unusually enterprising for his area. He bought a threshing machine and did custom threshing for the farmers in his locality, one of the more profitable sidelines for farmers. He wrote humorous or satirical articles for the local newspaper and became a critic of trends in public education. He very much deplored the types of education that lured young men away from the farm or inculcated in them more urbane or cosmopolitan, or what he believed to be irreligious, values.

Butler was a member of a small Primitive Baptist church, one with only monthly preaching. This was a very tiny sect, both in Tennessee and nationally (even in 1960 it claimed only 72,000 members). It derived from southern Baptists who, in the mid-nineteenth century, objected to mission activity. The Primitive group expressed a type of hyper-Calvinism that approached fatalism—God has ordained who will be saved, and human efforts are not only futile but blasphemous. The sect repudiated revival techniques and rejected Sunday schools. It was, in some respects, the most anti-evangelical of any Protestant denomination. Its members were the least likely of those of any sect to join the crusading evangelicals who led organized fundamentalist organizations. Ironically, almost all the reporters who covered the Scopes trial referred to Butler as a fundamentalist. Uniformly, those who covered the trial were illiterate on most issues involving American religion.

Butler, like so many Tennesseans, had little knowledge about Darwin or evolution until "educated" about the issues by people like Bryan, who addressed the Tennessee legislature in 1924. Also like so many other Tennesseans when confronted with the issue, Butler's reaction was almost reflexive—intense opposition to any exposure of Tennessee children to views that he believed so clearly contradicted the Christian Bible. Sensitized to the issue, Butler served on a legislative committee that supervised special schools operated by the state, and he found even there textbooks that contained what he believed to be evolutionary theories. Apparently on his own, he wrote a bill to take care of the problem and, in his innocence, probably expected little opposition to it. As a legislative effort, his bill had many problems, but given the context it is reasonably clear what he meant to achieve.

According to the caption attached to his bill, it prohibited the teaching of "the Evolutionary Theory" in any schools, colleges, or universities supported by the state public school funds. Section one of the bill prohibited any teachers in such schools from teaching "any theory that denies the story of the Divine Creation of man as taught in the Bible, and to teach instead that man has descended from a lower order of animals." Section two stipulated that teachers who violated section one were guilty of a misdemeanor and liable for a $100–$500 fine.

As drafted, the bill was not very clear. No one evolutionary theory had broad acceptance in 1925, and every version of the Bible contained

more than one story of divine creation. Many avowed Christians believed that the biblical stories were consistent with certain types of theistic evolution, and this included even some of the leading fundamentalists, who used the day-age or gap theories to reconcile the two. It
remained unclear what "teach" meant. Did it mean that a teacher could
not even tell students about evolutionary theories or answer student
questions about such theories, or did it mean that teachers could not
teach that such theories were true (this was what Bryan wanted)? In
order to violate the law, did a teacher have both to deny divine creation
and support descent, or was either of these sufficient for conviction (the
bill connected the two prohibitions by "and" and not "or")? If a teacher
excepted humans, or even the human "soul," from any hereditary tie to
lower animals, could she use evolutionary theories to explain the origin
of all other forms of life? Defense attorneys at the Scopes trial even
argued that the bill, as worded, did not preclude teaching that humans
descended from apes, for apes and humans are part of the same "order"
according to standard biological classifications, and thus the primates
cannot be a lower order.

In all probability, most Tennessee legislators would have preferred not
to have to vote on the Butler bill. They feared embarrassment for the
state. But confronted with a choice, all but five members of the house
voted for it, some out of conviction, some out of fear of constituent
reaction. They could hope that the state senate would reverse their vote
or find some way to table the bill. In the senate, the judiciary committee
at first recommended rejection. But a series of delays allowed the bill to
become an object of debate and controversy. It is clear that a vast majority of voters, however ill-informed about the issues at stake, favored such
a bill. A vocal minority opposed it. Thus the pressures built and legislative fears ballooned, until early March 1925, when the committee re-
versed itself and recommended passage; after extensive debate, most serious, the bill passed the senate on March 13. A reluctant Governor Austin
Peay signed it into law on March 21. Debates in the assembly, as well as
an analysis of the distribution of votes, shows some slight different between rural and urban legislators, but not enough to explain passage.
What became most clear was major divisions among Tennessee church
members and ministers.

The divisions among Christians matched those that accompanied the
struggle just then climaxing within northern denominations, but with
one major difference. Modernists had had little influence in Tennessee.
White Christians were concentrated in four groups: the Methodist Epis-

copal Church, South; the Southern Baptist Convention; smaller but widely dispersed Presbyterians in three denominations; and Restoration churches, most now in a separate fellowship of Churches of Christ, fewer in Disciples of Christ congregations. Blacks were largely in three Methodist denominations and two wings of National Baptists, but as far as the record indicates black Christians were not involved in any legislative lobbying. From all that we know, a larger proportion of black Christians than whites would have favored the Butler Act. The only organized Christian opposition came from larger, city-based mainstream congregations, those with more affluent and more highly educated members. These were most often Methodist, Presbyterian, or Disciples, but with a few Baptists plus a sprinkling from such thinly represented denominations as the Episcopal Church. But a majority of ministers and laity in the mainstream churches, statewide, represented rural or small town congregations and overwhelmingly supported the Butler Act.

In 1925 Tennessee was an impoverished southern state, with per capita incomes at less than 50 percent of national averages. It lagged behind all but two or three states in educational expenditures and had one of the highest illiteracy rates in the nation. In the twentieth century it had struggled to catch up, to develop a viable system of public education. The resistance was high, particularly in largely rural counties. Not until 1909 did the state offer any funding for high schools, and only then for counties willing to develop them. It first required counties to levy taxes to support secondary schools in 1917 and, in 1921, finally mandated that each county establish at least one high school. In 1913 it first required school attendance up to age fourteen, or the normal age of completing the eighth grade, but had difficulty enforcing such a law in many rural areas. The net effect of such educational polices was that, until the twenties, most well-educated Tennesseans had only an eighth grade certificate, and even many elementary school teachers had little if any secondary education. Butler was all too typical.

This was about to change in 1925, as the legislature struggled over the most important school reform package in state history, one supported strongly by Governor Peay. Although severely amended, this package finally centralized the Tennessee school system, with major statewide funding, equalization formulas, and mandated eight-month school terms. Also, the state university and teachers' colleges received new funding. One clear reason that Peay signed the Butler Act was his desire to gain legislative support for his reform package. This may also have swayed favorable votes in the state senate. Equally important, it dampened the resistance to the bill that one would have expected from the faculty of the University of Tennessee. Apparently, most bitter opponents agreed with Peay—the bill would remain an unenforced indicator of deeply held religious opinions in the state, and nothing more.

Had it not been for Roger Baldwin's young and aggressive American Civil Liberties Union (ACLU), Peay would probably have been correct in his predictions. The ACLU was concerned about the fate of academic freedom, as several states were considering anti-evolutionary bills of one type or another. Its academic freedom committee wanted, as soon as possible, a test case in Tennessee, and in press releases carried in most city newspapers, including Chattanooga, advertised for some teacher in Tennessee willing to violate and thus challenge the law. The ACLU agreed to assume all costs for such a test case. In a story that has almost become a legend, four or five men in Dayton decided to accept the ACLU offer (to the despair of most Tennesseans), and they asked John T. Scopes to volunteer as the guinea pig. He was only twenty-four and had just completed his first school year as a well-liked, unmarried high school science teacher and coach. One of the conspirators, George W. Rappleyea, was formerly from New York City and had managed the remaining properties of a bankrupt coal company in Dayton. He resented the Butler Act, in part because he believed that some version of evolution was true. In the next few months he became better informed about the issues and more radical in his outlook. The other men had varied views, most unmatured, about the issues, but they wanted to get Dayton on the map. Small retail merchants had dreams of large crowds and great sales (largely unrealized, since few distant visitors came to Dayton). Rappleyea telegraphed the ACLU and began the complicated process that led to the Scopes trial of July 10–21, 1925.

Scopes, after some persuasion, agreed to become the defendant. He resented the Butler Act, but on his own would never have agitated the issue. He came from a rather independent minded Kentucky family, had an eclectic degree from the University of Kentucky, and had taught general science rather than biology at Dayton. But in April he had subbed for the high school principal in the standard biology course and had helped the students review their textbook, though he could not later remember talking about Darwin or evolution. But the textbook, one adopted by the state and sold at the local drugstore, did have a rather extended but general discussion of the subject. At least students were supposed to have read about something called "evolution," and with careful tutoring were able to testify in the trial that Professor Scopes had taught them about the subject. They were reluctant, because they liked him so much that they did not want to do him harm. Note that in Dayton, a well-staffed high school was as valued as a college or university today.

The trial became a great circus, publicized around the world. Journalists soon referred to it as the "monkey trial," and even local citizens tried to capitalize on this title. The levity was not the fault of the state prosecutor, A. T. Stewart (later a U.S. Senator) or the Tennessee lawyer the ACLU selected to defend Scopes, John Randolph Neal, a brilliant but increasingly eccentric former professor (the university, in effect, had fired him) at the Law School of the University of Tennessee in Knoxville. The problem came from the outside volunteers. First, with the support of Riley's World's Christian Fundamentals Association, William Jennings Bryan offered his services to the prosecution, and he basically turned out to be a pain in the neck so far as the legal process was concerned (Bryan's son and three local attorneys also assisted in the prosecution). In reaction to the likely role of Bryan, an old antagonist, Clarence Darrow, by now a rather notorious Chicago labor and defense lawyer, offered to help the defense. H. L. Mencken, the cynical and pungent Baltimore journalist, urged Darrow to take on this not unwelcome task. Also volunteering for the defense was Dudley Malone, a famous and fashionable divorce lawyer from New York City and a Roman Catholic. The ACLU, with some reluctance, finally accepted both offers and also sent along one of their attorneys, Arthur G. Hays. In turn, these lawyers assembled a group of expert witnesses. To the joy of local merchants, the city hosted around twenty famous people by July 10, plus up to two hundred reporters. A handful of cranks, both pro- and anti-evolution, provided extra local color for the often bored reporters.

The involvement of Bryan and Darrow helped turn the Scopes trial into one of the first great media extravaganzas of the twentieth century, with over two thousand newspapers including articles on the trial and with direct radio broadcasts by a Chicago station. But the sensationalized reporting, and the fame of Darrow and Bryan, helped sabotage the goals of the ACLU. Bryan was not a practicing attorney, and thus he offered no real help to the prosecution. Darrow was all too famous, not only as an avowed agnostic, but as one who had recently used theories of social determinism to defend two rich, youthful, and unrepentant murderers, Nathan Leopold and Richard Loeb (he helped them avoid the death sentence).

What the circus-like atmosphere soon concealed was how very serious were the issues at stake in the trial. The ACLU wanted to convince either the jury at Dayton or the Tennessee Supreme Court that at least some forms of evolutionary theory were compatible with Christian belief. This was what Bryan emphatically denied, as he tried to bring all the populistic arguments from his fundamentalist crusade into a case that the ACLU had hoped to defend on narrow legal grounds. Darrow was already such a controversial figure, and so outspoken in his rejection of any form of theism, that he promised to be a type of red flag to the very jury, and audience, that the ACLU needed to win over at Dayton. Darrow's views, when combined with the usually inaccurate reporting and continuous insensitive assaults upon the religious beliefs of Tennesseans by his friend Mencken, created the tension and conflict that jeopardized the defense strategy, as events would demonstrate. This was true even though Darrow, at least most of the time, tried to prove that good Christians had no reason to oppose the teaching of evolutionary theory. He downplayed his religious beliefs, unlike Mencken, and went along with the line of defense developed by Neal and Hays and supported by two sets of experts, one made up of mainstream Christians of a liberal or modernist persuasion, and the other of well-placed scientists who were at least nominal Christians.

As far as the evidence indicates, Bryan was, in the days before the trial began, the only fundamentalist at Dayton (others soon came). That is, Bryan was the only evangelical Christian who had joined in an open battle against modernism. Yet reporters generally referred to almost everyone in Dayton as fundamentalists, which only meant that many attended local churches and, at least for the most part, believed the Bible to be true and, on most issues, agreed with the views of Bryan. What was soon clear was that local citizens had not been involved in the evolutionary debates. Many were open, glad to learn more. At least the minister of a local Methodist Episcopal Church was a bit of a "liberal," and it was he who had Rappleyea teach in his Sunday school. This was one of many northern Methodist congregations in what had been a largely unionist east Tennessee.

Dayton, compared to most small southern towns, was a clean, somewhat progressive county seat of Rhea County, in the fertile valley of the Tennessee River, although in sight of Walden Ridge, which formed the eastern boundary of the impoverished Cumberland Plateau. Coal had flourished and then declined, but the local farmers did well with fruit and strawberries. A major federal highway ran through Dayton, and the Southern Railroad connected it to both Knoxville and Chattanooga.

The local citizens bent over backwards to be hospitable and even a carping Mencken had to admit that Dayton was a pleasant town. In the trial, the locals seemed as open to the defense arguments as to those of the prosecution, and gave the most prolonged applause to an eloquent defense of freedom by Malone. Even Butler left his threshing crew to come to Dayton, ostensibly to write articles for a newspaper. He was gracious, friendly, badly wanted the court to hear the expert witnesses for the defense, and professed a desire to learn more about evolution.

It is impossible to gauge the views of local citizens on the issues at trial. Most of the jury, and probably most of the people who attended the trial, were from the county, not from the town. Most attended small rural churches, a majority Methodist and Baptist. Typically, ministers served more than one congregation, with preaching as infrequent as once a month. The rural ministers were not seminary trained; many did not have any college education. It was different in Dayton, where the churches were not large but had full-time and educated pastors. The reports from the participants in the trial indicate anything but a town caught up in evangelical fervor or rigor. At least half the young people attended weekly dances at a resort up on Walden Ridge. Scopes attended different churches on Sunday, but was not.a member of any one and not personally devout. This seemed true of many of the men who gathered at Robinson's Drugstore, and who conspired to have the trial in Dayton. Yet reporters, looking for that strange breed of people called "fundamentalists," did locate a congregation up on Walden Ridge that matched their image—with an illiterate minister who, if the reporters were correct, believed the earth was flat. No one ever bothered to identify the denomination. Likewise in Dayton, some reporters visited a black Pentecostal congregation and confronted a type of near ecstatic worship that almost scared them out of their wits.

In retrospect, it is easy to sympathize with the local people. They tried so hard to be good hosts, bending over backward to be kind even to Mencken. Many temporarily moved from their homes to provide comfortable lodging for the famous guests. They were unprepared for the widely disseminated caricatures and insults directed toward them in the press, images of ignorant and intolerant representatives of an Appalachian subculture who had suppressed people like Scopes. Even when guests did show their appreciation, such as many of the visiting experts, they could still be a bit patronizing toward the local people, for they came to help enlighten them, to bring them into the modern world. As Governor Peay had feared, the trial opened Tennessee and the people of the state to widespread ridicule. Actually, the people in the area were as innocent of any intentional malice, as diverse in their local eccentricities, as parochial and prejudiced in outlook, and as confused about evolutionary theory as were rural and small-town evangelical Christians in all parts of the United States. But one has to acknowledge that it was the greed, and the desire for national publicity, on the part of the local conspirators who sought the trial that brought these uninvited and often unfair tribulations to the city and county.

The trial began on a Friday. The prosecution had a simple plan—to prove that the people of Tennessee had a right to control the curricula of public schools. The case thus involved only one question: Did Scopes violate the Butler Act? Despite the textual problems with the wording of the act, the prosecution argued that the intent of the statute was clear enough to enable a jury to decide the issue of guilt or innocence. The defense used more of a scatter-gun approach. The goal of the ACLU was to appeal the case to higher courts, although the defense lawyers would have welcomed a ruling by the local judge that the act was unconstitutional. They did not really expect such a ruling. They cited several constitutional scruples. The statute was too vague, thus placing teachers in jeopardy of a loss of liberty or property (their salaries) without due process, as required by both the state constitution and by the Fourteenth Amendment of the federal constitution. It was unreasonable, in the sense that it asked teachers to reject common and well-established knowledge, comparable to a requirement that they teach children that the world is flat. It seemed to violate sections of the Tennessee Constitution that provided for a limited separation of church and state, mandated support for literature and science, and protected freedom of speech and press.

The Scopes trial involved eight days of circuit court sessions at the often sweltering Rhea County courthouse, but it seemed longer because of two weekends. Presiding was Judge John T. Raulston, an elected judge from Franklin County, but a judge often insecure, intimidated by all the famous lawyers, and desperate to uphold a sense of fairness. On the opening Friday morning the court secured a new indictment from a grand jury because of possible irregularities in an earlier grand jury action. During the afternoon, the prosecution and the defense examined a panel of jurors and agreed on the twelve men who would try the case. In some ways, the answers given by the jurors, mostly local farmers, made up the most revealing part of the whole trial (most newspaper reports emphasized that they were all fundamentalists). In actuality, what was soon apparent was how innocent they were about the whole Darwinian-Fundamentalist controversy. They were largely Baptists and Methodists, with one from the Disciples of Christ, but not all were faithful in church attendance and none revealed any profound knowledge of Christianity. They seemed sincere and fair-minded, and some suggested a bent for independent thinking. Had the defense been able to confront jurors with its expert witnesses, it is quite possible that they would have exonerated Scopes. Because of the way the trial played out, they had no alternative but to convict, as the defense admitted and desired (in behalf of an appeal to a higher court). The jurors were thus a pawn in a larger drama beyond their control, and they were also the only twelve people in Rhea County who had to miss most of the exciting events in the trial, which took place while the jury was excluded.

On Monday, before the jury was sworn in, the defense moved to quash the indictment of Scopes on the constitutional grounds cited earlier. Before debate on this motion, Raulston excused the jurors. During Monday afternoon the prosecution lawyers tried to counter the constitutional points raised by the defense, with some of the most important legal sparring taking place during this session. Darrow ended the day with a long, eloquent defense of the quash motion. This was his only prepared speech during the trial. He thus got a jump on Bryan and provided the first good copy for the press. In part, he concentrated on the constitutional objections already planned by the defense. He chose to focus upon the establishment clause in the Tennessee Constitution, construing it as essentially similar to the clause in the First Amendment to the federal Constitution (he of course ignored other parts of the state constitution that considerably qualified and weakened this clause). The state legislature had clearly supported the establishment of religion by the way it intervened to dictate the content of instruction in the schools.

Even as Darrow pleaded for religious tolerance, he could not help but reveal his own distaste or even contempt for the religious views of most of the local citizens in the courtroom. This set a tone for the whole trial, one that informed most of the reporting in large city newspapers. Darrow talked about the different creation stories in the Bible, ridiculed its credentials on scientific issues, and noted the hundreds of different Christian creeds in addition to all the world religions. He could not conceal his disillusionment with organized religion and attributed much of the bitterness, hatred, cruelty, and warfare of the past to its influence. He did try, at times, to distinguish Tennesseans, or at least those with common sense and goodwill, from the invading, outside fundamentalists, such as Bryan, for until these outside agitators indulged their form of demagoguery Tennesseans had permitted the teaching of evolution. He saluted the locally despised Christian modernist (one, he said, "who dares to be intelligent") who accepted evolution and who believed in a God who did not make the world in six days but was still at work making it better. Even as Darrow made some effort to establish rapport with the audience, his friend and ally Mencken not only wrote a stirring summary of Darrow's speech, but made very clear that the ignorant audience never understood his logic and that it was such "fundamentalists" from "upland Tennessee" who were persecuting an "infidel Scopes."

On Tuesday morning, the defense objected to a Tennessee custom—a prayer before the opening of court each day. Raulston would not give in on this point, but he did agree that the local ministerial association could select a different minister for each day. The association carefully tried to achieve diversity by selecting a Jewish rabbi and a Unitarian minister on two of the days (a gesture all but ignored by the press). On Wednesday, Raulston took the whole morning to read his response to the constitutional challenges. He accepted, in each case, the arguments of the prosecution. Although without experience in such a complex case, he wrote a persuasive argument that the Butler Act was not inconsistent with either the Tennessee or the United States Constitution.

The real trial, before the seldom-seen jury, began on Wednesday afternoon. Nothing dramatic happened. Malone itemized the arguments to be offered by the defense and included a preview of the type of testimony expected from expert witnesses. The state used the high school principal and students to prove that Scopes had indeed taught a theory of human descent from lower animals and that he had used a textbook that included evolutionary theory. The students gave studied answers, based on careful prompting before their testimony. Mild questions by the defense elicited an admission that they had suffered not at all from learning about evolution.

When the prosecution rested, the defense called as its first witness one of its assembled experts, Maynard M. Metcalf, an eminent zoologist who had, until the last year, been teaching at Johns Hopkins University. As soon as Hays had asked the questions needed to identify Metcalf's extensive credentials as a scientist, and turned to the questions about evolution, Stewart strenuously objected. The state, throughout, had argued that the jury could understand the intent of the act, which Raulston had ruled constitutional, and that "expert" testimony about evolution or the

Bible was out of order. The defense responded that this was the only type of evidence that could undermine the state's case. They had to prove that evolution, as a fact about natural history, was as established as any other form of reliable knowledge and that such a fact was not necessarily inconsistent with an enlightened understanding of the biblical stories of creation. Raulston was perplexed and in a bit of a dilemma. If he denied such testimony, the trial would end. The Dayton merchants would lose money; reporters primed for a great standoff between Darrow and Bryan would be bitterly disappointed. He deferred judgment on admissibility, once again asked the jury to leave, and then allowed Metcalf to continue his testimony largely, it seemed, for the benefit of the press.

On Thursday, Metcalf prepared to resume his testimony before the court, but Stewart insisted that the court first rule on the issue of admissibility. Despite some misunderstandings over an earlier bargain with the defense attorneys, Stewart now moved to exclude all expert evidence about evolution or the Bible. The act simply prohibited teaching human descent, and all the evidence presented to the court suggested that Scopes did just this. The arguments about admissibility were extensive, with Bryan's son opening for the state. In the afternoon, and for the first time, Bryan took the floor. He was supposed to argue against the inclusion of experts, but he quickly wandered far afield, and soon, instead of addressing the judge, who alone could decide the procedural issue, he lectured the audience.

Bryan rambled. He drew upon old speeches. He ridiculed educated experts, appealed to the common sense of ordinary people in Tennessee, and insisted that Darwin was the real devil of the piece. Although later evolutionists had often criticized Darwin, or dismissed natural selection, they were still teaching the doctrine of evolution. He quoted from Darwin's *Descent* and lampooned the textbook used by Scopes. He ridiculed experts who would try to reconcile Genesis and evolution, for they were completely irreconcilable. Teaching of the hypothesis of evolution would not only challenge the religious verities of students, but withdraw the only support for virtue. He associated Darwin with Friedrich Nietzsche, with German atrocities in World War I, and with the amoral outlook that he believed Darrow had exhibited in the Loeb-Leopold case. The members of the jury were better experts on the Bible than any number of scientists, most of whom did not even believe in God. He did not want to give such people a platform. He ended with paeans of praise for the Bible and with the simple question at stake in the trial:

Did Scopes violate an act that may have displeased the so-called experts but clearly reflected the wishes of the vast majority of Tennesseans?

Bryan's rambling sermon led to the most eloquent and coherent address of the trial. Dudley Malone had worked for Bryan and the State Department during World War I and referred to him as his old chief. Malone won his audience by a dual appeal—to fairness for a defendant and to the need to be open to truth. According to his understanding of the Butler Act, the prosecution had to prove that Scopes violated both conjoined prohibitions in the act. That is, to be guilty, he had both to have taught a theory in conflict with the Bible and one that traced human descent to lower orders. He granted that the prosecution had proved the second, but not the first. He stressed two mind-sets, that of scientists who are ever open to new truths, and that of dogmatists who viewed truth as something revealed and unchanging. The dogmatists had always tried to suppress truth and, as so many others at the trial, he appealed to the silencing of Galileo by the Church. The defense simply wanted to present eminent scientists and theologians who believed that Genesis and the fact of evolution were not in conflict, that the Bible was not a textbook in science, and that at points of conflict between a literal Bible and the best of contemporary understanding, one had to reject a literal interpretation. If what Scopes taught was, according to the understanding of the ablest minds in the country, consistent with a proper use and understanding of the Bible, then Scopes was not guilty. To prove this, the defense had to expose the jury to the testimony of such experts. He stressed the dedication and the sincere Christian commitment of these underpaid teachers and scientists who came to Dayton at their own expense, and he shamed the prosecution for its seeming fear of what they might tell the jury. The jury, like the young people of Dayton, might have an open mind and benefit from being able to confront new knowledge. It was only simple justice to let the defendant develop his theory of what the case was about and to present the only type of evidence that could possibly prove his innocence. To prohibit this evidence was to leave Scopes with no means of defense, helpless before a court that so defined the issues as to prejudge the outcome.

Malone ended with a tribute to truth:

The truth always wins and we are not afraid of it. The truth is no coward. The truth does not need the law. The truth does not need the forces of government. The truth does not need Mr. Bryan. The truth is imperishable, eternal, and immortal and needs no human agency to support it. We are ready to tell the truth as we understand it and we do not fear all the truth that they can present as facts. We are ready. We are ready. We feel we stand with progress. We feel that we stand with science. We feel that we stand with intelligence. We feel that we stand with fundamental freedom in America. We are not afraid. Where is the fear? We meet it. Where is the fear? We defy it. . . .

Malone's eloquence moved the applauding audience. He persuaded them, as he persuaded Butler, that they should hear the experts even if they did not agree with them. He had appealed to the basic beliefs and values of his audience as much or more than had Bryan, and he left the prosecution in the seeming position of falling back on legal technicalities to win its case. Even Bryan told Malone it was the best speech he had ever heard.

The prosecution, of course, did not accept the defense's contention that Scopes would be innocent if the defense could prove evolution consistent with the Bible. Stewart argued that the clear intent of the legislature was to prevent the teaching of descent, which the legislature had deemed inconsistent with the Genesis account. He admitted that nothing in the act prevented teaching about the evolution of all other species except humans. Thus he argued that the only use of expert testimony open to the defense was evidence that proved that evolution did not entail human descent. Judge Raulston, at the beginning of the Friday session, announced his decision to exclude any expert evidence that strayed beyond the narrow limits suggested by Stewart. Heated arguments ensued, including some rude remarks from Darrow that led to a later citation for contempt and then an apology from Darrow.

The defense won one small victory—Raulston agreed that it could place statements in the record detailing what its expert witnesses had planned to present to the jury. He also granted the defense an early adjournment on Friday morning, to enable the experts to have the weekend to prepare their statements. On reconvening on Monday morning, Hays read not only these carefully prepared statements before the court (not the jury), but summarized what the defense hoped to prove by other witnesses not present at Dayton, all in order to support its expected appeals to higher courts.

The exclusion of expert testimony was arguably correct from a legal standpoint. It simplified the task of the prosecution and assured conviction. But it precluded what could have been an extended, informative airing of issues before a perhaps befuddled jury. Had Raulston granted the defense's theory—that teaching descent alone was insufficient for guilt but that it had to be paired with teachings inconsistent with the Bible—then he would have had a good reason to admit expert testimony on both the Bible and evolution. This would have opened a can of worms. Not only would the prosecution lawyers have been able to examine the defense experts, but to introduce counterexperts of their own. John Roach Straton waited expectantly in New York for an invitation to come and beard the evolutionists. In fact, the whole ongoing fight over fundamentalism in the northern mainstream denominations might have moved to Dayton. If Bryan's praise was any indicator, the prosecution might have eventually persuaded George McCready Price, a Seventh-day Adventist and self-proclaimed geologist (he was in Europe) to come to Dayton and there present a view later called "scientific creationism" or "flood geology." The trial could have gone on for weeks. Stewart knew this, and he also knew that the prosecution would not be able to introduce experts with anything close to the credentials of those who had already gathered at Dayton.

After a weekend of labor, the defense team announced the purpose of their expert testimony. They wanted to prove that the Bible teaches the difference between soul and body; that God is spirit; that the human spirit but not body is in the image of God; that the subject of the Bible is ethical and spiritual, not material; that modern scientists are concerned with the structure and development of living bodies, not religious or ethical issues; and, finally, that the Bible clarifies that God created human bodies from the dust of the earth but does not clarify how he did it. Actually, this summary of a typical modernist conception of the Bible proved a poor guide to the expert statements, which were much less and much more than the defense promised. Most of the experts addressed the scientific issues, not the biblical ones. A Hebrew scholar did note translation mistakes in the Authorized or King James Version of Genesis 1, and suggested that a better translation would make the creation story more consistent with a developmental perspective (in most respects, the scholars who have worked at recent translations have not agreed with his view). A Methodist clergyman from Chattanooga expressed a liberal view widely prevalent in his denomination, that the Bible vindicates creation but does not reveal how it took place. He argued that only with the eating of the fruit of the tree of knowledge of good and evil did humans emerge and that no scientific theory could account for this. Evolution explains physical developments; the Bible explains the origin of spiritual qualities. This emphasis upon two realms of truth supported the type of apologetic offered by most of the experts. In a rather brief statement, Shailer Mathews, dean of the Divinity School at the University of Chicago, summarized what he advertised as a modernist approach to Christianity (see Chapter 4 for his full views).

Some experts addressed rather peripheral issues. An educator from the University of Chicago stressed how essential evolutionary theory was to all theories about human development, and thus critical to the training of teachers. A soil scientist argued that only an evolutionary perspective could explain the evolution of soils, since the work of primitive bacteria began to form the organic deposits necessary for soil formation. A Chicago anthropologist emphasized cultural evolution and racial differences. He cited what was known about the evolution of humanoid types, or what might be called the "ascent of man." Two geologists offered brief but informed essays on strata, guessed wrongly about the age of the earth, and also surveyed the early evidence on the immediate progenitors of humans. The one witness who briefly testified before the jury, Metcalf, emphasized what all the experts acknowledged—they were there to prove the almost universal acceptance of evolution, not to defend any one theory about how it occurred. Few mentioned Charles Darwin.

Kirtley Mather, a geologist from Harvard, accepted the day-age theory and rightly stressed that evolution involved no cause, no force or power to explain natural history, while God was such a force or power, but one that had to use processes and methods. Scientists who clarify these processes add to human knowledge about their God. This idea of the progressive revelation of an immanent deity was the most central theme of modernists. Mather was as good at one-liners as Bryan; he stressed that his knowledge of rocks had led him to a better understanding of the Rock of Ages and quoted from the old two-revelation theory (the Bible and nature) made popular by Henry Ward Beecher in the immediate aftermath of the publication of Darwin's *Origin*.

Horatio H. Newman, a geologist from the University of Chicago (Darrow's residence in Chicago helped account for the prevalence of experts from that city), offered an extended textbook survey of all the subjects that tended to confirm the fact of change, of evolutionary development, which was in all fields a "law of nature." He offered about as sophisticated a survey of biological evolution as one could write in 1925. He did not mention the Bible or religion. From the present perspective, what seemed strange about his testimony were major underestimates of the earth's age (from only 100 to 500 million years) and only the most rudimentary genetic knowledge.

With the expert statements on record, it seemed that it was time, finally, to bring back the long-absent jury and complete the trial. Since a guilty verdict was now assured, most reporters and visitors, including Mencken, had left Dayton on Friday and did not hear the expert statements. But the trial did not end as it should have. Darrow and the defense attorneys had worked out a final strategy, and they sprung it on a naive judge. They first successfully protested an outdoor sign (the trial had moved outdoors) asking people to read the Bible and then asked to include various versions of the Bible as evidence along with the King James, which Hays persisted in calling the St. James version. This was all a ruse to introduce the problem of biblical interpretation. As this debate began, Hays asked to call Bryan as a witness, to appear as a biblical expert and to add testimony that might be helpful in the defense appeal. Stewart rightly protested such a procedure, not only at first but continuously. Raulston was never more a fool, or a glutton for press attention, than at this point, for he accepted the request. Bryan could, as a lawyer should, have refused, and that would have been the end of it. His ego intruded, and he accepted the challenge, although the jury was still out and what he said had only the standing of the prior expert statements. He was not sworn in, but took the stand for what became a disgraceful interlude, the only completely senseless and even cruel part of the Scopes trial. Darrow did all the questioning.

Bryan's testimony allowed two old antagonists to have a final go at each other. Both were old men, Darrow at sixty-eight and Bryan at sixty-five, but Darrow was in better health. Bryan had used every opportunity during the trial to bait Darrow and to misinterpret his beliefs. Now was Darrow's turn. The issue was the Bible. The questions almost all came from an earlier, published list of questions that Darrow had addressed to Bryan in a newspaper but with no response. Unlike in the testimony of the experts, nothing very new or original developed during the afternoon circus. Darrow was well-read, had a thirst for bits of information from all fields of study, had kept his mind honed not only from courtroom appearances but from seminars and discussion groups among intellectuals from the University of Chicago. He was a complex man, sad and lonely in some ways. He often delighted in shocking simple people, and he seemed to relish all the local publicity about his agnosticism. Yet, as much as Bryan, he yearned to be on stage and carefully cultivated every audience with his folksy style. In his way, he wanted to be loved. He was also at heart a preacher and, in fact, had briefly served as an interim minister for a Unitarian congregation in Madison, Wisconsin. Not consistently, but on some occasions he professed an almost fatal-

istic form of determinism, which denied any concept of human responsibility. The environment determined all.

Bryan was beset by diabetes, and possibly a hardening of his arteries.
He was not senile. He was alert at the trial and in good form in his one
extended but rambling presentation, but notably he largely drew upon
older speeches and did not display any intellectual agility. In his last years
his reading was very limited, his knowledge of advanced thought all but
nonexistent. He was not quick in his thinking and seemed very forgetful
in this, the last week of his life. Despite his self-image, he knew almost
nothing about the Bible. Neither, for that matter, did Darrow, who had
a sophomoric awareness of internal inconsistencies and some grasp of
biblical criticism. His questions for Bryan were mostly the old chestnuts
from the eighteenth century, reminiscent of Thomas Paine—the fish or
whale that swallowed Jonah, the sun that stood still for Joshua, the
source of a wife for Cain, and, above all, the problems that beset the old
chronology worked out by Bishop Ussher, largely on the basis of biblical
genealogies. Bryan fell into a trap by using this chronology to date such
events as the flood. He did not have the presence of mind to make clear
that these dates were not a part of the Bible, but were included only as
marginalia by some publishers. This lapse was symptomatic of Bryan,
who had to confess no knowledge of any number of issues raised by
Darrow's questions. He was not even able to define an agnostic, after
stating that agnosticism was one of the weaknesses of Buddhism.

Nothing has been more misinterpreted than this Darrow-Bryan inter-
change. One immediate response of journalists, including those from the
New York Times, was that Darrow completely crushed and humiliated
Bryan. This led to the widespread misapprehension that the questioning
hastened or even caused Bryan's death. Actually, the exchange was very
frustrating for both men and, in the case of Darrow, led to much grief.
Almost everyone, including some of his associates, thought that he had
deliberately and cruelly taunted and ridiculed a famous old statesman.
The ACLU tried, unsuccessfully, to drop him from the team of lawyers
involved in the appeal process. Bryan was frustrated because of his inadequate responses and his belief that other people considered him an igno-
ramus. He at least looked forward to his planned questioning of Darrow.
In the view of the audience, Bryan probably won the debate, in the
sense that he persuaded more people than did Darrow. The post-con-
frontation evaluations varied according to the outlook of those who
reported. Bryan was tired; it is not clear that he was devastated. The
most misunderstood aspect of the questioning was Bryan's statement that

he did not believe the days of creation were twenty-four-hour days. Some in the audience were indeed shocked, but this had long been a view held by many in the fundamentalist camp. It was not a concession won by Darrow's persistent questions, but one of several examples of Bryan's nondogmatic and often generously inclusive view of Christianity, which troubled some fellow fundamentalists. Only a small, largely Seventh-day Adventist group of creationists still argued for an earth only six thousand years old.

The trial resumed on Tuesday. Stewart finally prevailed over Raulston, who would not allow the farce of the previous afternoon to continue, and excluded Bryan's testimony from the record. With no further evidence to offer, the defense asked Raulston to bring in the jury and instruct it to bring in a verdict of guilty. This left no occasion for closing arguments, which further frustrated Bryan, who had written his closing statement. This planned address (he gave copies to the press) was essentially a summary of all that he had been saying about the evils of Darwinism and evolution for the last five years. After more procedural sparring, the jury finally returned, and the judge so charged it that a guilty verdict seemed obligatory. But just in case, Darrow also asked the jury to bring in a guilty verdict, explaining that this was necessary for an appeal to a higher court. One technical issue proved important later. Raulston told the jury that if it was satisfied with a minimum fine, it could leave that to the judge, which apparently had been the local practice in moonshine cases. Stewart reminded him that the state constitution required a jury to assess fines of over $50, but this did not persuade Raulston to change his normal practice. The jury left, deliberated for nine minutes, and returned with the guilty verdict. Raulston imposed the minimum $100 fine. Scopes made a brief statement, protesting the unjust fine and promising continued efforts to oppose a law that violated constitutional guarantees and his freedom to teach the truth. Almost everyone involved made statements, and Darrow even declared this case, reflecting a new tide of opinion that led to a testing of every fact of science by a religious dictum, to be a return to witchcraft trials. Raulston denied all defense motions except the right of appeal and had a "brother Jones" pronounce the benediction before adjournment.

Legally, the Scopes case ended only in January 1927. As planned all along, the ACLU supported an appeal to the state supreme court, but its board was deeply divided over an unsuccessful attempt to remove Darrow from the defense team. Darrow gave the closing arguments before the Tennessee Supreme Court in May 1926. Scopes was not in attendance. Several new lawyers were involved on both sides, but Neal and Hays were both present. One of the five judges at the hearing died before the remaining four judges gave their decision. It was a very mixed, even confusing decision. Two of the four judges ruled that the Butler Act was constitutional and that Scopes violated it. But they stressed that what the bill proscribed was only the teaching that humans descended from lower types and, therefore, that much of the evidence in favor of evolution was irrelevant, since it involved more than the origin of humans. Teachers were free to teach about the evolution of all other species. A third judge agreed that the act was constitutional, but he accepted the defense contention that even the evolution of humans could be consistent with some interpretations of the Bible. The act only proscribed theories of evolution that attributed the beginning of life to material causes and denied a divine first cause. By this interpretation, Scopes was not guilty of violating the act, and it seemed that the act placed such minimal limits upon the teaching of evolutionary theory as to be meaningless. A fourth judge found the Butler Act too vague to be valid. Since two judges out of four upheld the conviction of Scopes, the defense seemed to have narrowly lost in Tennessee and was in a good position for an appeal to the United States Supreme Court. Not so.

The Court found that Raulston, as Stewart had feared, violated the state constitution by assessing the $100 fine, which was the prerogative of the jury. Not only did it reverse the decision of the trial court, but it further urged the state attorney general not to retry the case. It cited the fact that Scopes was no longer a state employee and the need to preserve the peace and dignity of the state. The defense was helpless. Its only recourse was to try to find someone willing once again to test the law. It never seriously tried. Only forty years later, in 1967, did the Tennessee legislature finally repeal the Butler Act, and not without some strenuous opposition. By then it was clearly unconstitutional because of post-1940 church-state interpretations by federal courts. The United States Supreme Court declared a closely related Arkansas act unconstitutional in 1968.

Despite the inconclusive nature of the Tennessee Supreme Court decision, the hearings before the court raised several of the principal issues at stake at Dayton. On one level, the Scopes trial vividly illustrated a developing clash between intellectuals and the larger public. This was not new. Tensions had always existed between the views of ordinary people and those of the few exceptionally gifted or well-educated people who probed the frontiers of thought and expression. But the gap in understanding and taste broadened by the 1920s. This was evident in literature, in the plastic arts, in new philosophical schools, in the revolutionary shifts in physics, in music, in changing moral standards, but perhaps, above all, in the intense battles over religious belief.

At Dayton, a local, regional culture suffered a type of invasion from the outside. Highly educated, cosmopolitan elites descended upon the village. Some were arrogant. Almost all were unintentionally patronizing. They found what they perceived as ignorance, or an unfortunate cultural lag, and with good intentions they wanted to begin an educational process, to bring the local citizens up-to-date on the complex issues involving evolution. They were quickly frustrated. They found a few local cheerleaders, Rappleyea and a Methodist minister in Dayton, mainstream ministers and the editor of the major newspaper in Chattanooga, a scattering of scientists at the University of Tennessee and Vanderbilt University, but no support from most ruling elites in Tennessee. They ran into a still homogeneous Protestant culture—not a monolithic culture, but one that still exhibited a type of solidarity when under attack. Lawyers, judges, and politicians rallied to its defense and, in so doing, made the state seem hopelessly backward and parochial to the visiting outside observers or witnesses who came to Dayton, whether theologians, scientists, or journalists.

In a sense, Tennessee still had a religious establishment. Its constitution prevented the state from giving any preference to any religious establishment or mode of worship. But the same constitution made belief in God and in future rewards and punishments a requirement of all officeholders. A legislative act required all public schoolteachers to read ten verses from the Christian Bible (universally the Authorized or King James Version), without comment, at the opening of each school day, ostensibly in behalf of improved morals. Opening school prayers were so customary as to seem mandatory. At Dayton, even the defense did not argue that the Butler Act was inconsistent with the federal establishment clause, because at this time the United States Supreme Court had not so extended the reach of the Fourteenth Amendment. The First Amendment stipulates only that the U.S. Congress cannot enact laws respecting an establishment of religion. It does not directly place such limits on state governments, and numerous states in 1925 still favored theistic religions. The establishment clause, at its adoption, served as a commitment to the states that the new federal Congress would not regulate state practices, for at the time three states still provided tax support for a favored Christian denomination. Thus, the defense had to argue that the

Butler Act violated the separation clause in the Tennessee Constitution. This argument, perhaps above all other defense claims, invited a shrill and angry response from the two lawyers whom the new state attorney general (Frank M. Thompson) hired to defend the state case.

In their appeal, the defense attorneys continued to insist that guilt under the Butler Act required a violation of both clauses—a denial of the biblical story of divine creation and teaching the descent of humans from lower orders. This strategy clearly entangled the issue of a religious establishment and raised the problem of what interpretative leeway a teacher might have for understanding Genesis 1–2. Both Raulston at Dayton and even more the state in its brief to the Tennesssee Supreme Court chose to ignore the biblical reference and to insist that the operative part of the law, the aspect that was clear enough to enforce, involved only descent. By adopting this strategic tactic, the attorneys for the state tried to finesse the establishment issue, since they found no direct entanglement with religion in the descent issue, although they admitted that religious concerns may have influenced legislators to support the bill (some religious conviction might influence support for almost any conceivable legislation).

The state attorneys did not believe the state constitution required a complete separatist position because it included religious tests for officeholding. What the state establishment clause did do was preclude favoritism to any sect. It did not require neutrality toward religion, for the constitution explicitly favored religion, although not any particular religion. But in their brief the state attorneys made clear that this support of religion meant support for "real" religions, those that involved a belief in God and in immortality. They denied that any true religion, past and present, had ever supported the idea of descent. Thus the very existence of religion, in any of its expressions, was inconsistent with the descent doctrine. And following Bryan very closely, they denied that any system of morality, even any ordered society, could survive without the support of religious belief. In this sense, they accepted the argument that the Butler Act was a bill to protect religious belief, but not in a way that favored any one sect. It favored all religious sects and set up a minimum protection for all of them. What it did not protect was the teaching, in the public schools, of beliefs that threatened religion and most likely would lead to atheism and thus jeopardize all possibilities for an ordered and free society. The attorneys frequently cited anarchy as the likely outcome of teaching that humans descended from lower orders of animals.

Perhaps this all rang true for at least 90 percent of Tennesseans, including those who were members of no churches but who still believed the Genesis stories. For them, what happened at Dayton had to be disturbing. Eminent people from the outside, as well as educated elites within Tennessee, made two points over and over again: Organic evolution and the descent of humans was now an accepted fact not only for biologists but for educated people generally (the defense had even used a note from Woodrow Wilson indicating surprise that anyone still rejected evolution); and a growing number of professed Christians not only accepted some form of evolution as verified beyond doubt but also argued that it was consistent with Christian belief and a correct or enlightened understanding of the Bible. In other words, only unenlightened, uneducated, or intellectually closed minds still said otherwise. Maybe, by strict constitutional standards, Tennessee had the right to preclude the teaching of descent even if it were true, but if this meant that it prevented its own children from learning the best of contemporary knowledge, knowledge accepted among the educated people of the world, knowledge that might soon be necessary for professional acceptance or even certain jobs, then it was in an embarrassing situation. Those who came to Dayton to defend Scopes did all they could to create such embarrassment, and they touched such a tender nerve that the state attorneys, even though they did not need to do so, devoted much of their brief to what amounted to a religiously loaded polemic, one that in retrospect seems much more embarrassing than the Butler Act, which, after all, reflected the innocent views of a good-natured farmer from Macon County, not the arguments of college-educated lawyers.

The testimony of the outside experts at Dayton did not become part of the record before the state supreme court. The state professed to ignore it, but in fact it haunted the state attorneys. The state, they argued, because of its constitutional requirements for officeholders, had a clear duty to prohibit teachings in the schools that would undermine belief in God and immortality. In fact, this was the highest expression of its police powers. They sensed that a worldview was at stake. From their perspective, all the imported experts simply had to be wrong, or else all the verities accepted by a vast majority of Tennesseans were in jeopardy. The state thus included much from Bryan's final but undelivered speech in its brief. The attorneys added their own sermons. They argued that no really great or outstanding scientist had ever advocated the idea of descent. No one had ever established, or would ever be able to prove, that humans descended from animals. The only ones to take exception to this made up a small, superficial group of would-be scientists, or well-intentioned, would-be rescuers of religion who had been suckered by these pseudoscientists. The vituperative labeling went on and on: scientific dilettantes and intolerants, near scientists, self-styled intellectuals, and blindly partisan propagandists. The Butler Act was a defense against "the systematic, disturbing, misleading, uncritical, unscholarly, unhelpful and untrue intrusion of such half-baked and ill-considered cant and fustian." Those who used such cant were part of an ultramodern intelligentsia with sinister goals. They were against all religions, or what was the only hope for the world. Above all, they were subversive, in the sense that they used their sophistry to wean children away from all respect for authority, away from belief in God and the moral constraints such a belief entailed. They supported an amoral, brutelike ethic, one that meant social anarchy. On and on they piled on the invective, as if such largely ad hominem arguments would somehow destroy all respect for such outside experts, who had no real credentials. They had to believe that no truly eminent scientists accepted descent. But pathetically, when they sought eminent scientists to support their side, they could identify only two "impartial and critically scientific" Roman Catholic scholars, not biologists, who had written polemics against Darwinism.

Scopes assumed a role that soon made him seem, for the outside experts at the trial, a martyr to the cause of personal and academic freedom. By the perspective of most reporters, as depicted to the larger world, Scopes had defied not just the new Butler Act but the whole conformist mentality of village or province. He was a part of the revolt against the village, one who tried to escape Main Street. He tried, but failed, to bring enlightenment, a wider perspective, to an orthodox, even totalitarian society. Of course, the local orthodoxy prevailed. The almost mythic fundamentalists, whom reporters found lurking everywhere in Dayton or even in Tennessee, became the devils of the piece, the epitome of mass society, the ignorant peasantry, the agents of populistic repression. In the language of H. L. Mencken, these Baptists and Methodists (sneer words to him) made up the "vulgar democracy" of America. Even as perceptive a critic as Walter Lippmann described them as ignoramuses and struggled to find a means of reconciliation between enlightened elites and the unwashed multitudes.

What the ACLU wanted to achieve from the test case at Dayton was added court protection for a type of academic freedom. This meant protection for those individuals who expressed ideas that were unpopular with a local or even a national majority. But even the ACLU recognized that the public school system was not an arena for complete freedom of speech. Teachers, as public employees, could accept terms of employment that limited what they did in the classroom, including what they said before students. As citizens, they still enjoyed all their protected freedoms outside the classroom. Thus, academic freedom was of a different order, even yet a difficult concept to define and defend. The crux of the case was the content of Scopes's teaching. Had he used the classroom to promote some personal political agenda, or to proselytize students in favor of his own religious beliefs, the ACLU would have been the first to protest. But from the perspective of Scopes, what he wanted to teach, but could not legally teach after enactment of the Butler Act, was accepted knowledge in a critical discipline. From his perspective, his commitment to teach the truth to students was threatened by the Butler Act. And, quite clearly, the Butler Act reflected, not a concern of parents about the best curriculum, but a desire to protect students from ideas that would challenge revered religious beliefs. As moves to prohibit teaching about evolution spread from state to state, and as an organized fundamentalist movement among evangelical Protestants seemed to be reaping victory after victory, the ACLU envisioned a wave of religiously motivated repression of the rights of conscientious teachers to do their work. The question was: What constitutional remedy could protect teachers, particularly in states in which an overwhelming majority of people wanted to protect their children from what they perceived as dangerous beliefs?

In a sense, whether humans had in fact descended from lower orders of life was not the issue. Neither legislatures nor courts are in a position to adjudicate issues of truth and falseness in biology or in any other discipline. Even if descent is an established fact, true in the sense that other empirically established hypotheses are true, the people of Tennessee might still decide that they did not want this "truth" taught to their children. And in all school systems, there is a recognition that children, at certain ages, are not yet ready to absorb or cope with types of knowledge. But since the Butler Act's proscriptions applied even to colleges, the phasing issue was not important in the Scopes controversy. The purpose of the bill was to protect all students in public institutions from the terrible effects of learning about, and possibly accepting as true, human descent. The state, in its brief to the Tennessee Supreme Court, made this point—that the legislature could rightly reflect the common understanding of the people of Tennessee, even if by some other standard the common wisdom was completely mistaken. But the attorneys for the state would not concede that descent was a fact, and thus they defended a Tennessee statute that only kept certain highly speculative theories out of classrooms. But, legally, they noted that they could defend the Butler Act even if it contravened widely accepted scientific views. After all, any number of state-selected textbooks undoubtedly contained errors of fact as well as unnoticed expressions of preference.

In effect, in 1925, the ACLU had no constitutional solution to the problem of restrictive state curriculum guidelines, even those clearly motivated by religious concerns. After 1940, a series of decisions by the United States Supreme Court forced the states to live up to the same standard for the separation of church and state that the First Amendment had originally placed upon Congress. Clearly, any requirement that teachers adhere to creation stories in the Christian Bible was now un-constitutional. Any individuals affected by such requirements, including teachers, could seek redress in federal courts. They did this in Arkansas in the 1960s, and the Supreme Court, in 1968, declared that state's anti-evolution law unconstitutional, even though it did not follow the one in Tennessee and refer specifically to biblical creation. Less clear is what recourse a teacher has if a state does not allow any teachings at all about human descent, with no overt religious reason for such a prohibition. The burden, in this case, would be to prove that this prohibition clearly involves a religious goal and amounts to favoritism for one particular religion.

At Dayton, Bryan used a ploy that has become a favorite of contempo-rary creationists. He noted that the separation or nonfavoritism clause in the Tennessee Constitution precluded teachings that favored Christian-ity over any other religion. But, he argued, the defenders of Scopes wanted to open the schools to clearly anti-Christian teaching. Of course, the defense tried to prove that nothing in the fact of descent need be understood as anti-Christian. But for some Christians, including all who believed in biblical inerrancy, there was indeed an undeniable conflict. Could one expect parents to allow their children to go to school and there confront such purported facts as were sure to lead them to doubt the religion taught at home? As Lippmann noted, this was a growing problem in an increasingly heterogeneous America. Not only did schools have to cope with people of diverse ethnic and religious back-grounds, or a context in which almost any curriculum might offend some parent, but perhaps of even greater importance, every American lived in a society in which a nonethnic and nonsectarian minority, an intelligentsia, was increasingly at odds with an older religious culture.

And these cosmopolitan intellectuals had enormous cultural influence, so much so that, over time, they would win almost all the cultural wars. Such intellectuals came to Dayton and lost, but the divided Tennessee Supreme Court decision came close to vindicating their claims. Within fifteen years, they were able to prevail in the federal courts. They prevailed, in part, because the judges were part of this intelligentsia.

Bryan's argument—that evolutionary theory was a counterreligion, or at least hostile to religion—has remained a perplexing ingredient in creationist appeals for equal time in the schools. In homogeneous communities, in which everyone shares a single religious tradition, none of these conflicts could arise. In small Tennessee villages, possibly even in small towns the size of Dayton, teachers, parents, and children affirmed roughly the same religious beliefs. No minorities challenged the working consensus on basic beliefs and preferences. High school teachers used the state-mandated textbooks on biology, possibly stumbled through the section on evolution, but did not grasp its significance until fundamentalist crusaders made an issue of such texts. And by then, even in Dayton, the consensus had already begun to break down. Scopes and Rappleyea did grasp the implications and believed that the schools should expose children to such important knowledge. They had no allegiance to the older consensus, had not been part of it, and thus could hardly understand the depth of opposition to something as well established as evolution. After all, the battles over its acceptance seemed to have died out over fifty years before. In the view of the intellectual elite in America, this was now a part of conventional understanding.

The attempt by Scopes's defenders to overthrow the Butler Act was, from a local perspective, an assault upon their communal values by outsiders or by an arrogant minority within Tennessee. The almost scurrilous attack on these arrogant outsiders by the state attorneys documented their resentment. In effect, it seemed to them that the defense team stood squarely against the democratic will. They were correct. They wanted to place such limits on majority opinion as to protect rights of self-expression by resented minorities. How could they justify such protections? One appeal, of course, was to standing law, as reflected in state and federal constitutions. If such laws provided protection for certain minorities, then only constitutional amendments could give majorities the power to effect their will. Beyond constitutional covenants, one could only offer some utilitarian or moral appeal. Justice, or equity, or the efficient functioning of government, or the long-term progress of a society, required policies to protect freedom for various forms of self-expression, including the leeway for teachers to communicate what they saw as truth to their students. But in the absence of constitutional protections already in place, one had to gain acceptance of such freedom either through successful persuasion of the larger public or through the use of coercive power.

A few people grasped this truth. In the North, most of the newspapers and periodicals that carried articles on the Scopes trial (almost all did, including daily coverage by the *New York Times*) led the cheers for Scopes and his defense. One clear exception was the *New Republic*. In four articles, it adopted a consistent editorial stance. It lamented the Butler Act. The people of Tennessee and their legislators were misinformed and were foolish to enact such an atavistic law. The state would suffer for its lack of wisdom and forethought. But it was for Tennesseans to make policy. They should repeal the Butler Act. Maybe more education would lead them to repeal. What the *New Republic* feared was a judicial resolution. It did not want the courts to interfere. Of course, in clear cases of constitutional violation, courts had to grant relief to litigants. This was not such a case. At best, the constitutional issues were blurred, and judicial resolution would reflect an unwanted assumption of authority by an unelected court. It would mean the imposition of elite outside values upon the state of Tennessee. Such a trend toward judicial sovereignty presented more dangers than did the Butler Act. Tennesseans had the right to make bad decisions, whatever the standard of adjudging what was bad, or else the United States did not have self-government. If the people of Tennessee, by and large, adhered to a type of Christianity that was inconsistent with evolution, then it made sense that they use such beliefs in adjudicating curricular issues. It would have made no sense for them to authorize the teaching of beliefs antithetical to their religion, exactly what Bryan had argued all along. It was only a minor issue in semantics whether evolution was antireligious or even a counterreligion. The point was that Tennesseans so perceived it, and so long as this remained the view of most Tennesseans, it was only reasonable for them to try to keep it from their classrooms. To do otherwise was to commit a type of religious suicide.

Scopes lost, but contrary to most public perceptions, almost no one at Dayton resented his role in the trial. He was a friend to people on both sides of the issue. Thus, his superintendent offered him an appointment for the next school year. He refused, because he had decided to attend graduate school in geology at the University of Chicago. The defense attorneys and the expert witnesses at Dayton began a fund to further his education. In two stints, he studied at Chicago, but never completed his dissertation and ended up working for an oil company for most of his career. He retained his friendship with Darrow, whom he came to idolize, even to the extent of echoing his form of environmental determinism.

Bryan died at Dayton the Sunday following the end of the trial. He died, not of heartbreak because of the trial, but because he had abused his body and gorged it with too much rich food. He was an instant martyr to the fundamentalist cause, but after a few years the loss of his leadership hurt the movement. The climax of the anti-evolution crusade came in the three years after Dayton, with both Mississippi and Arkansas enacting laws modeled in part after the Butler Act. Other state efforts failed, and support for such legislation faded after 1929. By 1926, it was clear that the fundamentalist factions would not capture any major northern denomination, and by the Great Depression it was clear that they would not be able to use legislation to suppress the teaching of evolution. Thus, in the depression and war years, and then in the great revival of Christianity in the fifties, crusading evangelicals, either as a subculture within the traditional denominations or in dozens of new splinter denominations that were fully evangelical in commitment, remained, if not invisible (they were quite visible at the local level), then submerged, at least in the perspective of the more cosmopolitan culture.

With each passing year, evangelicals developed greater institutional strengths. They nurtured stronger colleges, led by Wheaton near Chicago (nondenominational), by a more confessional and doctrinal form of conservatism at Calvin College (Christian Reformed), by the Moody Bible Institute and several splinters from it, and soon by over a hundred regional Bible colleges or institutes or small denominational colleges. They even founded a small, struggling college at Dayton, one named for Bryan. They developed numerous transdenominational organizations, including the Inter-Varsity Christian Fellowship, the Campus Crusade for Christ, and the Fellowship of Christian Athletes. In 1942, delegates from several, mostly small evangelical splinter denominations formed the National Association of Evangelicals. Today, it represents almost fifty denominations, including holiness, Pentecostal, Calvinist, and Wesleyan denominations, and even a few sects with Anabaptist, Adventist, or Friends heritage. Evangelicals, some from the Pentecostal tradition, have almost dominated radio and television ministries. They have also published literally hundreds of periodicals. But most important of all, the evangelical factions within the Southern Baptist Convention eventually all but captured that denomination and its huge publishing, missionary, and educational assets. It is now the largest Protestant denomination in America, and a vital core of wealth and strength for the evangelical cause and for biblical inerrancy, although one should not ignore major resisting and moderate factions that still battle for the soul of that denomination.

In another sense the fundamentalists were also more successful than they at first realized. Laws or legislative resolutions that condemned textbooks that taught evolution, joined with the three state acts prohibiting its teaching, had an intimidating effect on the publishers of biology textbooks. Most dropped all direct references to Darwin or to evolutionary theories. This meant that the responsibility of introducing this subject matter remained with teachers, most without much advanced work in biology or genetics. Only with *Sputnik* in 1957, and a renewed national concern about scientific training in America, did publishers once again include extended sections on evolutionary theory. In a sense, they caught up with the best texts of 1925. But once again, such content in textbooks aroused growing opposition from evangelical Christians, few of whom any longer used the label "fundamentalist." The issues had to be different. The legal context had shifted. Thus the new crusade involved not efforts to keep evolution out of the schools but attempts to get creation back in. The only constitutional way to do this, as was soon evident, was to persuade the courts that creationism could be a scientifically viable theory, not a thin cover for Christian doctrine. Once again, this led to well-publicized "fairness" laws, mandates for textbook content, and two famous trials in Arkansas and Louisiana. So far, these modern creationists have lost all their legal battles, but they too have intimidated some school boards and textbook publishers. The story goes on, and may have no early ending.

Reading Guide

The most recent, most scholarly story of the Scopes trial and its legacy is in an excellent book by Edward J. Larson, *Summer for the Gods: The Scopes Trial and America's Continuing Debate over Science and Religion* (New York: Basic Books, 1997). Its notes include most of the primary and secondary literature on the trial. Ray Ginger wrote the first, and still in some ways the most readable, popular history of the trial, *Six Days Are Forever: Tennessee v. John Scopes* (Boston: Beacon Press, 1958). A more detailed blow-by-blow account is in L. Sprague de Camp, *The Great Monkey Trial* (New York: Doubleday, 1968).

Kenneth Bailey, in a 1949 M.A. thesis at Vanderbilt University, first offered the full story of the enactment of the Butler Act and followed this with a Ph.D. dissertation, "The Antievolution Crusade of the Nineteen-Twenties," Vanderbilt University, 1953. Willard B. Gatewood, who wrote a book on the anti-evolution controversy in North Carolina, compiled a still useful anthology, *Controversy in the Twenties: Fundamentalism, Modernism, and Evolution* (Nashville: Vanderbilt University Press, 1969).

Even yet, the best source on the Scopes trial is the actual transcript of what occurred. The best published version is *The World's Most Famous Court Case: Tennessee Evolution Case* (Dayton: Bryan College, 1990). This transcript is the source of all quotations from trial participants included in the above essay. The literature on the major participants is rather extensive. Bryan, of course, has dozens of biographers, but the one most closely related to the Scopes trial is Lawrence W. Levine, *Defender of the Faith: William Jennings Bryan, the Last Decade, 1915–1925* (New York: Oxford University Press, 1965). Clarence Darrow, a much better lawyer than writer, gave his version of the trial in *The Story of My Life* (New York: Grosset & Dunlap, 1932). John C. Livingstone has written the most scholarly biography of Darrow: *Clarence Darrow: Sentimental Rebel* (New York: Garland, 1988). Over twenty years after the trial, an all-but-forgotten John Scopes, assisted by James Presley, wrote his memoirs, with greatest attention to the trial, *Center of the Storm, Memoirs of John Scopes* (New York: Holt, Rinehart & Winston, 1967).

4

A DIALOGUE AMONG
CHRISTIAN INTELLECTUALS

In the 1920s, no Christian intellectuals were more often in the headlines than John Gresham Machen of Princeton Theological Seminary, Harry Emerson Fosdick of Union Theological Seminary, and Shailer Mathews, longtime dean of the Divinity School at the University of Chicago. Each was personally involved in the battles over fundamentalism. They also exemplified the broad spectrum of Christian responses to new scientific knowledge and to biblical scholarship.

Machen was an ideal spokesman for a type of confessional orthodoxy, in this case Presbyterian or, more generally, Reformed or Calvinist. Fosdick, a charismatic preacher as well as a seminary teacher, became the most eloquent, and by far the best-known, spokesman for what he called "evangelical liberalism." He was not nearly as radical, philosophically, as Mathews, who epitomized what both he and his most hostile critics called "modernism." At least for those who remained within the traditional evangelical churches, Mathews was on the far radical extreme in his philosophical and theological commitments. All three of these Protestant intellectuals wrote popular books to promote their own platform in the twenties and, often without express name-calling, clearly maintained a dialogue with one another.

For several reasons, it makes sense to begin with the orthodox perspective. Machen not only opened the dialogue in 1923 with a brilliant polemic, *Christianity and Liberalism*, but set out the issues at stake with greater clarity and logic than his two protagonists. Although Machen did not fit the mold of popular fundamentalists, he did agree with most of their goals. No one offered them such sophisticated intellectual ammunition, for among the leaders of the fundamentalist crusade no one else had his scholarly credentials or his logical acumen.

Machen was an odd bedfellow of most fundamentalists. A sophisticated but shy man, he loved the theater, smoked and drank with colleagues, and never had any respect for the dispensational premillennialism so pervasive among self-proclaimed fundamentalists. Politically inept, uncompromising, rigid, he was never able to work well with others, including his more moderate colleagues at Princeton.

Machen was born in Baltimore in 1881. He came from a professional family and enjoyed excellent educational opportunities. His family was part of a confessional Presbyterian tradition, one that had, before the Civil War, become identified as Old School. Young Machen completed his B.A. in the classics at Johns Hopkins University, then moved on to the Princeton Theological Seminary, a seminary identified with his own developing doctrinal outlook. There he studied with Benjamin Warfield, who in turn was the student of Charles Hodge, the founder of what many called the "Princeton School" of theology. He also gained an M.A. from Princeton University. He then spent a year in two German universities, only to return to his Princeton Seminary, there to begin as an instructor and only slowly to rise to full professor. His scholarly work, admired for its exactitude even by modernists, involved Paul and the problem of the virgin birth of Jesus. In addition to his books, Machen defended a type of confessional orthodoxy in numerous articles in the *Princeton Review.*

In *Christianity and Liberalism*, Machen departed from his usual labors as a New Testament scholar and Calvinist apologist. He was, as it turned out, the last distinguished defender of the Princeton theology, the roots of which went back to Paul and Augustine as well as to John Calvin and other Geneva theologians. Machen became America's leading defender of the doctrines formulated at Dort and Westminster. But by 1923 he was soul sick about developments within his own Presbyterian Church in the United States of America and about the growing success of types of liberalism and modernism in American evangelical Christianity generally. Thus, he temporarily set aside intramural or sectarian controversies to become an advocate for the great doctrines of the Church. His Presbyterian loyalties continued to shape some of his arguments, but to the best of his abilities he now wanted to defend the essential beliefs of Christianity present in all its traditional expressions, including even Roman Catholicism and, perhaps harder for him to swallow, the Arminian tradition as best represented in America by the Wesleyan churches.

Machen defended a specific, doctrinal, supernatural, theistic, salvation religion, or what he believed alone deserved the label "Christianity." This religion was rooted in a biblical cosmology and shaped by a series of providential historical events, climaxing in the atoning death and the resurrection of Jesus of Nazareth. The essential, defining doctrines of Christianity, and thus of the historic Church, were under attack as never before. It was most dangerously threatened by those who, through deceit or fuzzy thinking, camouflaged their rejection of essential doctrines by use of the old language of orthodoxy (he had Mathews in mind). These internal subversives had rejected all or almost all the essential and defining doctrines, beginning with the Christian God. Machen, as had Hodge and Warfield before him, granted that the beliefs of these self-professed liberals did constitute a type of religion, one often warm and sentimental and superficially appealing, but this religion was not Christian, unless one used the word "Christian" for any new religion one cooked up to cater to modern sensibilities. Thus, Machen, over and over again, begged all those who had rejected the heart themes of the Christian tradition, who could not without qualifications affirm the traditional creeds and confessions of the Church, to be honest and separate rather than continue their effort to erode the Church from within. Despairingly, and prophetically, he often sensed that it would be the orthodox who would have to leave the increasingly corrupted northern mainline denominations.

Machen approached these issues with two important convictions. First, new scientific knowledge, in several fields, had transformed the modern world. The all-important question was whether Christianity could survive in a scientific age, not primarily because of the specific new knowledge and new tools but because of a philosophy that had accompanied the new science, or what Machen called "naturalism." Religious liberals were infected with such naturalism even when they verbally seemed opposed to it. By naturalism, Machen did not necessarily mean some form of mechanistic or deterministic materialism, but a denial of any form of supernaturalism. Supplemental to this acknowledgment of the achievements of scientific inquiry, Machen departed from his liberal protagonists, who generally greeted such new knowledge and lauded the progress that humans had recently achieved, by a deep sense of declension. He saw all around him, not progress, but moral confusion, distorted values, vulgarized arts, and a steady loss of freedom to such collective institutions as the modern state.

Logically, systematically, Machen catalogued the content of a new religious liberalism. He began with doctrine. Liberals often dismissed the historic creeds of the Church or lamented divisive doctrines. In a tradition that traced back to Horace Bushnell, they defined religion as a way of life, not a set of doctrines, or made experience the foundation of religion. They thus saw creeds and formulas as suggestive, not decisive. Some even said the more the better, even when they contradicted each other. Liberals embraced soft, sentimental, and basically non-Christian affirmations, such as the fatherhood of God and the brotherhood of man, when it was clear to Machen that God, in any other sense than creator, was a loving father only to Christians and that Christians and sinners were, in no useful sense of the word, "brothers." Behind this liberal eschewal of doctrine was a sinister purpose: to convince lay Christians, even all the way down to those who read corrupted Sunday school literature, that what one believed was relative to time and place, and religiously unimportant, while sentiment and feeling were all important. But this was really only a cover for a new set of liberal presuppositions (really doctrines) that were all consistent with naturalism.

Machen's response to nondoctrinaire liberals often involved truisms. He correctly pointed out that Christianity was a historical religion, one keyed to events that took place in the past. For example, it rested on beliefs about what Jesus taught, what he did, and on his claims about his own divine status and role. The first Christian literature (the unchallenged letters of Paul) was full of doctrine. One has only to read Romans to be aware of this. Thus, Machen easily made his point—a Christian has to adhere to doctrines and, by that very fact, be exclusive. An inclusive religion cannot be Christian. But this leaves the problem: Which beliefs are obligatory, which optional? The liberals clearly lessened the number of essential beliefs, at times almost to the vanishing point. But orthodox Christians, in different historical traditions, so differed on doctrinal issues that one might wonder which, among the variants, was essential. Machen granted this point but argued that widely divergent Christians did not disagree about the central doctrines of the Church, which he tried to define in the major part of his book. Liberals had rejected some, or even most, of these essential doctrines. He was not as narrow as some of his critics suggested. He believed premillennialist fundamentalists were wrong, mistaken in reading the Bible and in their beliefs about last things. He had always bemoaned the soft, sentimental, easy doctrines of Arminians and saw liberalism as one all too likely outcome of such sentimentality. He, of course, was an heir of Luther and Calvin and bemoaned the many errors of Roman Catholicism. He believed in the plenary inspiration of the Bible and deplored fellow scholars who were more selective in their judgments about the Scriptures. But in each case he acknowledged that these erring brethren were indeed Christians, heirs of salvation, because they all affirmed the essential doctrines, doctrines inextricably bound up with their response to God. But such a gesture toward other Christians begged the issues: What is critical in the way of belief? Why are Roman Catholics redeemed Christians and liberals not so?

Although he never put it this way, Machen really believed that liberals had rejected belief in the only existing God. In effect, he accused them of creating new gods to fit their own taste and desires, or gods more consistent with a "scientific" understanding of the universe. Machen still affirmed theology as the science of God. Theologians have God as the object of their knowledge. He admitted that liberals, in many cases, sincerely believed in some higher power, in some creator behind or present within history, and even in some cases in a god that was vaguely personal or responsive to humans. Liberals professed to "feel" his or its presence and continually talked about god as father to humankind. But such vague and irenic gods had little relationship, except verbally similar names, to the awful, transcendent God of Christianity, a God indeed providentially present in his creation but always more than, and prior to, any of his handiwork. The Christian God was much more than a vague world force, or immanent presence, or a mind or spirit concretized in history. The Christian God was all powerful, all knowing, the source of all things, and, although a God who normally governed the universe through proximate laws of his own design, a God who, at special times and for his own special purposes, directly intervened in history. That is, the God of Christianity was a God of miracles.

Along with their pantheistic or sentimental gods, liberals had, quite consistently, rejected the Christian view of humanity. They had lowered the immense gulf between God and humans, ignored the inherent alienation of humans from God, and thus evaded the awful judgment of God upon all humans. They had so elevated their conception of humans as to deny that humans were under an awful condemnation, full of guilt, and thus in need of divine mercy. Christianity is a religion of the broken-hearted, of humans who, in moments of greatest insight, come to realize and to confess their sinfulness. Only such contrite humans are in a position to respond to the unmerited grace of God. Liberals had all but abolished sin, in the sense of an alienating pride and rebellion. They had turned salvation into moral achievement and often had such an elevated sense of human worth and competence as to rejoin the pagan philosophers of ancient Greece. In a sense, they had practically deified humans and turned the Kingdom of God into some future utopia. For them, religion had become a means to live a joyous and happy life. Obviously, for such liberals, the older doctrines of original sin and of unmerited grace made no sense. Neither did the doctrine of the atonement. For Machen, the orthodox view of God and man, and thus the need for an atoning savior, were essential beliefs of Christianity. Deny them, and one was not, could not in honesty claim to be, a Christian.

Machen acknowledged that God revealed himself in nature. But nature did not reveal a plan of salvation. Thus the saving knowledge of God came directly from himself, in the form of Scripture. And it was only through Scripture that humans came to know about critical events related to their salvation, most critically the events surrounding the life of Jesus. The revelation in the gospel is indeed complemented by direct human experience, by the work of the Holy Spirit, but this experience is not in itself sufficient without the guidance of the Bible. Machen not only found in the Bible an "infallible rule of faith and practice," for him an essential Christian belief, but further believed the whole Bible inspired by God, without error. Honest Christians disagreed. He would not join fundamentalists and exclude from the Church those who rejected his very carefully qualified doctrine of inerrancy (I do not have the space to develop the many subtleties here), but as a whole he gave credibility to fundamentalists on this point. What was essential was that one accept biblical authority, that one rest all critical doctrines affecting salvation on its authority. Liberals were un-Christian because they rejected the ultimate authority of the Bible for all matters of faith and practice. Liberals, of course, saluted the Bible, referred to it as divine, found in it critical insights about a developing understanding of God, rejoiced in its stories about Jesus, but still did not accept its binding authority. How could they, when they no longer believed in the God revealed in the Bible, in the miracle-working Christ of the New Testament, or in the utterly fallen and sinful humanity that is one of its major themes?

At the heart of Machen's theology was the redeeming Savior. The most critical doctrines of Christianity involve Jesus as the promised Messiah or Christ. By definition, a Christian is one who believes that Jesus was the atoning Christ, even if Christians still disagree about the subtleties of the Trinity or the exact nature of the human and divine elements in Jesus. Machen, with unneeded overkill, spent much time demonstrating that Paul, and early Christians, so perceived Jesus. The creeds of the Church rest on this view of Jesus. Early Christians, as contemporary Christians, did not merely believe in the faith that Jesus revealed, as liberals so often averred, but they had faith in Jesus. He was, for them, much more than a moral guide, a man of wisdom and insight, an example of God's love, or other such mushy liberal celebrations. But liberals had no need of an atoning savior, did not believe in miracles, and thus they had created their own self-serving images of Jesus. Some of the images fit, but they were selective and diminished his status. For the critical belief about Jesus involves his divinity, not merely his moral teachings or sacrificial conduct. For Machen, nothing was more clear than that Jesus himself affirmed his messianic role (liberal scholars such as Mathews admitted this). Liberals were, at best, embarrassed by Jesus's miracles, his harsh judgments upon humankind, and his claims of special authority. Yet, deceivingly, liberals talked of Jesus and of the Christ all the time. One might even describe their beliefs as a Jesus religion, but what they ignored was the one critical issue—the deity of Jesus, which was a necessary precondition for an atoning sacrifice that could appease the awful justice of God.

This implicates salvation doctrines. Since liberals no longer affirmed a God of wrath and judgment, no longer believed in an utterly helpless and sinful humanity, and no longer believed in an atoning savior, the Christian scheme of salvation was irrelevant to them, even beyond their comprehension. They believed the death of the Christ was an exemplary sacrifice, a model for humans to follow. But by stressing its effects on humans, they ignored its critical role in salvation—how it affected God and made possible his mercy toward humans, who vicariously were able to gain reconciliation with God, not on the basis of their righteousness (they had no such), but on the righteousness of the Christ. This salvation was only for those of faith, and even faith came from God.

Uncomprehending liberals established a new plan of salvation, one more pagan or Greek than Christian. They substituted a gospel of Jesus, of sacrifice and service, for the gospel of the cross. They all but ignored damnation, or rejected any belief in hell, flirted with a de facto universal-

ism, and looked forward to unending progress toward a kingdom
achieved by reform. They were joyful, well adjusted, even happy. They
preached helpful, even therapeutic sermons. They were above all irenic
and, in America, made religion a tool to overcome new social problems.
Here, Machen's own cranky political views often subverted the intended
generality of his critique. In many ways, he anticipated the later, neo-
orthodox critics of an irenic liberalism. Some of his lamentations found
a later echo in Rienhold Niebuhr. But his fear of collectivism, his distrust of politicians and the state, led him not only to stress that repen-
tance and conversion had to precede an improved society, but to limit
the range of such reforms primarily to the family or very local institutions. This libertarian bent separated him from most fundamentalists,
who fought throughout the twenties for an effective enforcement of
national prohibition and who freely entered the political arena to gain
their goals for the larger society.

Machen's final charge against liberals involved their view of the
Church. Here, again, Machen's own developing battles within the Presbyterian Church too often shaped his arguments. He was bitter. For him,
the Holy Catholic Church contained all Christians, all people of faith.
Such Christians had an obligation to gather in visible congregations for
worship, including the sacraments. Such congregations were, by definition, exclusive in their membership. Only Christians are part of the
Church. But humans are not the ultimate judge. Congregations should
establish confessions of faith and use these as a basis for admitting members. No congregation can prevent hypocrites from affirming such a
faith. They have to leave judgment to God. But something very sinister
was happening in the mainstream, avowedly evangelical churches of
America. Individuals were affirming the required creeds, avowedly making the correct confessions of faith, when they clearly did not believe
what they confessed. They did this openly, for they made clear, in other
contexts, how much they qualified the older and intended meaning of
such confessions. Liberal Presbyterian ministers accepted ordination and
subscribed to the Westminster Confession, yet in their pulpit or at the
lectern in Presbyterian seminaries, or even in the councils of the Church,
made clear that they did not really believe half of what they subscribed.
Instead of ensuring a clear identity for a congregation, or for a denomination, so that members would know the required doctrines and commitments, they so loosened the meaning of confessions as to admit almost anyone to the Church. A type of loose inclusiveness had become
fashionable. And the Church was becoming a den of hypocrites. Machen

begged such hypocrites to redeem themselves with a little honesty. They could form their own religious organizations (the word "Church" would not fit), and compete with Christian churches. Such was his skepticism about the larger culture that Machen was sure they would gain a large membership. Or they could join the Unitarian movement, a religion "without an authoritative Bible, without doctrinal requirements, and without a creed." Machen specifically urged faithful, evangelical Christians to stop all contributions to liberal congregations or to agencies of the Church dominated by liberals. By 1923, one such agency was his own Princeton Seminary.

Machen rarely named his liberals, although he did refer to Fosdick. What he created was an ideal type. In all details, it probably fit no one person. But it was close to the mark for someone like Mathews, who in a few cases rather clearly provided a negative model for Machen. Machen frequently stressed that he was not attacking liberal religion. It was often appealing, as were its leading proponents. He only wanted to make clear that liberal religion was not, in any historically informed sense, Christian. This tactic was a bit disingenuous, for Machen could barely conceal his contempt for many liberal beliefs. Even when he granted the popularity of its doctrines, he was in a sense condemning by faint praise. As critics charged, and as Machen freely admitted, he defended a Christianity that was, not static, but grounded in past historical events, in ancient Scripture, and in certain clarifying decisions made by the early Church councils. The basic features of this received religion were timeless and not subject to human alteration, although the exact nature of the human response would change through time. Such a stance made him the perfect representative of religious orthodoxy, meaning a complete allegiance to developed doctrines and practices.

Machen's doctrinal position led him into problems at his own seminary. Within the Church, Princeton had become the lone bastion of Old School confessional orthodoxy, or a position identified with Hodge and his successors. Machen was the ablest representative of this tradition in the twenties. A majority of the seminary's faculty remained conservative, and thus the seminary had continued to attract ministerial students who identified with this now venerable tradition. But by 1920, Princeton (the seminary was not part of Princeton University) was clearly out of step with both larger theological trends and with the more inclusive posture of the denomination. Machen thus symbolized the inflexible old order, and in a way that typed the seminary and threatened its prestige and relevance in the circles of major Protestant seminaries. It was out of step, deliberately so from the perspective of Machen, for he believed that it alone among academically respected seminaries upheld the traditional doctrines of the great church.

The president of the seminary since 1914, J. Ross Stevenson, wanted to make it more representative of the denomination as a whole. This did not mean the dismissal of people like Machen, but bringing in balancing new voices and new points of view. In 1926 Stevenson delayed Machen's appointment to a new chair until the General Assembly, at his request, had investigated the whole administration and direction of the seminary. This led to what Stevenson desired—a full reorganization, a new single and more representative board, and thus a seminary now calculated to reflect the whole spectrum of views within the denomination. Machen fought the reorganization, appealed to the General Assembly, but lost. Thus, sure that Princeton could no longer be a clear voice for traditional Calvinism, Machen resigned from Princeton in 1929 to form a new Westminster Theological Seminary, taking with him three sympathetic faculty members and twenty students.

The formation of Westminster complied with the logic that Machen had pushed all along. A church, and a seminary, should have a clear identity, stand for something clear and unambiguous. Westminster did this, becoming the last bastion of Old School Presbyterianism and of the Princeton school of theology. Perhaps unfortunately, the new seminary attracted students primarily from regional bastions of fundamentalism and was soon clearly identified with fundamentalism more than with the scholarly rigor and integrity that Machen preferred. In reaction to the increasingly centralized and bureaucratic Princeton Seminary, Machen, an extreme libertarian on almost all issues, established a faculty-dominated form of administration for Westminster, which in time invited internal factionalism. Meanwhile, in reaction to what he saw as the dictatorial as well as liberal policies of his denomination, Machen helped organize an independent mission board, one clearly controlled by his faction within the church. This move lost him the support of most former allies, who still remained loyal to the denomination. The General Assembly, now with an actionable issue, declared the new missionary board to be schismatic and ordered all Presbyterians on it to withdraw or stand trial. Machen of course refused to resign, and after a trial in 1935, he was suspended as a minister. This led him, in the last two years of his life, to organize a new denomination, the Presbyterian Church of America (because of a legal challenge to this name, the denomination became the Orthodox Presbyterian Church in 1939, but this after Machen's death in 1937).

Even before this, in 1936 one of Machen's former students at Westminster, Carl McIntire, led a revolt within the fledgling denomination, separating and eventually forming the small Bible Presbyterian Church. It is a bit ironic that McIntire left, in part, because Machen did not require premillennial beliefs at Westminster and because he demanded moderation, not abstinence, on alcoholic drink. The vulgar fundamentalists were ready to take charge of a movement to which Machen had given his life. McIntire, less a scholar than Machen, a radio evangelist, became an almost demagogic leader of the forms of Presbyterian fundamentalism that survived into the post–World War II era. He adopted as his most hated targets both the National and the World Council of Churches (he formed a competing council in each case).

In most respects, Harry Emerson Fosdick was at the opposite pole from Machen. He symbolized Christian liberalism. He was at the center of all the fundamentalist controversies of the twenties, the bête noire of the orthodox. By 1925 he was, by far, the best-known liberal minister in America, even in a sense a celebrity. He became a friend of the rich and the famous. His inspirational sermons, published in a series of books, became best-sellers. He lectured in packed churches and auditoriums all over the United States and in Europe. In a sense, he was the liberal counterpart of Billy Sunday. In most respects he exemplified Machen's ideal typical liberal and turned the label "liberal" into his badge of honor.

Fosdick was raised in an almost stereotypical Victorian family. Born in 1878 in Buffalo, in a literate, Baptist, Republican family, he grew up either in Buffalo or in a nearby village. His father was a high school teacher, not affluent but cultured and socially secure. In the summers young Harry moved to a grandfather's farm in Chautauqua County. The family was close, loving, and devout but not fanatical. Young Harry confessed a saving faith at the precocious age of seven and was immersed as a Baptist. When outside Buffalo, the family attended both Presbyterian and Methodist congregations. Harry absorbed a rather loose but vital evangelical orthodoxy. He was deeply if sentimentally religious, very serious, but frightened by some revival preachers (not Dwight L. Moody, whom he always admired).

After his first year of college, at Colgate, Fosdick spent a troubled year back home. He had embraced evolutionary theory as a college freshman and was surprised when his father confessed that he had long since accepted it. Gradually, he came to doubt parts of the Bible and rebelled against almost all aspects of his childhood religion. But back at Colgate, he rather quickly repented his rebellion and, influenced by theologically liberal professors, began to recast his former beliefs in such form as to correlate with modern knowledge. In effect, he embraced a new religion, but one that he still called Christianity. He now rejoiced at his liberation from the literalism, legalism, and biblicalism of a now unbelievable orthodoxy. Before he graduated from Colgate, he had decided to become a Christian minister, in order to bring his liberating message to other troubled or confused Christians. Note that his revolt was intellectual, not ethical. He retained the moral standards of his youth, although he later rejoiced in certain amusements condemned by his youthful Baptist pastors—secular music, the theater, and golf.

He spent his first graduate year at the familiar Colgate Seminary, then won a scholarship at Union Theological Seminary in New York City in 1901. Union, formerly Presbyterian but now legally independent (it disaffiliated in 1893 rather than dismiss Charles A. Briggs, who in a famous controversy and heresy trial suffered suspension by his denomination), was one of the most daring seminaries in the United States and brought Fosdick into contact with excellent scholars and theologians. He would never be a theologian himself, would remain frustratingly vague on many issues, but in a quite general way he embraced versions of nineteenth-century idealism. He had to drop out one year because of a severe mental breakdown, a dark period that he later accounted as an important balance to an almost impossibly happy youth. At Union, he first became aware of the severe economic problems of a large city, did his first preaching in missions to the slums, and became an advocate of what he called the "social gospel." He would be much influenced later by fellow Baptist Walter Rauschenbusch.

After graduation, Fosdick first gained ministerial experience as an associate pastor in a Baptist congregation in the city, then gained his first full pastorate in Montclair, New Jersey. Here from 1904 to 1915 he honed his skills as a preacher. He also gained a degree of fame. He lectured widely, wrote polished sermons, published many of these in books for a popular audience (one on the assurance of immortality, and a three-part series on the meaning of prayer, faith, and service). In these writings he was generous in outlook, nondoctrinaire, but inspiring. In 1915, after some part-time teaching of homiletics, Union invited him back as a full-time professor of practical theology, a position he held until retirement. His ministry, henceforth, would be on a part-time basis. In effect, he became a Sunday preacher, with other staff taking care of most ministerial duties.

After a few years of guest preaching, in 1919 Fosdick accepted an unusual invitation from a newly reorganized First Presbyterian Church, one that included as members several Union faculty. Although he was not Presbyterian, and could not as a Baptist gain fellowship in the New York Presbytery, Fosdick became a guest preacher, ostensibly under the regular minister but, because he did most of the Sunday preaching, the de facto minister of this affluent, largely professional congregation. Unfortunately, this appointment paralleled the beginnings of an organized fundamentalist movement and deep divisions in both the Presbyterian and Baptist denominations (see Chapter 2 for this story). He soon became a very visible and aggravating symbol of liberalism to the orthodox ministers in New York.

Fosdick did little to deflect the attacks. In 1922 he preached a now famous sermon, "Shall the Fundamentalists Win?" He begged for tolerance and inclusiveness. He wanted to prevent schisms in the Church. But he denounced fundamentalists as illiberal and intolerant, blind to new knowledge and quick to lock out of the Church anyone who tried, honestly, to accommodate such new knowledge. They ignored the fact that even Jesus believed in a progressive understanding of revelation. He itemized the doctrines in dispute: miracles and particularly the virgin birth, a Bible literally dictated by God, a legalistic and substitutionary atonement, and premillennial expectations. But Fosdick so oversimplified the fundamentalist position as to make it look stupid, and he thus elicited very effective, even devastating counterattacks from orthodox intellectuals. He ended with his usual plea for an "intellectually hospitable, open-minded, liberty-loving, fair, tolerant" Christianity. Because of this fighting sermon, Fosdick was now a marked man, the symbol of heresy to fundamentalists.

In 1923 the Presbyterian General Assembly, under conservative control, asked the New York Presbytery to take needed steps to assure orthodoxy in its pulpits and published a minority report that itemized five doctrinal points at issue (all clearly ones that Fosdick rejected). His congregation refused to dismiss him. Then in 1924, in a mandated policy, the General Assembly made church membership a condition of Fosdick's continuing appointment. This would have required him to subscribe to the modified Westminster Confession, and despite desperate efforts on the part of friends, he refused and thus resigned his ministerial position. In his final weeks at the First Church, mobs tried to gain seats to hear him preach, and his final sermon in March of 1925 left his congregation in tears.

His departure from First Presbyterian allowed Fosdick to join in the creation of a church after his own heart. After much negotiation, John D. Rockefeller Jr. persuaded Fosdick to become head pastor of his own Park Avenue Baptist Church. The congregation accepted his special terms—that the membership be completely open, with no creeds or formal confessions, and that the congregation, as soon as possible, build a new church, one better equipped to serve the varied needs of the poor and afflicted (it had its own effective employment agency during the Great Depression). After six years, this became the Riverside Church, perhaps the best known in New York City. Its home was next to Union Theological Seminary and Columbia University, in what became an impoverished area of the city. Fosdick dominated this church until his retirement from its pulpit in 1946. He still lectured widely, developed a popular radio ministry, published best-selling books, and befriended presidents and statesmen. He became affluent, even wealthy, with incomes from the seminary, his congregation, and his book royalties. His family lived well, with a summer home on an island off the coast of Maine and frequent trips abroad. His congregation was only nominally Baptist (it sent delegates to the Northern Baptist Convention) and as inclusive as any in America. Fosdick would not head a church that required immersion, and thus baptized members any way they wanted. Soon, almost all denominations were represented in his still largely affluent congregation, but a congregation that launched dozens of human services to aid mostly nonmembers. Fosdick never repudiated Christian liberalism, but he was much influenced by neo-orthodoxy in the 1930s. He acknowledged the myopia of many liberals, but believed until he died that his type of liberalism alone enabled many of the most intelligent and knowledgeable Americans to remain in the Church.

It is not easy to describe Fosdick's exact beliefs, or why he celebrated what he called liberalism. Perhaps it is even more difficult to explain in what sense he remained a committed Christian. After his period of doubt in college, he professed never again to doubt the existence of a god, some underlying meaning and purpose to existence, and some form of human immortality. Even Machen granted the sincerity of these affirmations, but then he always asked in what sense such a generalized religiosity constituted a form of Christianity. Fosdick had his answers, but they were not always very clear.

Fosdick was not primarily a scholar, but a preacher. Yet, in his teaching at Union, he contended for years with one subject, a subject that informed his work with aspiring ministers: how liberals should understand and use the Bible. His two most scholarly books involved biblical history and revealed years of careful study and a very sophisticated grasp of work in biblical scholarship. Knowing what he did about the Bible, he simply could not understand those who insisted upon biblical inerrancy. Unless blind to scholarship, they had to be dishonest. For Fosdick, the Bible was full of inspiring writings, most of all in the New Testament. But it recorded the religious expressions of people for almost a millennium, expressions shaped by a changing social context and prevalent understandings of the world. Much of this was literally unbelievable in the twentieth century. Fosdick did not choose to disbelieve it; he simply found it unbelievable because it was inconsistent with so much else that he believed. He admitted that future generations would bring different experiences to bear on life and conceptualize their world quite differently than progressives in the early twentieth century. The net effect of this understanding was a necessary historicizing of the Bible and of the whole Judeo-Christian tradition. It made almost irrelevant, even diverting, such questions as whether God really made the world in six days, Noah survived a worldwide flood, or Jesus was born of a virgin. In a literal sense, of course not. Who could affirm such outdated beliefs?

However the fundamentalists defined the essential beliefs of the Church, Fosdick could not affirm any of them. The Bible was full of truth but not true in much of its detail. He could not give any credence to the two very different nativity stories in Matthew and Luke and found incredible the idea of a virgin birth. He found any penal or substitutionary version of the atonement an insult to the God he believed in. He even interpreted the resurrection of the Christ in purely spiritual terms, whatever that means, and not as a resurrection of the material body.

What were his positive beliefs? His philosophical bent was idealistic. He referred to himself as a neo-Hegelian as a youth. He was attracted to the personalized idealism of the ablest, and most liberal, Methodist philosopher and theologian, Borden Parker Bowne. His inclination was always to refer to God as Spirit, not a very helpful term but one that he used to disassociate God from materiality. It was Fosdick who gave support to the widespread argument, among those who insisted upon the reconciliation of Christianity and Darwinism, that physical scientists dealt with the material universe, not with a spiritual realm that was more central to religious faith. Just as Fosdick rejected any physical resurrection, so he most appreciated the Gospel of John and the late Epistles of

Paul (Ephesians, Colossians), or books that seem rather far removed from the Jewish belief in a bodily resurrection. In this outlook, Fosdick was the farthest removed from Adventists, who denied any separable soul or spirit, or from premillennialists, who looked forward to an earthly kingdom ruled by Jesus. But by the fact of his etherealization of Christianity, he was hard pressed to be very specific about his theological views.

Fosdick reminded one, at times, of adherents of the ancient Brahman religion of India. He also echoed themes from Horace Bushnell. Ultimate reality, even though he usually characterized it in vaguely mindlike ways, was beyond human comprehension. He admitted that his early Hegelianism was overly confident or dogmatic. The foundation of religion is human experience. But humans, being self-conscious, always try to describe and explain experience, and thus they conceptualize their religious experience. Christians have done this from the time of the New Testament. They have thought, and then rethought, their basic doctrines. At each period, their conceptualizations have reflected, not the ultimate reality of God, but the fashionable beliefs of their day, and these in turn have reflected much about the social institutions of an age (all positions defended by Mathews). Like Bushnell, he saw all conceptual schemes as relative to time and place. This is an elusive position at best. For example, in his autobiography, reflecting back over a busy lifetime, he admitted the lack of any systematic theology. Instead, he suggested that Christians should take the "best" insights in all prior formulations, but recognize the incompleteness of each. Obviously, the ability to recognize the best implies criteria that Fosdick never enunciated. Possibly, he should have said those aspects of past formulations that are most consistent with present experience, or what he often called "Christian" experience. It is likewise hard to imagine the criteria that allowed one to know that all such conceptualizations are incomplete or partial, since such a judgment seems to implicate at least some sense of the larger whole.

In a series of lectures, published in 1922 as *Christianity and Progress*, Fosdick, in a scholarly context, came closest to defining his conception of God. He made clear, as he did in his sermons, that he was a monotheist. He saw humankind as struggling to come to a better understanding of an existent God, not as the creators of their gods. He used terms like "creative reality" and "power from whom all life proceeds" and "universal spiritual presence" to characterize God. He described God as the soul of all creation. This rather elusive God was the creator of both matter and mind, or the physical and the spiritual. But the spirituality revealed in humans offered a better analogy for God's being than did the physical universe, despite all its wonders. Most often, Fosdick offered functional definitions. The liberal God was not a God aloof and afar, but a God involved with human struggles for righteousness, captain of a well-fought crusade. He was a God who moves throughout the world calling people to join in a progressive crusade for righteousness. He was a God of progress and change, who fought in and for and with humans against social evil, and who, by his support, guaranteed an ultimate victory. Yet such a fighting God was always also a personal God, a father or brother to all those on the moral battlefield.

Fosdick, above all else, repudiated any form of dogmatism, any affirmation of certainty, in one's talk about God or religion. He was so open, so inclusive, that critics charged him with vacuity. He rejected all forms of sectarianism, struggled to prevent schisms, for such divisions, more than anything else, prevented the message of the Christ from influencing modern life. He had ministered, he said, primarily to people whose experience had duplicated his own. They grew up in an orthodox family and church. In time they found this religion unbelievable and felt devastated as a consequence. They moved toward rebellion and a complete rejection of Christianity. Such "ruined" people came to Fosdick, and his open or free Christianity literally saved their lives. It dissipated unfocused guilt. It gave them hope. It brought them back into the Church of Christ. It assured them of forgiveness and salvation. This was the role of liberal Christianity, a religion whose function remained the same as that of the nineteenth-century evangelicalism that he still revered. Evangelicalism was a newly formulated form of Christianity in the early nineteenth century. It spawned new institutions. Liberal Christianity showed the same responsiveness to new needs in the twentieth.

But what is this Christianity? First of all, it was an experience of a spiritual reality beyond the material world, or a God who needed and loved humans. Next, it was the experience of sin and guilt, and the need and reality of forgiveness by a power greater than our own. This involved a confrontation with the Jesus revealed in the Gospels, and the inspiration one found in his life, in his confident relationship to God the Father, and in his sacrifice and forgiveness. In 1922 Fosdick itemized the meaning he found in the life of Jesus, who exemplified the "fatherhood of God, [the] friendship of the Spirit, the sovereignty of righteousness, the law of love, the glory of service, the coming of the kingdom, the eternal hope." This Christ inspired one's own commitment to sacrifice and service, and provided hope for the ultimate realization of our highest ideals. Finally, religious experience contained intimations of immortality, an immortality that Fosdick seemed always to assume but did not dwell on, for he did not want consolations about the distant future to divert humans from their present responsibilities in this world. Fosdick came at these essentials, or what he called the "eternal verities," in many different ways. In his sermons, he often sounded very traditional, with much of the language of an older evangelicalism.

Fosdick resisted the argument that such an open-ended liberalism was little more than a religion of consolation and moral effort. Throughout his writings, he also included a minor chord—on human weakness and sinfulness. He always tried to introduce an element of realism into what was, usually, an irenic outlook, or what he referred to as a modern Christianity closely tied to a belief in progress. But despite the minor chord, he would not concede the older, darker views of humanity. Orthodox doctrines of human depravity simply had no resonance in a modern age. An awesome or fearful god could no longer inspire belief. Sin, in his descriptions, came close to a lack of moral strength, not some awful separation and alienation from God. As a more somber neo-orthodoxy gained ascendancy even in such liberal seminaries as Union, Fosdick made one claim that is still persuasive. It was that the liberals, early in the century, had dissipated an older, almost idolatrous biblicalism and, in this sense, made it possible for the new versions of orthodoxy to thrive in the mainline churches. It was liberals, after all, who retained as church members the educated and thoughtful audiences who, by the thirties, were most receptive to the reemphasized themes of sin and grace by theologians like Reinhold Niebuhr. Without liberalism, the older orthodoxy, with its version of biblical inerrancy, with its stubborn refusal to come to terms with unquestioned knowledge about the universe, would have permanently alienated these people from Christianity.

By Machen's criteria, Fosdick was not a Christian. Instead of embracing the historic doctrines of the Church, he refused to endorse any precise doctrines at all. His new god bore little resemblance to the supernatural and transcendent God of the Church. He did not begin to probe the meaning of sinfulness in humans, or appreciate the awful gulf that separated them from God. He did not worship the Christ as himself a deity. He repudiated any substitutionary view of the atonement. He was so open and inclusive as to leave no room for a clearly defined Church. Nor did he clearly see the Church as the ark of salvation (Fosdick once defined the Church, not as a means to escape divine wrath, but as an instrument to bring personal and social righteousness to the earth). Only on one point did Fosdick challenge Machen's view of liberals. By no stretch of language was he a philosophical naturalist. This was not true of Shailer Mathews.

In many ways, Shailer Mathews's youth resembled that of Fosdick. Born in 1863 in Portland, Maine, he was over a decade older than either Machen or Fosdick but outlived Machen. Like Fosdick, he spent summers on the farm and grew up in an orthodox and abstentious Baptist home. His father was a merchant, prosperous but not wealthy. Yet Mathews had all the advantages of such affluence, including an excellent high school education and then college years at Colby. Here he became a convert to evolutionary theory and began to think critically about his own religious beliefs, but according to his memory he remained pious and involved in revivals and youth work. He was most influenced by a young sociology professor, Albion W. Small, later his colleague at the University of Chicago.

Without strong commitments to the ministry, Mathews attended Newton Theological Institution, a still orthodox Baptist seminary but one that employed some able biblical scholars. In his senior year he secured a temporary ministerial position in a small, rural Baptist congregation. He was moderately successful but decided to become a teacher rather than a preacher. He secured a position back at Colby, in rhetoric and elocution. After a year, when Small became president, Mathews moved to history and political economy. He spent two years of leave in Germany, studying history and economics, not theology, but converted to the new institutional economics, with its policy orientation and loosely socialistic commitments. During his seven years at Colby he continued as a faithful Baptist but remembered some crises of faith based on various new scholarly findings. To his surprise, he received an invitation to join the faculty of the new Divinity School at the University of Chicago in 1894. He was reluctant, felt unqualified to teach courses in the New Testament, but was inspired by all the hopes for this new university. He would spend the rest of his academic career in the Divinity School. The school was nominally Baptist but free of church control. Mathews remained a member of the northern wing of Baptists for the rest of his life, helped develop a new, more centralized Northern Baptist Convention in 1908, and served as its president in 1915–16. During the battles over fundamentalism he became the most prominent representative of a liberal or modernist position within his church. He came to Dayton to defend this modernism at the Scopes trial.

At Chicago, Mathews adapted his historical and sociological outlook to New Testament studies. Gradually, he had moved to what most deemed a liberal outlook, influenced in his case by evolutionary theory, an immersion in historical and critical methods, and the enormous influence of those who now advocated a social gospel. His first scholarly book, after his move to Chicago, was on the social teachings of Jesus (1897). He later revised this book and published two others on the relationship of Christianity to economic and social reform. His more technical scholarship was on aspects of the New Testament, including a book admired even by such conservative scholars as Machen, on the messianic elements in the New Testament. But Mathews would not have much time for detailed scholarship. He became, not a preacher or lecturer like Fosdick, but an academic statesman and a very serious advocate of what he called "modernism." For a few years he edited a serious journal on religion and reform, *The World Today*, and in 1908, after moving to the field of historical theology, he became the dean of his Divinity School. He helped assemble a small group of biblical scholars and theologians that even yet are remembered as the Chicago School. They made Chicago, along with Union, an outpost of liberalism. If any one issue distinguished the Chicago theologians, it was their effort to integrate what they called science with Christian theology, or even, in a sense, work out a scientific theology, or a theology grounded in a type of naturalism rather that the earlier forms of idealism. His colleague, Henry Nelson Wieman, went beyond even Mathews in assimilating Darwinian theory and a pragmatic method to theology.

In 1924, in *The Faith of Modernism*, Mathews tried to provide a popular refutation, point by point, of Machen's *Christianity and Liberalism*. In this important book, Mathews summarized much of his earlier scholarly work and tried to present it in as palatable a form as possible. He hoped to persuade moderate and conservative Christians that, even if they could not accept modernism, they should give it a fair hearing and grant a degree of acceptance to their fellow Christians who embraced it. In these hopes he largely failed. But more than anyone else, he gave some specific content to the modernist label. In fact, in subsequent historical perspectives, it has largely been his work that has remained definitive of a modernist movement.

Mathews often faced the charge of hypocrisy. Critics noted that, in his lectures and sermons before lay audiences, or in the councils of his Northern Baptist Convention, he sounded like an orthodox, evangelical Christian. Yet in his more scholarly work he was a radical critic of almost all forms of orthodoxy. How could he have it both ways? Actually, Mathews did believe he could have it both ways and spent years trying to persuade others of how he did it. If he was duplicitous, it was in his failure to make fellow Christians aware of how he used traditional language. They easily misunderstood his position, but Mathews correctly could point to his extensive clarifications in what he wrote.

Fortunately, as a Baptist, Mathews did not have to subscribe to any confession. Also, the historic creeds (Nicene, Apostles') were not normally a part of Baptist worship. But even if they had been, Mathews might well have recited them with no sense of deceit. He wanted to be a part of a Christian movement stretching back to the time of Jesus. He saw Christianity as a great world religion, with certain core beliefs, but otherwise a religion that had rationalized its beliefs according to the assumptions and beliefs normative in each of seven stages of Western history, and also a religion shaped, at all times, by what he called the current social mind. In this sense, he completely historicized the doctrinal and theological aspects of this historic faith. Mixed in with the living faith of Christians, expressed in attitudes and commitments, in prayer and worship, were often elements of earlier formulations. For some simple Christians, these earlier doctrines continued to satisfy, to provide needed tools for understanding their living faith. Mathews was glad to offer fellowship to such Christians. But these doctrines were anachronistic, increasingly barren imports from older social and intellectual systems. When the orthodox tried to make these anachronistic beliefs normative, or even obligatory, for informed modern Christians, they not only forced honest people out of the Church, but they ensured the gradual drift of an increasingly fossilized Christianity into irrelevancy. Such, he believed, would be the result of Machen's version of Reformed orthodoxy.

Mathews was sure that modern Christians lived in a new and very different age. This meant that Christians had to rethink the formulations that expressed their faith, to ensure that they fit the assumptions, and the tasks, of the twentieth century, and also to make them honest and believable by youth who had absorbed these assumptions or struggled with those tasks. To do so was to follow in the path of Christian intellectuals from Paul to the present. In almost all respects, past formulations of Christian doctrine, often necessary for apologetic and defensive purposes, reflected an existing political system and existing metaphysical, physical, and historical beliefs. Mathews traced, in great detail, the doctrinal parallels between a god that demanded sacrifices and Mesopotamian tyrants, or the monarchical and sovereign god that fit the modern nation-state, or even a creditor god that fit early capitalism. In the modern era, Christian intellectuals simply had to recast their understanding of the core Christian beliefs, and it was the goal of modernists to do just this.

What was most distinctive about the present age, for Mathews, was the new understanding of our world made possible by what he called "science," as well as the enormous "social" problems created by the technologies such new knowledge made possible. In fact, at times, two words became a litany for Mathews, "science" and "social." He used both ad nauseam. Mathews had no doubt that moderns lived in the wake of revolutionary new knowledge, developed in the physical, biological, social, and historical disciplines. Although he did not claim any finality for such knowledge, he had little doubt of its truthfulness, at least in the sense of its practical payoff. It worked. Beyond the ongoing inquiry, the advances of understanding in every area of human curiosity, Mathews applauded the rational-empirical methods that informed such inquiry. Christians could not ignore either the knowledge so far gained or the methods that ensured further progress. One at all conversant with the new age had no alternative but to recast the core beliefs of Christianity to fit modern science as well as what he referred to as modern democratic politics. For Mathews, this meant a great deal more than finding some way to reconcile biblical stories with modern geology. It meant new ways of conceptualizing the core beliefs, such as the one most central belief of all, in God. Any god acceptable to modern intellectuals had to be a god not only consistent with the universe revealed by scientists, but a god so conceptualized, and so rationalized, as to be verifiable by the scientific method.

Anyone who would understand the early twentieth century would do well to explore the range of images that almost everyone associated with the loaded word "social." The word was ubiquitous. Mathews used it all the time, but rarely defined it. He embraced what he called a social gospel, appealed to a social mind, talked of social reform. He cut his academic teeth in sociology, and as so many, like his mentor Small, had soaring hopes for this new discipline, not just for a new body of knowledge about human groups, but as a tool that opened up new ways of curing—what else—social problems, possible through the new practical field of social work. Behind this verbal excess lay Mathews's understanding that humans are social animals, since even language forms in a group context. He believed individuals are "largely," but not completely, conditioned by the various groups around them. He lived in the wake of

World War I, and in a context of concern about economic inequality and exploitation, and thus saw that the only way to begin to deal with the problems of peace and social justice had to be, not appeals to individuals, but efforts to reform social institutions. To Mathews, a new emphasis upon groups of people, upon distorted institutions, or the so-called social gospel, reflected the new task of Christians. Thus, modernist Christianity had to be both scientific and social.

One refrain was constant in Mathews's books—the need to distinguish what is permanent or genetic or persistent from the incidental or contextual or transient in Christianity. He referred to such dualities dozens of times in his modernism book. This was not a new strategy. In 1842, Theodore Parker, the radical Unitarian and transcendentalist, preached a sermon entitled "The Transient and Permanent in Christianity," in which he labeled transient all human creeds and doctrines. The sermon scandalized even his fellow Unitarians. In the same sense, Mathews astonished most contemporary Christians by the wide range of orthodox beliefs that he relegated to the transient superstructure of Christianity. What Mathews had most trouble clarifying was what remained in the core.

A belief in a god was common to all Christians, but not distinctive to Christians. Mathews affirmed a Christian God with at least two essential or defining characteristics. First, God was in some sense the creator, or at least the guiding force, behind the evolving universe. He professed to find scientific justification for this belief, with Darwin a key to his proof. But this cosmic God was also personal, a loving father, the source of some type of human salvation. The proof of these characteristics was biblical, in the sense that the Bible provided enough historical information about Jesus of Nazareth to vindicate a belief in a personal, loving God. Mathews could not find the logical tools to make the cosmic and personal attributes of God coherent. He never tried. He found no need for such. He believed the Christian community had always affirmed such a god. This was the foundational assumption of a world religion, always implicit, the starting point for doctrinal elaboration.

Mathews believed that informed people, in the twentieth century, could not believe in a transcendent or supernatural deity. From Genesis myths to New Testament miracles, one indeed found such a god in the Bible, a god that made sense in past ages. No more. Mathews wrote a very insightful book—*The Growth of the Idea of God*—on changing conceptions of God from primitive religions and the ancient Hebrews to the present. The book revealed Mathews's implicit, undoubted monotheism. He wrote as if all the references to a god or gods had a unitary but opaque focus. They represented progressive steps toward a better understanding of God, not merely a spectrum of gods created by the human imagination. In a sense, he even saw God himself behind each new theological emergent, for the gods affirmed by humans in different ages exemplified a type of progressive evolution, a prototype of what is going on at a cosmic level.

The contemporary understanding of God had to be scientific. Mathews believed he had found such an understanding. It was not new to him. In brief, he found in Darwinian evolution, not a challenge to belief in a god, but a type of proof. While he was in college, Francis E. Abbot, an ex-Unitarian minister and one of the founders of the avowedly non-Christian Free Religious Association, published *Scientific Theism*. In it, he argued that the success of scientists generally, and the insights of Darwin in particular, had made it clear that our universe was not only fully intelligible (although not yet fully known), but that it revealed intelligent guidance. After Darwin, the best model for the universe was not a machine but a purposeful organism. His proof of all this was the continued success of scientists. For Abbot, such a scientifically vindicated god had no relationship to the supernatural deity of Christianity. Thus, his new god justified a break from all past orthodoxies and the formation of a new religion that required no deference to any biblical authority, but one based on free inquiry. Possibly Abbot was more honest in this admission than Mathews. Mathews insisted that new insights required, not the rejection of Christianity, with its deep and abiding roots, but simply a complete recasting of the superstructure. He even argued that modernists would rather die than concede that they were not Christians. This reflected the depth of his loyalty to what he always called the Christian movement.

Simply stated, Mathews defended the following cosmology. Through time, the unfolding universe spawned more and more complex organisms. Darwin explained the progression. In time, these led to humans, or organisms with mind and thought. Such an outcome could not reflect chance. It had to reveal some immanent purpose. Although Mathews called this belief "scientific," and celebrated scientists for revealing a more profound understanding of God, it is difficult to find anything like empirical proof for his view. His belief in some immanent purpose seems at one with earlier design arguments, although in this context he ended with a god who was not above or outside nature, who did not create a universe, but whose very reality was involved with the unfolding of nature. Of course, this cosmic god (he did not see it as some divine mind) was abstract and without any personal characteristics. But like Aquinas, who believed he had logical proof of a prime mover but not of the biblical Jehovah, Mathews had to consult Scripture and his own vital experience to make the transition from a cosmic god to a personal, loving, fatherly deity. This step involved Jesus and the only core beliefs beyond theism essential to being a Christian.

Jesus involved the Bible. Mathews affirmed the usefulness of the Bible. It is essential to Christianity, when rightly used. Respect for the Bible requires that one approach it with all the modern tools of historical method. When one does so, any belief in inerrancy is absurd, but the Bible does reflect the writings of inspired individuals. Mathews often reviewed what we know about the Bible—the likely authors, the time of composition, the worldview that conditioned different parts of it, the diverse canons and the complicated path to canonization, and, above all, the richness and enormous diversity of the various books. In this literature a modern Christian finds critical information about the history of his religion, inspiring people who expressed a timeless religious attitude, and lofty ethical guidelines. Here is the product of a religious movement, not an authority for religion. Here is the record of ever developing insights about God, insights that should nourish faith today. Above all, the New Testament contains unimpeachable primary sources (the major letters of Paul) about early Christian views about Jesus and, in the four Gospels, at least some authentic insights from other early apostles. Without this information, a modern Christian could not affirm a personal and loving God. In this sense the Bible is essential to Christianity. It alone provides knowledge of a Savior.

When Mathews talked about Jesus, he seemed closest to orthodoxy. He never tried to turn Jesus into merely a social reformer or moral example. For Mathews, above all else, Jesus was a revealer of the nature of God, or what Mathews often called God's resident spirit. He accepted, from his own scholarship, the messianic image Jesus had of himself, but he minimized the more apocalyptic passages in the Gospels. In his evolutionary cosmology, Jesus exemplified the ultimate goal or end of evolution—a perfected human, full of goodwill and love, living with others in harmony and peace and justice. This was not a new idea, but one often expressed in the wake of Darwin's *Origin*, most forcefully in the United States by the Berkeley scientist, Joseph Le Conte. Mathews, of course, emphasized Jesus not only as a model for individuals, but as one who offered the ethic needed for a fully just social order.

Beyond these affirmations, Mathews was suspicious of almost all orthodox views about Jesus. He found the weak Biblical support for a
virgin birth unconvincing. He emphasized the contextual needs that led
to the gradual elevation of Jesus to a person within the Trinity (he did
not necessarily deplore this doctrinal development, but believed it
largely irrelevant to the twentieth century). He emphasized the passion
of Jesus, but believed completely outdated all the doctrines related to
this, such as that of an appeasing sacrifice or a substitutional atonement.
These were all contextual and transient beliefs, most tied to the now
outdated image of God as an all-powerful, judgmental sovereign. When
Jesus came outfitted in such anachronistic images, he was at risk of becoming irrelevant in the modern world. Thus, the modernist effort to
reintroduce him with new images and formulations was a rescue opera-
tion. The survival of Christianity depended upon such modern recasting.

Mathews, one feels with some trepidation, affirmed Jesus' resurrection. From the letters of Paul, he was persuaded that this belief was
widely affirmed by the earliest Christians. It was basic. Thus Jesus over-
came fear, despair, sin, and death, and in this sense provided assurance
that humans could do likewise, that a God of love offered such salvation
to them. Jesus illustrated a salvation given by a loving and forgiving God,
but his death was not a cause of such salvation. Mathews used some
strained language to talk of the resurrection. He said that Jesus showed
himself to be alive after the passion. Mathews doubted any resurrection
of the material body. Paul, in the first New Testament writings, did not
clearly affirm this. All that seemed undoubted was some form of continued personal identity, even as Jesus continued to live in the same sense
that the human dead remain alive. What Mathews was sure of was that
the resurrection, however understood, was consistent with known physical laws, or laws that will become apparent in the future. Not only did
Mathews discount all biblical miracles, but he was unwilling even to
appeal to nonlawful events for this one central "miracle" of Christianity.
Jesus helped vindicate Mathews's elusive belief in human immortality.
Mathews never tried to fill in any of the details.

Jesus revealed, not necessarily a scheme of salvation, but an illustration
of how God saves. Religion fulfills a personal need for help from a
superhuman power upon which one feels dependent. Jesus made clear
that a God present in the evolving universe is also a God who offers
such help, at least to those who humbly seek it. From Jesus they gain
insight into such a God, gain support, comfort, and guidance. They
express such faith in a loving community, which is the Church. Salvation

means a readjustment or realignment of a person with the immanent will of God, a bringing of one's own will into line with his abundant love and goodwill. It means overcoming one's lower and bodily and selfish urges, which is what Mathews meant by sin. Such salvation redeems not only the individual, but will, of necessity, find expression in the larger society. Utopian as it sounds, such salvation can lead toward complete justice and peace. If the God revealed by Jesus is taken seriously, one's whole life will be transformed. The individual goal is to be a complete, harmonized person like Jesus. The social goal is what Jesus meant by the Kingdom of Heaven, a good society or republic attained here on earth at the end of an evolutionary process.

Mathews preferred an image of salvation that had no relationship to past versions of hell and heaven. He also repudiated the governing king image of Reformed dogma. God, as the ultimate cosmic force, is not outside the processes of nature. He (the pronoun derives from the father image, not from any cosmic status) is in the process, guiding it, but not apart from it. If one uses the word "nature" to refer to all reality, then God is part of nature, albeit the intelligent and purposeful part. Since he is directing a process, humans can more easily relate to him as a leader, a guide, and not a master. In some sense, human goodwill, expressed in social institutions, helps God, or at least is his means for fulfilling the ultimate promise of evolution. Faith in such a God not only empowers individuals for service, but gives one an assurance that, in the long term, such noble efforts are not in vain. Mathews was a cosmic optimist. He found in evolution his own version of a theodicy.

With this all too brief summary, one can understand what Mathews meant by modernism. He stressed that no one set of beliefs, no doctrines or theologies, unified modernists. Yet, at various times, Mathews tried to at least provide some common views affirmed by all modernists. His much quoted confession, in *The Faith of Modernism*, in light of the above discussion, may now almost make sense. It is worth quoting in full, for it is the fullest expression of a modernist creed that I have ever read:

> I believe in God, immanent in the forces and processes of nature, revealed in Jesus Christ and human history as love.
> I believe in Jesus Christ, who by his teaching, life, death and resurrection, revealed God as Savior.
> I believe in the Holy Spirit, the God of love experienced in human life.
> I believe in the Bible, when interpreted historically, as the product and the trustworthy record of the progressive revelation of God through a developing religious experience.

I believe that humanity without God is incapable of full moral life and liable to suffering because of its sin and weakness.

I believe in prayer as a means of gaining help from God in every need and in every intelligent effort to establish and give justice in human relations.

I believe in freely forgiving those who trespass against me, and in good will rather than acquisitiveness, coercion, and war as the divinely established law of human relations.

I believe in the need and the reality of God's forgiveness of sins, that is, the transformation of human lives by fellowship with God from subjection to outgrown goods to the practice of love exemplified in Jesus Christ.

I believe in the practicability of the teachings of Jesus in social life.

I believe in the continuance of individual personality beyond death; and that the future life will be one of growth and joy in proportion to its fellowship with God and its moral likeness to Jesus Christ.

I believe in the church as the community of those who in different conditions and ages loyally further the religion of Jesus Christ.

I believe that all things work together for good to those who love God and in their lives express the sacrificial good will of Jesus Christ.

I believe in the ultimate triumph of love and justice because I believe in the God revealed in Jesus Christ.

One could hardly conceive of a confession more at odds with the doctrines commended by Machen. Mathews freely acknowledged as much and believed it was therefore all the better. Machen found little in this modernist platform, save certain loaded words, that justified the label Christian. Mathews was willing to bet his life that this was an updated, intellectually tenable, modern formulation of a Christianity that had gained respectability through a series of such reformulations in each changing era of Western history. It was part of the Christian tradition, a unique virtue of a religion with such universal appeal that conscientious and honest intellectuals had kept a religion vibrant, responsive, alive through such doctrinal reformulations. Only atavistic radicals, those out of tune with their own age, had resisted such changes. Fortunately, these reactionaries always lost out. In the great, ongoing, never fully transparent course of evolution, it was God that ensured victory to the progressives or modernists. By the same logic, of course, the next major stage of world history, the next revolution in human thought, would require new formulations of a type in no sense predictable by Mathews.

Mathews was no more prescient than Machen. In time, both of their positions proved very ephemeral. By the end of the twentieth century it was clear that the most vital, expansive forms of Christianity embraced neither Mathews's modernism nor the rigid confessionalism of Machen.

Both are now period pieces, largely forgotten. Modern evangelicals are usually more soft, more irenic, more accommodating than Machen. Yet, unlike Mathews, they still affirm an inspired Bible, believe in a transcendent and providential God, appeal to biblical miracles, emphasize personal redemption above social reconstruction, have limited faith in scientific inquiry, and are skeptical about the potential for human progress.

Reading Guide

The above essay involves key books by the three protagonists. The first is John Gresham Machen's *Christianity and Liberalism* (New York: Macmillan, 1924). Except for some key articles and essays, Machen composed no other book of this type. The only full biography of Machen is by a scholar very much in his Calvinist tradition, Ned Bernard Stonehouse, *J. Gresham Machen, a Bibliographical Memoir* (Grand Rapids: Eerdmans, 1954). A brief but perceptive biography is in Charles A. Russell, *Voices of American Fundamentalism: Seven Biographical Studies* (Philadelphia: Westminster Press, 1976).

Harry Emerson Fosdick was, both in his day and ours, much better known than Machen. His one book that best engaged the controversial issues of the twenties is *Christianity and Progress* (New York: Fleming H. Revell, 1922). The book that best fits his teaching at Union, and one very revealing of his brand of liberalism, is *A Guide to Understanding the Bible: The Development of Ideas within the Old and New Testaments* (New York: Harpers, 1938). Most helpful in understanding Fosdick is his *The Living of These Days: An Autobiography* (New York: Harpers, 1956). By far, the best biography is Robert Moats Miller, *Harry Emerson Fosdick: Preacher, Pastor, Prophet* (New York: Oxford University Press, 1985).

Shailer Mathews was a prolific author. Obviously, the book most pertinent to this essay is his *The Faith of Modernism* (New York: Macmillan, 1925). His view of God is clearest in *The Growth of the Idea of God* (New York: Macmillan, 1931). For his approach to social Christianity and a critical introduction to his theology, see his *Jesus on Social Institutions*, Kenneth Cauthen, ed. (Philadelphia: Fortress Press, 1971). Mathews wrote a rather pedantic but at times revealing autobiography, *New Faith for Old: An Autobiography* (New York: Macmillan, 1936).

5

BEYOND THEISM

With Darwin's *Origin of Species*, the challenges faced by any orthodox form of Christianity began to shift away from salvation doctrines, or other distinctive doctrines of the Church, to the foundational cosmology of Genesis. In the preceding chapter, articulate spokespersons for Christian orthodoxy, liberalism, and modernism joined in a continued affirmation of belief in a god. Because of their monotheistic assumptions, they each believed that, somehow, their competing conceptualizations of God had a single reference. In retrospect, clarity is best served by noting the quite different gods they espoused. Each protagonist fought to gain acceptance of his God, or what each believed was a correct but necessarily limited description of the only true God.

For many, the important issue was not which one of several competing gods fit reality, but whether a belief in either a supernatural or an immanent god any longer made sense. Could anyone, in a post-Darwinian world, justify such a belief? Theism was now at stake. And those who felt themselves most attuned to the full implications of a Darwinian understanding of nature joined Darwin himself in rejecting any transcendent god (any god outside or beyond nature) and any purposeful divine mind or force within nature (and thus any cosmic teleology). In so doing, they challenged Christians at a deeper level than did eighteenth century rationalists, who continued to believe in a creator god and in life after death. In fact, their worldview was as dependent upon a god as was that of orthodox Christians.

In the late nineteenth century, several intellectuals openly expressed their atheism or, more often, their agnosticism about any form of theism. Actually, as William James pointed out, the two positions were practically similar, since in either case the advocate did not believe in a god and did not gain any of the possible benefits of such a belief (for James, some of these benefits came, not from a responsive god, but from the mere fact of belief itself). In England, in the wake of the conflicts over Darwin, a group of English intellectuals in 1869 formed a famous discussion group, the Metaphysical Society. It sponsored a running debate between traditional theists or metaphysicians and what many saw as overly positivistic young men, such as Thomas Huxley, William K. Clifford, and Leslie Stephen, all of whom proudly claimed to be agnostic about any propositions that one could not submit to some type of empirical proof. To believe any such propositions was dishonest and immoral. Much more popular in England than this hardheaded agnosticism was that of the self-proclaimed philosopher of evolution (Darwin deferred to his great mind), Herbert Spencer. Spencer denied any human ability to know any reality that is beyond experienced phenomena. Humans have no way to describe any transcendental realities, no way to justify any conceptual ontology. At the same time, a belief in some unknown and unknowable reality behind phenomena seemed, to him, indubitable. Such an "Unknown" was scarcely a god, at least in any traditional sense, but many of Spencer's disciples, most notably John Fiske in the United States, so developed the possible religious implications of this Unknown as to make it a fairly functional substitute for the traditional Christian God.

In the United States, the French positivist, Auguste Comte, gained a handful of American disciples. Positivists saw traditional religious beliefs as an atavistic carryover from a past age. One American agnostic, Robert G. Ingersoll, gained a small following, in part because he was conventional on most economic and political issues, as well as a successful lawyer and a very persuasive lecturer. Always, in America, there had been men and women who quietly dissented from the normative Christian beliefs of their society. It is impossible to count them or to explore the nature and the depth of their skepticism. But such village skeptics, as much as a well-known Ingersoll, were not very threatening or dangerous. They often gained a type of begrudging tolerance, perhaps largely because no one believed they would convert many youth to their views.

In fact, they often served as a needed foil for young men who engaged them in debate and, by the local verdict, always won a victory for God and truth. Clarence Darrow was an excellent example of a type of village skeptic, not a commanding intellectual himself, but one who loved to beard the orthodox. Notably, before 1900, few influential American intellectuals openly defended a nontheistic position, whatever their private doubts. Every aspect of the existing culture worked against such views.

The cultural atmosphere changed early in the new century. Gradually, trends in psychology and philosophy, as well as in geology, biology, and anthropology, undermined theism. An emerging intellectual elite, often after traumatic periods of rebellion against their childhood religious faith, found the old verities no longer appealing or, more correctly, no longer believable. Some revolted against the old, with the most notorious of these in the twenties being H. L. Mencken and Harry Elmer Barnes. Others, such as Walter Lippmann and Joseph Wood Krutch, found theism unbelievable, but lamented what humans had lost along with their gods. Some tried to rescue the heart of the old religion, to find rich and inspiring versions of naturalism to replace it. By far, the most influential advocate of such a naturalism was John Dewey, arguably the most influential American intellectual in the twenties and thirties. From his home in Europe, George Santayana, an expatriate, wrote at great length on religious issues, largely for an American audience, and made his unique form of atheism broadly appealing even for deeply religious persons. Finally, in a strange twist on the reactions to the Scopes trial, John Crowe Ransom, the poet and literary critic, as well as an antimodernist Southern Agrarian, sang the praises of what he described as an orthodox god, but doubted that such a god existed.

Before exploring these nontheistic perspectives, I must point out that in the 1920s these views were not nearly as widely accepted, or as politically useful, as the views of Protestant liberals and modernists. As demonstrated in the Scopes trial, those who tried to reconcile evolution and Christianity best expressed what one might call an establishment viewpoint. They gained the best press. But, perhaps above all else, they seemed to offer a way of averting serious, rending cultural warfare. Fundamentalists tapped deep veins of belief still ascendant among the population as a whole. Their anti-evolutionary crusade undermined the authority of the cultural leaders by mobilizing a type of populist insurgency. Assaults on the schools, on some version of academic freedom, could balloon into state restrictions on free speech and press. Reconcilers wanted to calm the troubled waters, to suggest that there was no real basis for cultural conflict, to vindicate the unity and harmony of all forms of truth, and, in a sense, also to protect their own class interests. In 1925 the goal of such intellectuals was to minimize the conflict between Darwinism and Christianity, or even to deny any conflict at all. This strategy was so pervasive, and so influential, that it has largely shaped, and in most ways distorted, the memory of the Scopes trial.

In a sense, the reconcilers in the twenties reflected the last and perhaps most anxious expression of Victorian hopes. They were as much defenders of an old order as were the fundamentalists. And, over time, they failed to persuade an increasing number of intellectuals. In fact, their arguments, as at Dayton, now seem not only less logical and less clear, but also more dated, than the simple affirmations of evangelical Christians.

The earliest reactions to Darwin paralleled the flowering of American philosophy. Much earlier than in the physical sciences, Americans caught up with the best philosophic work being done in Europe. We now refer to the turn of the century as a golden age in American philosophy and still list the six ablest or enduringly influential men (Charles S. Peirce, Josiah Royce, Alfred North Whitehead, James, Dewey, and Santayana) as our classic philosophers. All were very much involved with the debates over Darwin, and all retained an intense interest in religion. Only two—Dewey and Santayana—openly broke with Christianity. Only they moved beyond any form of theism. But they were soft rebels at best, and both sought ways of preserving some of the heart values of the older religion in an age in which its foundational beliefs were no longer tenable.

At least until the twenties, the philosophers with most influence were those who, in one way or another, joined those who tried to reconcile Darwin, and the modern sciences generally, with Christianity. Both Peirce and Royce opted for a type of objective idealism, although for Peirce this was a very idiosyncratic type of evolutionary idealism. His often brilliant and original metaphysical speculations would later inform many twentieth-century theologians, particularly those who emphasized what they called process theology.

Royce was the ablest American advocate of a form of absolute idealism, modeled after admired German models. But Royce's absolute mind, whose existence he seemed never to doubt, supported a theodicy that encompassed the more dark and somber aspects of human life. Royce found, in doubt and error, an irresistible sense of a larger and inclusive mind that was, in the highest sense, one's own true self. In human relationships, and particularly in forms of loyalty, he found assurance that our highest values cohere with the intentions of the divine mind. But as in all forms of idealism, his assurance of such a higher mind rested upon what he believed to be the necessary presuppositions, or entailments, of human experience and human consciousness. His God, although in many respects colored by Christian and particularly Pauline images, had little resemblance to the Jehovah of Genesis, and Royce had small respect for traditional orthodoxy or for the work of most theologians. Even before he died, such philosophical idealism was under what proved a deadly critique by both analytical and continental philosophers, and is now almost without advocates.

William James became famous for his exploration of the experiential aspects of religion and for offering a defense of a vague form of theism. He defended, above all, the legitimacy of belief in a god or gods (he preferred a plurality of gods). But his vindication of such beliefs usually involved, not formal proofs of the existence of gods, but the possibly beneficial effect of the belief itself—the solace or moral self-confidence that might accrue to the individual. In late life, James found in types of extrasensory experience a possible, but never conclusive, proof of the actual existence of some form of pooled and higher consciousness. Notably, his defense of theism was very flexible and nonspecific and, in its generality, had no clear tie to traditional Christian doctrine, although he conceded that most American Christians would fill in the details of their God in such a way as to reflect a type of Arminian Protestantism.

Alfred North Whitehead directly influenced many theological modernists. Unlike a Dewey or a James, he had few ties to the biological sciences or to psychology. He began his career as a mathematician in England, and one very conversant with the revolution taking place in the physical sciences. After losing a son in World War I, he moved to America and to Harvard University in 1924, at the age of sixty-three. He devoted the rest of his life to philosophy and published in 1925 the very influential *Science and the Modern World*. In 1929 he would publish his most comprehensive and demanding work in philosophy, *Process and Reality*, a book that had enormous influence on American process theologians. Alone among the classic philosophers, he reacted specifically to the Scopes trial. The *Atlantic Monthly* solicited a Whitehead article titled simply "Religion and Science." Yet his credentials did not lead to an essay with much rigor or clarity. In many ways it reflected modernism in its most elusive form.

Even as Whitehead wrote his essay (1925), John Dewey and George

Santayana began publishing a series of books that reflected their most mature philosophic outlook. They were contemporaries of Whitehead, Dewey sixty-six and Santayana sixty-two. Dewey published his most comprehensive, and most ontological, book in 1925, *Experience and Nature*. In 1927, Santayana wrote *Scepticism and Animal Faith*, which was an introduction to his last great substantive contribution to philosophy, his four-volume *Realms of Being*. The outpouring of such major philosophical works by Whitehead, Dewey, and Santayana, in a period of only a decade, has remained without any precedent or repetition in American history. But clearly, of the three philosophers, Dewey would have the broadest impact upon American culture, and possibly even upon religion.

As in the case of any significant philosopher, the isolated treatment of one subject, such as religion, is always misleading. This was particularly true of Dewey, whose philosophy was so comprehensive as to relate and almost unify every field of human thought—ontology, scientific method, the history of Western thought, educational philosophy, cultural studies and political theory, art and esthetics, and religion. Dewey, a child of Vermont and its provincial university, enrolled in the new graduate programs at Johns Hopkins University and completed in 1884 one of the first doctoral degrees in philosophy awarded by an American graduate school. He cut his teeth on German idealists, particularly Hegel. But in his teaching, at Michigan and then Chicago, he gradually rejected the ontological foundations of such idealism—the belief in some divine mind immanent in history. He early developed the methodological outlook that he called instrumentalism, or a view that the only ultimate justification for our more rigorous knowledge claims is practical and moral—the way cognitive beliefs enable people to adapt to the world that they directly experience. Such a view seemed consistent with a Darwinian outlook, and Dewey was effusive in his praise of Darwin's influence upon philosophy, although self-serving and often mistaken in his reading of Darwin.

Gradually, Dewey moved away from, or beyond, the liberal Congregationalism of his youth. One finds no point of rebellion, no clear moment when he left the Church. By the twenties he was the leading spokesperson for a type of naturalism (he liked the term). In *Experience and Nature* he tried to describe the more generic traits of reality, which he called "nature," or those traits revealed in human experience (we have no other clues). He reflected in this book a form of natural piety, a sense of awe, wonder, fear, and ultimate trust in his dealings with a reality that humans can never fully conceptualize. He also noted, over and over again, the elements of flux and indeterminacy in nature, along with aspects of regularity and necessity. Humans, with no assurance of any ultimate or enduring success, maneuver between these poles, finding in flux the possibilities of change, in regularities the basis of conceptualized knowledge and some ability artfully to predict and direct events in nature, but never with any complete assurance of success. But, clearly, he denied the relevance of, or any operative content to, any supernatural or metaphysical realm beyond or behind nature. In this sense he was a complete naturalist, although by focusing on implications in Darwin he celebrated a nature that was much more rich and fulfilling than one suggested by the limiting, abstract, but useful conceptual nets that typified the physical sciences. Nature, at least wherever it spawned language and self-consciousness, did exhibit purpose and direction but no overarching purpose.

Dewey, more than any other philosopher, became the guru of various types of religious humanism. For many, he seemed the embodiment of "secularism," whatever they meant by that label. But he feared that those who followed him into a form of naturalism would end up with a disruptive and superficial form of scientism. He sensed that modern scientific knowledge had been destructive and disruptive, helping destroy a former sense of at-homeness in the universe. He did not want his naturalism to suggest irreligion. Just the opposite. Thus, in a not always rigorous book, *The Common Faith* (1934), Dewey defended what he believed had been the heart of past religions, or an attitude toward life and action that was deeply pious and supportive of great moral courage. He wanted to preserve this religious attitude, even when one could no longer, with honesty, believe in the gods and in all the certainties of the past. Against the advice of colleagues, he even retained the word "God." But unlike such philosophical contemporaries as Alfred North Whitehead, he meant by "God" no person, or mind, or even force behind the natural world. Instead, he used the word for what some people, possibly after a long lifetime, were able to attain: a type of courage and strong character. They attained this when they were able to develop, and live, a cohering group of ethical ideals. As Dewey used the term "God" it stood, not for any one set of ideals, but for a type of unity (essentially an esthetic idea) that could reconcile and harmonize such ideals and lead to a type of beauty. His use of the word "God" was unfortunate, in the sense that it departed completely from most conventional uses and proved confusing to many readers. But Dewey wanted to preserve con-

tinuities with his Christian past and to portray a very broad, encompassing, and esthetically rich type of naturalism as an appropriate substitute
for the enduring values present in the Semitic religions. In this sense,
even he was a type of reconciler, although not so perceived by the orthodox.

In a very distinctive sense, George Santayana also tried to do justice
to the Christian past. In some ways, he was more loyal to it than any
philosopher with American roots. Santayana, born in Spain of a Spanish
father and a mother who was of Spanish descent but an American citi-
zen, lived in Spain until age eight. He then moved to Boston to be with
his mother (the parents had separated). Here he grew up, always in some
sense an alien in America, or at least he so remembered. A brilliant
student at Harvard, he eventually completed a Ph.D. in philosophy, and
taught in Harvard's eminent philosophy department until 1912. At this
point, he gave up on a heretofore brilliant academic career and moved
to Europe (he never returned to America even for a visit). Already, in
his numerous books, in esthetics and poetry as well as philosophy, he
had continually explored religious themes, but there is no evidence of
any participation in Roman Catholic worship, although this was his
nominal heritage and a beloved half sister was a devout Catholic.

In his mature philosophy, Santayana rejected all the gods. He was a
professed materialist, atheist, skeptic, and behaviorist, labels that most
people do not identify with Christianity. Yet he always paid honor to his
Christian and Roman Catholic heritage. By his materialism and atheism,
Santayana tried to do justice to the existent world, to the source of all
dynamism and change. With loyalty to Lucretius (he fed extensively on
the classical heritage), he called this the "realm of matter." In no sense
was it personal. It reflects no mind or spirit behind its movements. In
fact, matter is the parent of spirit or consciousness, which is tied always
to the human brain and inconceivable apart from its material base. What
matter consists of is always open, a project for the scientific workshops,
which fill in some of its workings, at least well enough to enable humans
to fulfill some of their animal needs. The only test for such knowledge
claims is how well they work. Nothing in human discourse carries any
certification of existence, but existence is a necessary posit for any active
and involved animal. In fact, when caught up in the urgencies of a
practical life, any animal assumes existence. Skepticism is an indulgence
of a playful spirit, but at times a complete or ultimate skepticism may
liberate us from the inordinate claims of existence. If one wants to correlate Santayana's materialism with Christianity, as he at times did, then

matter stands for God the Father, the source of all things, including even consciousness. Only an atheist is properly pious, for an atheist acknowledges the power of matter and never falls into the impiety of idealists, who have inverted the order of being by making mind the directive force in the world. This is a form of arrogance, the ever appealing lure of Lucifer (rebellion), for the dependent daughter, mind or spirit, usurps the place of the parent.

Santayana acknowledged the dependence of humans upon matter. He did not by that fact love it. Matter, at least here and there, gives rise to consciousness or mind, which is born of matter and is nondynamic. Mind records, even values, but does not control the world of matter. Individual minds think. That is, they entertain and manipulate meanings, or what Santayana referred to as universal, nonexistent essences. Practical people (all people at times) focus on the types of thought, the concepts and generalizations, that record natural energies. We call these, when artfully developed, sciences. But Santayana found more delight in the free play of mind, in imagination and contemplation. He deemed this the most characteristic or becoming life of the spirit. Thus, spirit, although born of matter, incapable of being without its material base, breaks free, in its imaginative flights, from any direct dependence upon the regularities of nature or the powerful demands of the human body. Spirit, in this sense, is from the world, in the world, but affectionally not of it. It is dutiful in acknowledging its parent, but otherwise free and with a life of its own. In Christian terms, the spirit is the Son of God, or Jesus. But it is a mistake to take these analogies too far. Santayana was, and remained, an atheist. He believed in no gods. The highest form of piety and spirituality required such an atheism.

His atheism did not lead Santayana to any devastating critique of Christian theism. Just the opposite. Christianity, as any mature religion, was a creation of countless generations of people, a form of mature poetry, and therefore beautiful, a wonderful and rich object for appreciation, so unlike the abstract theories of scientists. Such religions often began with then contemporary understandings of nature and history, usually expressed in the form of stories. The originators did not consider these narratives to be fictions. In time, as human knowledge increased, these stories could no longer be taken literally, at least by people conversant with the products of the scientific workshops (Santayana never doubted their usefulness and their truthfulness, so far as they went). By his perspective, most of the stories in the Bible, stories that made up the very heart of what he called the Christian epic, were now mythical. The orthodox, including the leaders in his own Roman Catholic tradition, often refused to concede their mythical status. They took them as literally true, as did American fundamentalists. For them, so long as they could remain blind to all manner of cognitive conflicts, such literalism was innocuous, unless they became deadly serious about the myths and tried to force them on everyone in a society. The myths of Christianity embodied much practical wisdom, including guidelines for living one's life.

Always the traditionalist, Santayana believed that one broke from these constraints at great peril. For most people, most of the time, the path to some measure of happiness lay within the received religious and moral traditions. Of course, in some practical contexts, those who tried to understand and direct natural events on the basis of the older myths were doomed to futility. But futility was a lesser evil than the one faced by dense positivists who, appalled at the unscientific nature of religious myths, never came to appreciate their beauty or to grasp their wisdom. The best, the most revealing, insight into a culture was in religious myth, not in scientific knowledge. One blinded to this truth was doomed to an unspiritual and vulgar life, one divested of all joy and laughter and moments of spiritual peace. Santayana remained a Roman Catholic atheist, but of course a noncommunicant. Literalists in his church would not accept his protests that he was loyal to the deepest insights present in Roman Catholicism. Unfortunately, many critics would brand Santayana's view as a type of esthetic Christianity. This was unfair, for such ignored what was as central in his respect for the Church as its beauty— its moral wisdom.

Among the dozens of intellectuals who tried to deal with the issues raised at Dayton, two avowed disciples of Dewey and Santayana offered less philosophically informed but novel alternatives—Harry Elmer Barnes and John Crowe Ransom. Barnes became a reference point after the Dayton trial. In the appeal before the Tennessee Supreme Court, the lawyers for the state frequently sneered at Barnes. He seemed to them something like a devil incarnate. Barnes was a popularizing, prolific, and never very profound historian and sociologist, often best known for his extreme revisionist views about World War I. As a child in upstate New York, he participated actively in a Methodist church, one supported by his devout mother, only nominally by a more skeptical father. Unlike Ransom, who also grew up a Methodist, Barnes not only repudiated but came to despise the religion of his youth. Yet, of the two, Ransom was on the way to a more sophisticated emancipation from youthful beliefs than Barnes, who remained a type of Methodist evangelical in behalf of a rather austere form of humanism.

Barnes did his undergraduate work at Syracuse University, his graduate work at Columbia University, where he was influenced by the philosophy of Dewey and by the broad historical works of John Herman Randall Jr. At a distance, he admired a pragmatic philosopher at the University of Wisconsin, Max Otto, and two Unitarian ministers who founded the American Humanist Association. Even more than Darrow, he read widely in all fields and helped popularize the latest work in biblical criticism, in psychology, anthropology, and sociology, and was at least conversant with the physical sciences.

In the wake of the Scopes trial, in 1929 Barnes published a series of essays drawn from often highly controversial lectures or articles that he wrote in the preceding five years. Entitled *The Twilight of the Gods*, the book gained a reputation as one of the most radical of the 1920s. It further established a notoriety that he first gained, nationally, by a lecture he delivered before the American Association for the Advancement of Science. Because of the context, his radical repudiation of almost all religions offended the Association's president, Henry Fairfield Osborn, a leading opponent of anti-evolutionary laws and one of the most prominent of the reconcilers (he almost came to Dayton). In retrospect, Barnes's lecture, as much as the subsequent book, seems horribly dated, a now neglected and very superficial period piece. But at the time his advocacy profited from his verve, his claim of a bold and courageous honesty, and his ability to provoke angry and defensive rebuttals from almost all sides in the so-called debate about science and religion.

Barnes believed that none of the foundational beliefs of traditional Christianity remained tenable for anyone informed about the rapid progress of human knowledge. What he called the "scientific faith" had thoroughly discredited any form of supernaturalism, any belief in a cosmic companion, any hope of human immortality. The beliefs of traditional or orthodox Christians were now an affront to intelligence. Barnes was not opposed to a secular and humanistic religion, whatever that might mean, but generally used the word "religion" to refer to orthodox Christians or even to devout modernists, who claimed to accept all scientific knowledge but still retained, in new verbal garb, much of the older beliefs, beginning with a belief in an immanental god usually justified by outdated forms of nineteenth-century idealism. What made his critique of traditional religion distinctive was his emphasis upon very recent advances in the social sciences. These had allowed a new, scientific understanding of religious phenomena, which in essence reflected a modern-day form of cultural lag, a survival of primitive people who needed to appease the deities that they created to explain the workings of an inscrutable and unpredictable nature. Scientists had enabled moderns to understand, predict, and in many areas gain control over natural events, but for reasons not entirely clear to Barnes, most people still adhered to at least some of the older magic and superstition.

Barnes was a complete radical. In a rather vague way, he favored some form of socialism and had hopes for the great experiment in the Soviet Union. He hated prohibition, wanted a complete and liberating change in sexual mores (not a single item, he said, in the sex mores of respectable Americans squared with either science or esthetics), believed the survival of the earth required birth control (not a widely accepted perspective in the twenties), and, above all, repudiated the outdated notion of free will or individual responsibility. Each person is a product of a society and its institutions, and is in no way able to choose contrary to the conditioned responses learned in such a social setting. In this rather vague determinism, he both joined and may have influenced Clarence Darrow.

Several of Barnes's tactics infuriated those targeted by his critique (almost all Americans). Barnes was an admitted elitist, contemptuous of the uninformed common people, who seemed perversely committed to a primitive and archaic mind-set and who could not think precisely and logically. They needed detailed social control by informed experts (this included, at times, advanced eugenics and sterilization). He ridiculed the religious beliefs of "Tennessee peasants." He constantly appealed to bogus authorities, such as all informed observers, truly literate scholars, advanced scientific opinion, or the contemporaneously minded. The reason the masses of people were so ignorant of the scientific method, and of advanced knowledge in several fields, was the persistence of orthodox Christian beliefs. For Barnes, any Christian who believed in a creator god, in human sinfulness, in an atoning Christ, and in the possibility of life after death was orthodox. He called them all fundamentalists. This included almost all Roman Catholics and evangelical Protestants and even some devout modernists. For Barnes, the persistence of religious superstition was a greater impediment to human progress and happiness than World War I.

In chapter after chapter, Barnes itemized the baneful effects of orthodox religion. In every case, he saw only the dark side, leading to an obvious bias or overkill. He had a deep, personal bitterness about his

childhood faith and loved to caricature Methodists above all other benighted Protestant sects. For him, all religions originated in a sense of
mystery or awe or fear that led to a belief in gods, gave birth to propitiat-
ing rituals or forms of worship, and eventually led to all the intellectual
rationalizations that one found in theology. He rejected the protests of
modernists that they had long since moved beyond such a religion.
Based on some early polling data, he tried to demonstrate that even
modernists kept much of the old baggage, or tried to have the best of
both worlds, and that they were, in any case, only a small, possibly half-
liberated minority in the churches. Most Americans remained orthodox,
but for Barnes anyone was orthodox who believed in a god, in the
existence of a human soul, in immortality, in sin and original sin, in a
real heaven and hell, in a spirit world beyond the physical, in prayer as a
technique for gaining benefits from a god, and in the reality of sacred
objects. He believed he could demonstrate that most Americans believed
in all of these unfounded doctrines. He could only rejoice in the elite
who had moved beyond such outdated beliefs and vainly hope that he
did in fact live in the twilight of Christianity.

What Barnes did, with a degree of scholarly integrity, was confront
his readers with a survey of biblical criticism, an introduction to functional and behavioral psychological theory, and some insights into the
work of cultural anthropologists. He was influenced by Sigmund Freud,
particularly his *Future of an Illusion*, but did not show much insight into
psychoanalytical theory. With a near vengeance, he tried to debunk the
Gospel accounts of Jesus, but acknowledged that Jesus probably lived
(we cannot know almost anything for sure about him). The few teachings that we may attribute to him are either completely irrelevant to
present problems or rooted in ignorance. He did show how varied modernists bent Jesus to fit their own conception of human excellence.

Barnes not only ridiculed modernists, but had no respect for those
who viewed Christianity largely in esthetic terms, as mythical and beautiful. As an object of contemplation, worship might have a type of
beauty, but meantime it supported all the baneful effects of ignorance.
He even doubted if the traditional churches, stripped of their supernatural justifications, could even put on a good show on Sunday morning.
The opera, theater, and movies did a better job. In an extreme example
of insensitivity, Barnes quoted Santayana's beautiful and poetic rendition
of the Christian epic, not as a way of grasping the central narrative of a
great religious tradition, but as a way of baring its intellectual sterility.

In spite of his distaste for almost all existing religions, Barnes was still reluctant to dispense entirely with religion, although he was not very clear in his positive recommendations. His new, secular religion reminds one of Comte's positivist cult in the nineteenth century. Barnes never clarified who would be the leaders in his new religion; it would certainly not be the existing clergy. It might well be physicians. Whoever the leaders would be, they could not make any cognitive claims. Scientists already offered all the insights and controls necessary to human well-being. Some group of people, never defined but addressed as experts on esthetics, were to provide all the judgments about beauty or the quality of experience. Thus, for Barnes, the only "function of a liberalized religion, divested of its archaic supernaturalism, would be to serve as the public propaganda adjunct of social science and aesthetics." The unidentified leaders of religion were to help focus the emotions of people, in behalf of "justice, honesty, pacifism, cooperation, kindliness and beauty." He constantly used such valuative words, but never paused to define any of them. In his terms, "science" was not good at mobilizing people. Religion would have to do that. It would be the backing for a new social ethic, the organizer of a new collective will.

When asked for more specific guidelines, Barnes demurred. His was the critical task of demolishing the enslaving older religions. But he did profess to find some examples of what the new, liberated religion might look like, among advanced or radical modernists who joined the Ethical Cultural movement or the newly developing humanistic wing of Unitarianism. He acknowledged that secular cults, with no avowed religious content, might take over the mobilizing role of former religions, and he cited both anarchism and Russian communism as examples. Had he written a decade later, he might have had to acknowledge fascism and Nazism as such secular cults and perhaps moderate his enthusiasm for them. In these views, Barnes was an almost caricatured example of a form of belligerent agnosticism, or what some would soon call secular humanism. Although his basic beliefs were close to those of Dewey, his sharp scientism represented the type of dogmatism and elitism that horrified Dewey.

John Crowe Ransom was much more under the influence of Santayana than Dewey. In the twenties, he was a poet in the Fugitive circle and professor of literature at Vanderbilt University. He would soon gain new fame as the chief ideologist for Southern Agrarianism and then for a new type of literary criticism. Since he lived in Tennessee, he was embarrassed by the events at Dayton and struggled to come to terms with what the trial meant. He was most aware of the response of his department chair at Vanderbilt, Edwin Mims, who published a book as a quick response to the pejorative national images of the South created by the Scopes trial, and particularly by the columns written by Mencken. In his *The Advancing South*, Mims spoke in behalf of a small, but he believed growing, group of southern liberals and progressives. They bemoaned the fundamentalists at Dayton and insisted that such fundamentalists did not speak for the whole South. In spite of the negative image they created, the South had made great progress. Mims surveyed the liberal voices crying out, with increasing effectiveness, in the wilderness of reaction and fundamentalism. He emphasized planners at the University of North Carolina, new literary lights at his own Vanderbilt, the few modernist ministers even in such a benighted denomination as the Southern Baptist Convention, and a group of journalists and politicians beginning to address the racial problems of the South. Of course, Mims noted the recent growth of cities and manufacturing, yet wanted the South to avoid the worst abuses of industrialism as displayed in the North. All in all, it was an effective polemic. But for Ransom, and for such colleagues as Allen Tate, it represented a capitulation to northern and industrial values. Ransom wanted an alternative response and ended up with a somewhat incoherent book in 1930, *God without Thunder.*

Ransom grew up as a Methodist. His father was a clergyman. With increasing doubts and a sense of inconsistency, he long continued his membership in a Methodist congregation. But by 1930 it was clear that he found himself doubting most of the biblical stories that lay behind orthodoxy. He was also alienated, not by any of the repressive or dogmatic aspects of Methodism that so offended Barnes, but just the opposite. As he knew it early in the century, and from his father's congregations, Methodism reflected a soft and sentimental form of Christianity. He yearned for stronger stuff, for more demanding gods. His doubts about his inherited religion, his inability to believe, did not give him any sense of liberation but rather a sense of loss. The death of a god is a tragedy for those who knew and trusted such a god. Thus, he deeply sympathized with, even envied, the traditional Christians at Dayton. He also identified with what he believed he found behind their resistance to Darwinian theories: a profound distrust for the modern, abstract, and potentially dehumanizing sciences. He cheered the fundamentalists when they, armed often with the wrong weapons, nonetheless gave battle against scientism and the type of industrial progress that it spawned, or themes that he turned into the preface and theme essay of the manifesto of Southern Agrarians, *I'll Take My Stand.* Perhaps even more critically, he still found types of truth and honesty in those who defended an older version of god and did not fall for some recent and indulgent substitute. It was clear that, for Ransom, if he could believe in a god at all, it would be an old-style god, a god of power and will and thunder, a god who demanded human obeisance to his desires, who authored evil as well as good, who elicited fear and awe as much as consent and love.

Not only was Ransom deeply suspicious of the scientists at Dayton, or what they stood for, but he was downright contemptuous of modernists, of those who tried to reconcile new scientific knowledge, and its method of production, with Christianity. Properly understood, the sciences supported some form of naturalism, or a naturalism that Ransom would ultimately and begrudgingly accept, at least in its more Deweyian form. Scientific inquiry, if one understood its presuppositions, subverted all forms of supernaturalism. And the received Christianity was a supernatural religion, and thus inconsistent with the worldview of honest scientists. John Dewey was correct. Yet, at Dayton, and in almost all publications, one met what Ransom so deplored in Mims: a loose, internally incoherent, anxious, and fashionable defense of modernism. Sentimental Christians, including well-placed theologians, joined with "apostate" or naive scientists in celebrating some unholy marriage of science and religion. Both groups sacrificed intellectual rigor in their attempt to glue together incompatible beliefs. Even Nietzsche was not quite as contemptuous of such efforts as Ransom.

Ransom made one such "establishmentarian" compromise the object of his ridicule. In 1923 Robert Millikan, the physicist and Nobelist, helped gather forty-five scientists, theologians (loosely defined), and public intellectuals to mediate the developing cultural wars. They signed a proclamation, or peace treaty, and did it to correct popular misapprehensions. The theologians celebrated the work of scientists and, in a sense, gave them their divine blessing. The scientists repudiated the materialistic or naturalistic or irreligious position often attributed to them. This Washington agreement was, in retrospect, a near parody of modernist assumptions, assumptions that were very close to the beliefs of one participant, Shailer Mathews. The agreement opened with an unexceptional statement about the goal of scientists: to develop, without prejudice, the facts, laws, and processes of nature. It followed with the purpose of what it called religion: to develop the conscience, the ideals, and the aspiration of humans (a position close to that of Whitehead). Both functions were necessary for the progress and happiness of the human race. It ended with a muddy reference to the sublime conception of

"God" furnished by science, a God consonant with the highest ideals of humans. This God had revealed himself or itself through countless ages in the development of the earth as an abode of man (a typical, immanental view of God), and in "the age-long inbreathing of life" into matter, culminating in man with a spiritual nature and godlike powers (a vague version of theistic evolution drawn from Mathews).

Except for the statement of the goals of scientists, Ransom found the language full of confusing mush. The identified and vague god seemed a very nice god, one who gradually shaped an earth to suit humans and who over time somehow turned matter into godlike people. Such a god was part of a gigantic hoax, a series of evasions of the very serious issues at stake. No religion with any appeal to the masses of people could get by with such an irenic theism. Ransom preferred the God of ancient Israel, and even identified the deification of Jesus in Trinity doctrines as an early watering down of such a lofty and all-powerful deity. He loved what he called an Oriental type of god, not the rationalized gods of the Occident. Without much understanding, he thought such a god still lurked in Eastern Orthodoxy, less so in Roman Catholicism, and scarcely at all in mainline Protestantism. Any religion worth believing would be overtly supernatural, with gods of miracles and direct interventions, or gods who could directly respond to human needs. Such gods might indeed depart from the most rigorous understanding of the world, or from the principles inherent in such understanding (philosophers rightly clarified these), but the gods would be concrete and mythical. Without any philosophical supports, the fundamentalists were at least sensible enough to know this and were correct in condemning the compromisers, who seemed to make up, at the time, virtually the whole American intellectual establishment.

In many ways, in this strange, yet perceptive book, Ransom painted himself into a corner, into a tragic dilemma. Much as he admired the orthodox and recognized the logical coherence and psychological power of their doctrines, he still did not, could not, believe what he referred to as the "myths" of Christianity. Without these, one lost the heart of a religion. Modernists could not admit this, wanted to have their cake and eat it too, and thus cooked up all the friendly new gods, none of which had any appeal to Ransom, who had whetted his sensibility to such an extent that his taste in gods was not easily satiated. Ransom lamented what was clearly taking place. Everywhere the inherited gods were falling. Scientists had led in the deicide. And theologians had, in effect, capitulated, by allowing scientists to strip the gods of all power so long as they would continue to honor their now all but empty names. In venerating Jesus, or elevating him to the status of a humanized god, the theologians had in a sense already rejected the thunderous God of Israel. The modernists no longer really believed in this God, however much they chanted his name, and in fact were, as illustrated by Whitehead's frequent reference to the cruel gods of the past, really ashamed of the old gods, and for the very characteristics that made them suitable gods. God had become a principle, pale and weak.

Ransom had no prescriptions, no cure for the vacuity, the lack of poetry, and the thinly concealed naturalism of the modernists, or for the blindness or repressive political strategies of fundamentalists. About all he could suggest, or futilely wish for, were some new, focused, concrete, awe-inspiring myths that were consistent with, but transcended, the new and irrefutable knowledge about nature, including Darwinian evolution. But as much as Santayana, he knew that authentic, believable myths grow out of centuries of human experience and an imaginative response to that experience. He hoped that, if the mainstream Christians of America, in Methodist, Baptist, and Presbyterian congregations, were able (so far they were not) to resist all the secularizing trends, they would return to a virile and concrete god, an orthodox god, one of thunder. In this hope, he to some extent anticipated the types of neo-orthodox theology that became popular in the thirties.

The most enduring, and at times pessimistic, response to the perceived death of the traditional Christian Jehovah came not from scholars and academics, but from two public intellectuals, Walter Lippmann and Joseph Wood Krutch. Both Lippmann's *Preface to Morals* and Krutch's *Modern Temper* became classics of the 1920s.

Lippmann and Krutch became deeply involved in the issues raised by the Scopes trial. Lippmann even consulted with the defense team before the trial, and in its immediate aftermath delivered a series of lectures at the University of Virginia, published as *American Inquisitors*. He devoted over half of the book to the Scopes trial and, in two carefully developed dialogues, tried to flesh out all the unresolved issues at Dayton. In one dialogue, between a rather naive modernist and a very realistic and perceptive fundamentalist, he broached almost all the themes of his subsequent *Preface to Morals*, probably the most influential book he wrote during his long career. Notably, the model for his fundamentalist spokesperson was John Gresham Machen, whom Lippmann admired as a "scholar and a gentleman." He believed Machen's *Liberalism and Chris-*

tianity was the best book to come out of the religious wars of the twenties.

In his *Preface*, Lippmann drew extensively upon his undergraduate work at Harvard, in the first decade of the new century, under both William James and George Santayana. At various points, even his language derived directly from Santayana's early, five-volume masterpiece, *The Life of Reason*. In James, Lippmann confronted a philosopher who defended theistic belief, who charted all the human comforts that derived from such belief, who suggested the despair and hopelessness that might accompany atheism, but who never confidently believed in any of the old gods himself. In Santayana, he confronted an open atheist, but one who valued, above all else, the free, disinterested life of the mind or spirit. At least for the few people who could break free from all the entanglements of the world, and from the often overpowering but selfish appetites of the flesh, Santayana, in these early Harvard years, recommended a type of rational morality, one with the flavor of classical Stoicism. Lippmann committed himself to such a lofty life of reason. His problem, and the central problem of the *Preface*, was whether such a lofty morality could appeal to more than a small elite. Despite his doubts, he argued that evolving conditions in modern society assured that it could, and thus he ended the *Preface* with more hope than despair.

Lippmann began with what he believed was a tremendous transformation, or revolution, in human thought. Such had been the effects of what he called the "acids of modernity" that anyone exposed to these acids could no longer believe in what he called a "theocratic god," or a god that created and governed the universe and who promised some type of eternal life for humans. Of course, prophets in the past had often rebelled against orthodoxy and, in time, had inspired major changes in belief. But now it was different. The acids were too strong. No one would be able to repair the crumbling doctrines of the Church, restore a stable orthodoxy. Only in intellectual backwaters, like Dayton, among people who were still isolated from modernity, could the old faith survive, and perhaps even here not for many more generations.

The acids were many. Lippmann spent half a book exploring them. New scientific knowledge was only part of the story. More basic was the scientific method, the mode of gaining new knowledge, which was at an opposite pole from an earlier reliance on revelation. Thus, the whole scientific mind-set was inimical to faith. In a sense the crumbling began with the Reformation, when Luther and Calvin rejected the authority of the pope and of tradition, and turned to a literal, not a richly allegorical, Bible as the sole authority. From this biblicalism, and the desire to know exactly what the Bible meant, came inexorably the higher criticism and its subversive effect on simple faith. Even the modern national state, with its monopoly of power, and modern business enterprise, with its premium on profits and the joys of consumption, ate away at an older world view. Today, it was not that people wanted to reject the old gods, but that they increasingly found them unbelievable. They were simply not congruent with all the other experience that made up modern life.

Lippmann was aware of what it meant for the gods to die. All the old moral guidelines fell. No one could hold on to anything that was certain. As the icons fell, a few radicals like Darrow and Mencken could find meaning in life by, in a sense, still leaning on the old verities that they were so gleefully mocking in their battles against backwater yokels. But when they won, then what? Moral anarchy and despair seemed inevitable, unless modern intellectuals could find some substitute for the old religion, some new and nontheocratic basis for ethical commitment. Lippmann wanted to indicate a possible pathway to such a new ethical order, and thus his "preface" to morals.

Protestant modernists did not offer a solution. If anything, they had made things worse. Lippmann was very harsh on modernists. His attacks on Fosdick stung deeply, for Fosdick thought Lippmann should be on his side. The modernists tried to create new gods to replace the old ones. They wanted to escape magic and supernaturalism, to outfit gods that were not an embarrassment to contemporary understanding. But in so doing they got rid of everything that made the old gods appealing to the popular mind. In most cases he found modernists uneasy, or elusive, in their god talk, or in their references to immortality (they believed in no physical survival, no real heaven). He wondered: Do they really, honestly, in their bones, believe in a god at all? So often, liberals and modernists used the word god as a blanket term for their own moral ideals. Thus, he fully endorsed Machen's devastating attack on modernism. But Lippmann realized that Machen was not typical of fundamentalists, who were rarely credible intellectuals, but usually bizarre and ignorant, given to crackpot ideas of all sorts. Machen was a rare example of brilliant people who could still, in honesty, defend Christian orthodoxy. Lippmann did not doubt that many modernists experienced awe, mystery, and wonder, or that many did honestly believe, as did an almost incomprehensible Whitehead, in some force or abstract reality behind phenomena. But as Machen pointed out, this was not a Christian god, not a lawgiver, father, or judge, and thus not a god for the common people, who craved moral certainties and salvation.

Throughout the *Preface*, Lippmann reflected a deep and unsettling ambivalence. On the one hand, he was an elitist, even occasionally arrogant. He at times had small respect for the ordinary people of America, with their ignorance, crass materialism, and superstitious myths. Yet, on the other hand, he knew that no philosopher kings could bring peace and order to a democratic America. No Marcus Aurelius lurked in the wings, and no such moral aristocrat could win an election in America. In opposition to his elitism was Lippmann's commitment to representative government, to allowing people to rule themselves. This commitment, so characteristic of the editorial stance of his own favorite journalistic outlet, the *New Republic*, meant that he had, somehow, to suggest a way for more and more ordinary Americans, who were sure soon to lose the old and anchoring religious faith that had kept them dutiful and orderly, to find a new foundation for hope and for moral assurance. In the not very persuasive second half of the *Preface*, Lippmann tackled this problem and found an answer in what he called the "higher religions."

Lippmann placed great emphasis upon ascetic discipline and disinterested service. In almost all the major religions he found at least a subtext, one that appealed to only a few rarified intellects, and thus themes that quickly lost out in any popular religion. He found these themes in the Stoics, in Buddhism, in Plato, and even in the Christian Gospels and the letters of Paul. Most often, Santayana was his guide. These enlightened sages soared above the literal beliefs of any popular religion. In Santayana's words, they knew that all dogma was mythical, that miracles were legendary, sacraments only symbols, scriptures merely literature, liturgy only poetry. Above all, they knew that salvation did not involve human survival, or some heaven to reward earthly faith or obedience. In fact, such higher religions involved none of the self-affirming desires of ordinary people. If one literally craved immortality, then one only illustrated one's selfish desire, as much as those who obeyed the commandments because a father god punished disobedience. Such prudential desires alone prevented one from attaining the ascetic self-denial, and the form of disinterested service, that characterized any higher religion.

Those who could embrace a higher religion relinquished any belief in a cosmic lawgiver and judge and any literal heaven. Lippmann was far from clear about the exact beliefs that characterized a renunciatory and disinterested religion. He seemed to leave open many options but did emphasize that such a religion of disinterest supported all the higher virtues—courage, honor, faithfulness, truthfulness, temperance, even love. Such a higher religion might be consistent with a belief in some higher metaphysical reality, such as the world soul, or Logos, of Stoics. It did not preclude a belief in an impersonal god, as illustrated also in the more spiritual utterances of Jesus in the Gospels. It did not preclude a mature belief in immortality, in the sense that humans, in their character, in the way they lived their lives, exemplified some ideal (in Santayana's term, some essence), which was formally eternal, unbounded by time and space. Above all, those who gained the insights of a higher religion renounced the prudential morality, the selfish affirmations, of ordinary people. They lived on a higher plane, one that allowed them to assess, without bias or passion, any moral situation and come to an informed and rational decision. Lippmann was not always clear about the end, the goal, of such a rational morality, except human happiness, which at times seemed to cohere with something like the common good or the public interest. His elite, unlike passionate and partisan inferiors, were in the best position to define what these elusive goals really entailed.

But all this analysis led to a dilemma. Lippmann knew that such an elite could not make policy in America. If a moral society were to survive the death of all the older gods, then impartiality, disinterested judgment, and a renunciation of ordinary desires had to become the working outlook of an ever growing body of Americans. On first glance, this seemed impossible. Realistic fundamentalists stressed this point. Lippmann asked if an enormous number of people were not "too young, or too feeble, too dull or too violent, too unstable or too incurious, to have any comprehension of anything but the simplest scheme of rewards and punishments." Yet these same people, who had lost the ancient certainties, needed to believe in them but could not, needed a heavenly commander but could not find him. They were mired in an adult dilemma but had childish dispositions. The higher religion, or a religion of the spirit, would suit their needs, but it was beyond their power to attain. Despite these obstacles, Lippmann found much already under way in American society that might, in time, lead to enough mature and enlightened citizens to achieve what he called the "Great Society" (a borrowed phrase later picked up by Richard Goodwin and made the centerpiece of a speech by Lyndon Johnson, thereby lending a label to a vast body of social legislation in the 1960s).

Lippmann began his hopeful analysis with an essay in psychology, on the healthy growth of children toward maturity. This meant, as one grew up, a move from an innocence that expects all needs to be assuaged, to more and more self-denial, to a renunciation of many desires in behalf of a few harmonious goals that cohere with reality. To live in the realm of the spirit is to outgrow all childish wishes. Lippmann, with an optimism not always matched by his analysis, believed that many circumstances in the modern world were conducive to such maturation. He came close to saying that a higher religion's time had come, that its widespread acceptance was almost inevitable. In the ages during which a few sages had discovered its wisdom, circumstances had foreclosed its wide acceptance. No more.

When Lippmann moved from an analysis of the breakdown of the ancestral order to present expectations, he shifted from the more ironic and disillusioned renunciations of his mentor, Santayana, to the more engaged and hopeful instrumentalism of his friend Dewey. With Santayana, he could stress that humans live in a world that has no regard for their desires, one in which what humans see as evil is actually a report on how they relate to the world around them, or what they value in it. But instead of a retreat from worldly involvement, Lippmann stressed that perceived evils, being relational, only posed problems that humans could work to alleviate. In a sense, evil is a challenge, not an inherent state of affairs. Mature people are those who develop the needed tools to change the world where it is open to direction and the wisdom to accept those aspects of existence not open to human direction. The tool for making needed repairs is scientific knowledge. But such knowledge is as important because of its method of discovery as for its problem solving. It involves disinterested and cooperative inquiry, and thus it is an example of the disinterested moral stance that Lippmann applauded in all areas.

Lippmann ended his book with chapters on recent trends in business management, government, and sexual conventions. In each, he saw irreversible developments that were consistent with, or conducive to, disinterestedness. In business, the very requirements of large, increasingly bureaucratic firms were not the individualistic or libertarian motives of captains of industry, but a new type of cooperation and technical competence. In government, the new need was not for more rules and regulations, which did not work, but for the arbitration of competing interests in a pluralistic society. Lippmann here applauded disinterested statesmen, those who did not represent any partisan or partial interest, but who helped show the people what their real interests were, even when their leadership was unpopular. In an age of birth control and liberated women, which Lippmann saw as revolutionary, the old sexual regime could no longer gain assent; but on grounds of long-term self-interest, or disinterested rationality, Lippmann believed that humans should continue most of the conventions tied to monogamous marriage. In each of these areas, he believed that existing institutions worked in behalf of greater rationality, not less, that the ideals of a higher religion were pregnant in events. In this sense he was an optimistic prophet or moral statesman. He could not fill in many of the details. It was too soon. But he was confident, as a moralist who did not preach or enforce rules but instead tried to clarify an ideal, that "what the sages have prophesied as high religion, what psychologists delineate as matured personality, and the disinterestedness which the Great Society requires for its practical fulfillment, are all of a piece, and are the basic elements of a modern morality."

At least in the twenties, Joseph Wood Krutch shared none of Lippmann's hopes. Born in Knoxville, Tennessee, close to Dayton, he suffered through the Scopes trial, much as did Ransom. A writer for the *Nation*, he sent his despairing reports on Dayton to this periodical. Unlike Lippmann, he soon gave up journalism for the academy. For most of his career, he taught literature at Columbia University, but he was never a scholarly specialist. He continued to publish thoughtful essays, aimed at a broad public audience. He later repudiated some of the skepticism of his first masterpiece, *The Modern Temper*, but never again would publish a book that gained as large or as enduring an audience. In his later years, and in retirement, Krutch became one of America's leading environmentalists.

A sense of loss, a mood of despair, permeated *Modern Temper*. In fact, Krutch indulged a rather sophomoric pessimism and milked it for all it was worth. The death of Christian versions of god was not in the forefront of his analysis. He assumed that these gods had died sometime in the nineteenth century, possibly in the aftermath of Darwin's *Origin*. Theism was only the first of the great human illusions to dissipate. Left, at least for a time, were other illusions tied to now unbelievable estimates of human ability and nobility. In chapter after chapter, Krutch laid bare such childish innocence. Darwin and Freud had led in the exposure. But Krutch seemed most influenced by Nietzsche and Oswald Spengler. Nietzsche had shown the innervating effects of too much knowledge, which left people unable to become vitally involved in any active life. Spengler had worked out a pattern of growth, maturity, and then decline and death, which applied to all civilizations. According to it, the highest development of knowledge and artistry came just before the inevitable decline of a civilization, which opened the way for some new barbarians to begin the long process all over again. Krutch gained a temporary fame in the cold war years because he had tentatively identified the next barbarians, those who would take over after the early fall of the West, with the Soviet Union.

In brief, Krutch felt that the world exposed by modern scientists offered no home for the human spirit. The new knowledge had undermined earlier beliefs in reason, free will, and beauty, eliminated any room for poetry, religion, and mythology. It was now clear that humans were fully part of nature and that nature exhibited no purpose, supported no human values, exemplified no higher meaning. Humans were all alone in the universe, aliens in a world that supported none of their highest aspirations. Krutch lamented what had happened but accepted the truths that scientists and social scientists had gradually revealed. He launched no crusade against new knowledge. He did not like it. He sometimes resented it. But he believed it. With a morbid fascination, he surveyed all its implications. One could not go back. Once exposed, the old myths lost all credibility. Unlike literary expatriates, Krutch revealed no particular distaste for America or American values. If anything, he envied those innocent Americans who still affirmed, with no hint of doubt, the old myths about the gods and about humans. But even the innocent would soon have to respond to all the assaults upon the human ego, upon human needs and feelings.

With the gods long since banished, Krutch explored the increasingly dismal prospects of some form of humanism that could replace older religions. In past heroic ages, such as classical Greece or Elizabethan England, humans had been able, with little reliance on any divine help, to exult in the possibilities of great achievement and fulfillment. But such a humanistic faith had rested just as much on illusions as had theistic religion. In the wake of Darwin, then of Freud, no honest person could affirm the older myths, not only about the gods but about humans. One by one, Krutch demonstrated how the older icons had shattered and fallen to earth.

One transient illusion had been a misplaced hope that all the new knowledge, with the mastery over nature that it allowed, would lead to a wonderful new world. Not so. Knowledge led humans into a trap. With a higher mental development, humans moved ever farther away from natural ends. Lower animals are fortunate. Intellect, at a certain point, becomes a curse. It undercuts simple human goals and values. It leads toward emptiness. It innervates, alienates, and eliminates the social virtues that even some animals reenact in their lives. When civilization becomes too refined, too reflective and self-conscious, too honest, it is on the way to destroying itself. It dies from the top, undercut by those who have advanced farther in their intellectuality and sensitivity and thus those who inevitably have moved toward skepticism and cynicism. In the final alienation and despair, civilization cannot defend against the new barbarians. The sciences offer no solace. One can find no goals, no meaning, in the products of laboratories. New technologies can keep more people alive. They can carry people at higher speeds to unsure destinations. But such knowledge clarifies no new ends even as it denies people the solace of older and now discredited illusions.

In his two most memorable chapters, Krutch lamented the death of romantic love and the impossibility of truly tragic experience. After the gods died, Victorians at least kept, for a brief time, their confidence and faith in love. Freud took care of this illusion. All the sacrificial devotion, all the poetic play, all the mysteries formerly attached to the mating game have given way to physical processes and the governance of hormones. Sex—accessible, free, and animalistic—is also empty, without value or even great significance. Of course, as Krutch conceded, romantic love was a human creation, a belated cultural artifact, one not embraced in some societies. The psychologists and physiologists were correct. But these reductive truths about love had destroyed one of the last values that gave life meaning. Love had rivaled the gods in eliciting human reverence, loyalty, and sacrifice.

The loss of love was only symptomatic of the loss of all illusions about humans. They are not in the image of any god. They are merely a part of nature. They are constrained by heredity, conditioned by society, and incapable of any inherent nobility and greatness. Thus, modern humans are incapable of understanding tragedy. Henrik Ibsen had replaced Shakespeare. The cathartic effect of tragic drama cannot apply to a people who no longer believe in human nobility. Our heroes are more pathetic than tragic. Without any sustainable belief in human possibilities, without confidence in life itself, humans have lost a sense of dignity and of direction. What they do has no enduring value. The universe no longer trembles when great men die. This lost faith in human nature is irretrievable. Once again, we know too much to give credence to it.

Living in a dull, vegetative, nonheroic age, modern humans have vainly sought some new certainty, some new purpose. Krutch noted the revival of metaphysics, the vain search for free will behind quantum indeterminacy, the vague gods manufactured by modernists or by

Whitehead, and the recourse to pragmatic truth, which for Krutch was no truth at all. All such strategies were pathetic, doomed to failure in a world without fixed purpose. The sciences had invaded and mastered one field after another. Nothing remained beyond their grasp. The human spirit had lost any leverage. All the human devices to conceal human insignificance had failed, and now nothing stood between humans and complete despair. Humans, who had created all the illusions, had also, at times joyfully but unwittingly, created the sciences that destroyed the illusions. At times Krutch seemed to resign himself to civilizational decline. In some sense, overly refined humans deserved their fate, just as the eager, vital, assertive, superstitious barbarians deserved to take over the world and live with their illusions until, finally, with maturity, they learned the truth. As he concluded, "Ours is a lost cause and there is no place for us in the natural universe, but we are not, for all that, sorry to be human. We should rather die as men than live as animals."

With Krutch, I conclude this survey of nontheistic perspectives. The books cited above feature the most visible and influential voices of the twenties. The only close competitor would be H. L. Mencken, who wrote a serious and almost scholarly book on theism (*Treatise on the Gods*) in 1930. It sold well. But its basic arguments were very close to those of Harry Elmer Barnes, with some Nietzschian twists. Mencken found the source of religion in primitive fears and anxiety, then traced its evolution and surveyed its varieties, all as a preface to a very iconoclastic description and history of Christianity. But unlike Barnes, he did not foresee the early twilight of the gods or, like Lippmann, anticipate any early victory by a religion of disinterestedness. Mencken believed that only a small elite of tough-minded people could face the world with equanimity, or maintain high moral standards, without affirming one or another of the many absurd religious systems that would continue to pander to the masses.

Reading Guide

It is difficult to identify either one or a few books that embrace the vast range of issues broached in this chapter. The literature on the classic American philosophers is vast. I made only brief references to Peirce, Royce, James, and Whitehead, and will not try to introduce any literature about them. Since I offered extended summaries of the religious views of Dewey and Santayana, I feel burdened to suggest books, but that is not easy. They wrote so much. For Dewey, the most comprehensive view of his philosophy is in *Experience and Nature* (La Salle, Ill: Open Court, 1925). His one book that focused specifically on religion is *A Common Faith* (New Haven: Yale University Press, 1934). Santayana was most revealing about his religious views in *The Idea of Christ in the Gospels* (New York: Scribner's, 1946); *Platonism and the Spiritual Life* (New York: Scribner's, 1927); *Life of Reason: Reason in Religion* (London: Constable, 1917); and, above all, in the preface and conclusion of his *Realms of Being*, 1 vol. ed. (New York: Scribner's, 1942).

For Harry Elmer Barnes, the key book is *The Twilight of the Gods* (New York: Vanguard Press, 1929). This bears comparison with H. L. Mencken's *Treatise on the Gods* (New York: Knopf, 1930). John Crowe Ransom's one book on Christianity is *God without Thunder: An Unorthodox Defense of Orthodoxy* (New York: Harcourt, Brace, 1930).

Walter Lippmann wrote two books directly responsive to the fundamentalist controversy and the Scopes trial: *American Inquisitors: A Commentary on Dayton and Chicago* (New York: Macmillan, 1928), and the much more influential *Preface to Morals* (New York: Macmillan, 1929). Joseph Wood Krutch published *The Modern Temper* (New York: Harcourt, Brace) in 1929, and returned to these same themes, although in a less pessimistic mood, in *The Measure of Man: On Freedom, Human Values, Survival, and the Modern Temper* (Indianapolis: Bobbs–Merrill, 1954) and *Human Nature and the Human Condition* (New York: Random House, 1959).

THE GODS STILL TREMBLE:
AN UPDATE

It is now three-quarters of a century since the cultural controversies of the twenties. That seems so long ago. Only a few very elderly people still remember. Soon, the citizens of Dayton should begin their preliminary planning for a great centennial celebration of the Scopes trial. It will undoubtedly be even more profitable, at least for local merchants, than what happened in 1925.

Harry Elmer Barnes was, in one sense, completely wrong in his confidence that, by the 1920s, he was finally and happily observing the twilight of the gods. By all the evidence of occasionally quite refined polls, as many people today as in 1925 believe in various versions of Jewish or Christian gods. Even for such issues as life after death or belief in angels, nothing seems to have changed. Church affiliation is higher than in the twenties (around 60 percent), and in fact higher today than at any time in American history except the 1950s. In the 1990s, the level of popular belief in a range of traditional Christian beliefs actually rose. Around 40 percent of Americans report weekly church attendance; over 20 percent actually appear in any given week, and around 20 percent of Americans have a very close and vital tie to churches. That is, their religion is the most important aspect of their life. They are the Christians who faithfully attend not only Sunday worship, but Sunday evening services and, if Protestants, midweekly prayer meetings.

In the fifties, almost all Christian denominations enjoyed a period of growth. Church membership soared to its highest level, as baby boom parents flocked to churches. But even then the most rapid growth was in new evangelical denominations, in the holiness and Pentecostal movements, and in such apocalyptic denominations as Jehovah's Witnesses and the Mormons. In the sixties, except for Southern Baptists, the mainline denominations (Congregational, Presbyterian, Methodist,

Episcopal, the more inclusive branches of Lutheranism, Disciples of Christ, and American Baptists) began to decline, at first as a proportion of the American population, then in actual members. This decline accelerated by the nineties, and seems likely to continue. The causes have been complex, including such overlooked factors as a low birthrate among largely affluent members. Such churches, latitudinarian in doctrine, increasingly formal or liturgical in worship, have clearly had a more narrow appeal than orthodox, ecstatic, apocalyptic, or puritanical denominations. John Crowe Ransom was correct in his prediction that loose, inclusive, and soft modifications of the concrete, dogmatic, mythical religions of the past would never have broad appeal among the masses. But from a comparative perspective, what is equally remarkable is how such inclusive, historic denominations have been able to appeal to such a large percentage of affluent, well-educated, highly professional people, or the very classes of people who have largely deserted the Church in most European countries.

Does this mean that the fundamentalists won? Of course, the answer depends upon definitions. Few of those in the most rapidly growing denominations like the label. The largest grouping contains those denominations that proudly claim allegiance to what they call "evangelicalism." The leadership of the largest Protestant denomination, the Southern Baptist Convention, has clearly aligned itself with these modern evangelicals and possibly reflects the views of a majority of its members. Four black Baptist denominations reflect the same evangelical outlook. These evangelicals not only continue the defining commitments of nineteenth-century evangelicals (crisis conversions, active proselytizing, warm and supportive forms of worship, and austere moral standards), but such twentieth century criteria as biblical inerrancy and premillennial hopes.

By most measurements, the second largest group of growing denominations is made up of Pentecostals, now with a claimed membership of over ten million, most at the low end of incomes and social status. Most Pentecostals share many of the doctrines of evangelicals but place much greater emphasis upon ecstatic experience. They alone make the gifts of the Spirit, including faith healing and speaking in tongues, critical in their beliefs and their worship. Pentecostals are much less likely than other evangelicals to become actively involved in politics.

In a class by themselves are the apocalyptic denominations—Seventh-day Adventists, Jehovah's Witnesses, and Mormons. These groups grew very rapidly after World War II and are still growing exponentially abroad, but some evidence suggests a recent slowing of growth in the United States. Roman Catholics, who make up more than a third of American Christians, and who once retained the loyalty of most members and enjoyed both high birthrates and heavy immigration, are now facing their own retention problems, even as they have become virtually a part of the mainstream. Rigidly orthodox or confessional churches, like Missouri Synod Lutherans or the Christian Reformed Church, or the very conservative Churches of Christ, have not grown rapidly but have retained more members than their liberal counterparts.

Such a survey of the continued strength of orthodox, evangelical, Pentecostal, or apocalyptic Christianity is not the whole story. Although church membership is high, such membership almost fully encompasses those who attend churches. In the nineteenth century, when Protestant membership requirements were reasonably clear and strictly enforced, and when churches exercised discipline over members, the total church community (including youth, unsaved adults in church families, and attending nonmembers who nonetheless shared in the overall belief system and might later come into the church) was often up to four times the size of communicants and might include almost everyone in a village or town. Not so today. Thus, even though the percentage of very devout Christians is comparatively high, they make up a self-conscious minority nationally and are more culturally isolated than ever before. Evangelicals know this. They often assume what seems a countercultural attitude. In other words, a hegemonic evangelical culture in the nineteenth century is now a defensive subculture.

This shift parallels another one. Cultural leadership is now largely outside the churches. This does not hold true for political leadership, which is often very representative of local or traditional and conventional beliefs and values. Today, the higher the educational attainment, or the higher the scores earned on intelligence or achievement tests, the less likely are individuals to be Christians, or, if Christian, to be in other than liberal mainstream denominations. Opinion polls that use highly nuanced questions reveal that belief in a personal, gendered, and omnipotent Jehovah has declined rather steadily in this century. This is clearly true among college students and college graduates.

The decline in traditional religious beliefs and behavior is most clear among American intellectuals. Intellectuals make up a very small minority, but an influential one. As the twentieth century ends, it seems clear that most of them have moved ever farther away from certain critical beliefs still accepted by the larger population. The long-term implications of this gap of understanding, or even whether or not it will stabilize, widen, or narrow over the twenty-first century, remains unclear.

However wide their philosophical disagreement, a growing majority of such intellectuals have relinquished a belief in any inherent purpose in the universe, any god that created it, any firm grounding for truth claims, and any external authority for moral preferences or values. Nothing inherent in existence or reality vouches for the accuracy of various claims about the world or about what is right and wrong. No reality beyond humans supports or assures the achievement of human ideals, for the nonhuman world displays no inherent purpose, seems to move toward no goals. At Dayton in 1925, both orthodox Christians and the visiting experts resisted such seemingly skeptical conclusions.

Such a lack of deference to any transcendent authority does not necessarily lead to any debilitating skepticism. It does not preclude very useful types of knowledge. In fact, contemporary intellectuals who deny any grounding or foundations for knowledge are often the very people who have done the most to refine the disciplinary conventions that enable the production of useful knowledge at an ever accelerating pace and with ever greater refinements of method. Such a lack of deference does not mean that such intellectuals have, or even could, dispense with goals and purposes that are critical to their very identity. It does not mean that they could dispense with shame and guilt, or refrain from adverse judgments about the actions of themselves or other people. They may be as attuned to problems of ethical principles and moral conduct as ever before, and often with a great deal more sensitivity and conviction than nonintellectuals. What they have surrendered are older ways of vindicating or justifying their truth claims and their preferences.

They have given up a great deal in this surrender. In the Christian West, what may seem most apparent is their loss of belief in any personal, creative, and providential god, or the very heart of the Semitic cosmology. Such a god is not necessary to a purposeful or cognitively transparent universe, but if such a god exists, it guarantees some purpose in the universe as a whole and some decipherable plan or structure in it. The sacrifice of such theistic belief, or to put it in more dramatic and tragic language, the death of the gods, removes any basis for a belief in what many gods had promised humans: life beyond death as well as future punishments and rewards. Such doubts preclude any appeal to divine law or divine justice. Theism has been so central to Western civilization that one might argue that, without it, the whole civilization is in jeopardy.

Using the term in its most literal sense, modern intellectuals have become "disillusioned." They have lost most of what they now see as the illusions of the past, illusions that, before recognition as such, provided great consolations. The illusions also helped inspire the types of inquiry, and the resulting useful knowledge, that so molded our modern world. The erosive forms of doubt that dissipated the illusions were not a product of what some call "science." Just the opposite. The sciences were a product of these illusions, most of all the belief in a universe that had structure and form and that moved toward purposeful outcomes. It was such a universe that demanded more and more human understanding.

The concern over the alleged conflict between two reified abstractions, science and religion, now seems a quaint obsession of the twenties. In the light of much more radical forms of skepticism in the present, the great prestige afforded scientific knowledge early in this century has proved as vulnerable as belief in the gods, as Joseph Wood Krutch predicted. In a sense that they did not understand, could not understand, at the time, the reconcilers in the twenties had a point. A common faith in a cognitively transparent and purposeful universe undergirded both the sciences and traditional forms of theism. Among intellectuals today, the highest proportion that still embraces some form of theism, usually Christian, is in the physical sciences and mathematics. The lowest is among humanists in major universities, where belief in any god, or a fervent commitment to a church, or a confident hope of immortality, makes one an oddity.

The forms of modern disillusionment reflect, not a product of new knowledge so much as new philosophical insights. Indeed, various forms of knowledge have helped erode one or another traditional belief, including those religious beliefs tied to antiquated understandings of the universe. But in a tradition going back centuries, Western intellectuals were able to cope with such iconoclasm, always doing the needed repairs and erecting new philosophical and religious support for a type of cosmic optimism. They, often without recognition, repaired the disheveled older gods.

In a sense, the repair work reached its apex in the nineteenth century. The last great bastion of human confidence, joined at times by arrogance, consisted of the forms of philosophical idealism that flourished in Europe and America. We now refer back, with nostalgia and, for some, a great sense of loss, to the last rationalizations of a universe that, in some sense, abetted our hopes, cared about our afflictions, and anchored our understanding. In fact, more than ever before, the gods of that century seemed to smile. Maybe that was the problem. They were self-indulgent gods, who failed to deliver on what seemed to be their promises. These promises were, in reality, only the most wayward and provincial fantasies or unrealistic aspirations of those who created them. As Nietzsche's madman shouted, God was dead, and, above all, the irenic idealists who had created all the new gods in their own image, had helped kill the old, personal, visceral, willful God of Christianity. Yet those who indulged in deicide were so dense, so uncomprehending, that they did not yet appreciate the horror of their actions.

For so many of the protagonists in the twenties, the challenges to older certainties were new. They were the first generation of thoughtful Americans to face up to them. Almost all the intellectuals surveyed in this book grew up in Christian homes and in evangelical churches. A few remained orthodox and tried desperately to hold on to the older religion as they understood it. Liberals and modernists tried to salvage as much of the older religion as they could. Rebels such as Barnes or Darrow or Mencken exhibited a type of sophomoric rebellion and, with an often arrogant pride in their own liberation, spent much of their energies in caricaturing and vilifying those who still affirmed the beliefs they had "escaped." More perceptive and more brilliant intellectuals, such as Dewey and Lippmann, accepted the loss of the old gods; glimpsed the human costs if not the tragedy of such a loss; and tried to find new, nonsupernatural beliefs that could sustain moral engagement and communal solidarity. A despairing Krutch believed all such hopeful strategies were doomed to failure. Santayana and Ransom illustrated a more tragic reaction. They still loved the myths, and the wisdom, present in traditional forms of Christianity. But in no literal sense could they affirm the foundational beliefs of the Church. Their lack of belief reflected not a choice, but an existential fact. They had regrets. They envied those who still, in innocence, believed the older doctrines. Above all, they celebrated the human truths that remained within the myths.

As this century ends, we are fully three generations beyond the twenties. What was new and unsettling then is commonplace now, at least among intellectuals. Those who battled in the twenties knew, from experience, what it had been like to live in a structured and purposeful universe. They remembered the awe, the fear, and at times the comfort of living in a world inhabited by gods. Thus they experienced the insecurity, and at times the elation, of knowing that the gods were all dying. The dying gods in their emergent new world were nonetheless still a vital part of their identity. For those who had for a time believed, and then found themselves not believing (it was never a choice) in a god, the most important fact of their existence was the God who was absent. His authority, his love and support, were gone. It was like the loss of a father. Indeed, such a loss opens up new areas of freedom and personal responsibility. But this is small comfort to one in the immediate aftermath of death. Today, fewer and fewer intellectuals confront such an experience. For them, the trembling gods of the twenties are long gone, forgotten and irrelevant. Few intellectuals today know the poignancy, the tragic sense of irreparable loss, that their grandparents suffered. It has been one of my purposes in this little book to make clear to modern readers some of that poignancy and tragedy.

INDEX

ABOUT THE AUTHOR

Paul K. Conkin is Distinguished Professor of History at Vanderbilt University, where he received his Ph.D. in history in 1957. He has received numerous awards, including a John Simon Guggenheim Memorial Fellowship, a Senior Fellowship from the National Endowment for the Humanities, and a University Fellowship from the National Endowment for the Humanities. He was president of the Southern Historical Association in 1996–97. He is the author of many books, including *American Originals: Homemade Varieties of Christianity*.